Judi Spall

THE HISTORY OF RETRIEVERS

Compiled from the scrapbooks of H. Reginald Cooke

JUDI SEALL

First published in 2001 by
Judi Seal

© 2001 JUDI SEALL

ALL RIGHTS RESERVED

No part of this book may be reproduced or transmitted in any form or by any means, electronic or mechanical, including photocopying, recording, or by any information storage and retrieval system, without permission in writing from the Publisher.

ISBN 0 9540417 0

Printed and bound in Singapore
by Kyodo Printing Co

10 9 8 7 6 5 4 3 2 1

Contents

Foreword by Randle Cooke.

Introduction.

1   Extracts from Volume One (1903-1908).

2   Extracts from Volume Two (1908-1911).

3   Extracts from Volume Three (1911-1916).

4   Extracts from Volume Four (1916-1923).

5   Extracts from Volume Five (1923-1925).

6   Extracts from Volume Six (1927-1932).

7   Extracts from Volume Seven (1932-1935).

8   Extracts from Volume Eight (1936-1941).

9   The Final Years (1945-1951).

Dedication

This book is dedicated to the Hon. Mrs Amelia Jessel, without whose help and support this book would never have been published. Sadly, she never saw the finished publication.

About the Author

Judi Seall's first love was horses. She competed and hunted with Blueprint, a grey gelding, and Riska, a bay mare. Until she met her husband Sam, the only dog she owned was her terrier Lucie.

The first Flatcoated Retriever Judi owned, was her beloved Kate, who, along with Sam, was responsible for beginning Judi's interest in gundogs. Since then, Judi has competed successfully in Field Trials, both with Labradors and Flatcoats.

Judi now shares her life with a team of dogs (including Raffle, the 11-year-old son of Kate) on Bereleigh Estate, where she and Sam now live.

Acknowledgements

I would like to thank the following people for their continued support throughout this project:

- Liz Barnes
- Randle Cooke
- Mark Jones
- Skinners Dog Food

Foreword

Henry Reginald Cooke (1859-1951), my grandfather, devoted his long life to the breeding and development of Flatcoated Retrievers. He became an acknowledged authority on the breed that has continued to this day.

Some years ago, I inherited what proved to be a veritable treasure chest of contemporary account, in the form of beautifully bound journals. These journals were complied by him over the years, recording much of the contemporary scene and all that he and his Retrievers achieved. The books consist of photographs, articles to sporting journals – to which, under the nom-de-plume of Partridge, he contributed – and many observations and records in his own hand.

The journals are currently on indefinite loan to the Flatcoated Retriever Society in the care of The Hon. Mrs Amelia Jessel, and through her good offices it was arranged for the journals to be copied for the Kennel Club's Record Library. It was also she who introduced me to Judi Seall, with her request to edit the journals, to which I was delighted to agree. The result is this remarkable book, to which I am honoured to have been asked to contribute a few words of introduction.

My Grandfather was a quiet, self-effacing man, as devoted to his dogs as he was to his family. As comes across in the journals' successive pages, his circle of friends spanned from the great shooting personalities of the day, to a host of keepers, handlers and judges associated with Field Trials and Shows. His training methods reflected his personality in his unrivalled breeding skills, knowledge of the sport, friendly encouragement and great patience. His Short Notes on Choosing and Breaking a Retriever, Short Suggestions for Judging at Retriever Field Trials and A Few more Short Notes on Retrievers serve to this day, for those fortunate to have a copy, as model text books.

As a boy I can remember watching him, for hour after hour, on the lawn at Dalicote, surrounded by probably half a dozen Retrievers of varying ages, all motionless in the 'Drop' position, but never taking their eyes off him or the dog currently being worked. My particular recollection is of how sparing he was, both in reproach and in reward. He was always gentle, but with very much a formal and professional manner. He gave few outward signs of the affection in which he held them all. The Retrievers never came into the house except once a week at lunch on Sundays, when perhaps four of them would lie 'Dropped', and again motionless, throughout the meal, around the big bow window. Opposite, on the wall, were six magnificent paintings of former Champions by Maude Earl, a leading canine artist of the day. One wondered if this arrangement was intended as an incentive to them for the fame that could be theirs in their turn!

The History Of Retrievers

From the accounts of Field Trial events in widely differing locations and in quick succession in the season, readers may wonder how the dogs were moved around, and, curiously, the journals make no mention of this. The answer, of course, reflects the excellence of the rail transport system, using steam trains in those days, which are now no more than a memory. The dogs generally travelled alone in the guard's van in large wicker hampers to be met by successive station staff, fed, watered and put on the next connecting train.

At home, HRC was most faithfully served by Jack Woolwrich, who also looked after the cars. For Woolwrich's two successive keepers, Cutting and Tansey, operations centred mainly on HRC's Riverside Kennels at Nantwich. For many breeders since, this Kennel name has been revered!

HRC's ultimate aim was the perfect Dual Champion. He pursued excellence, looks, conformation and temperament in all his Retrievers, alongside a rigorous working performance. He would seldom enter a dog competitively unless its credentials were sufficiently strong in both. HRC's dogs won the Cruft's Challenge Cup for the Best in Breed in 1907, 1909 and 1911, outright in the three years running to 1916 (the cup remains a treasured possession in our family), and also practically every important Field Trial in the country. Over the years, in light of this record, it is difficult to single out individual names, but perhaps Riverside Champions Kim, Toby, Bess, and, above all, Dual Champion Grouse, all deserve special mention and remain the stuff of legend in any Flatcoat pedigree.

This book will be of much specialised interest, both to Field Trial contendors and show exhibitors of the Retriever breeds. More generally, it provides a remarkable picture of contemporary country sporting life in the United Kingdom at the turn of the century – dare one say of a happier, bygone age. I doubt if my grandfather ever imagined that the contents of the journals he kept over so many years of his long life would ever be shared with successive generations of Flatcoat lovers, but it would have given him immense pleasure – and indeed perhaps has – to know that, through Judi Seall's initiative and efforts, this will now be so. I thank her on behalf of us all.

Randle Cooke

INTRODUCTION

In 1996, on behalf of the Kennel Club, I was approached by The Hon. Mrs Amelia Jessel and asked if I would be prepared to produce collages, photographs and relevant information for a new stand at Crufts. The stand was to be called The Working Gundog Forum, and was to have sections for each of the Gundog breeds. Having agreed to help, I was given the opportunity to borrow the journals kept by H. Reginald Cooke from 1903 until just before his death in 1951. H. Reginald Cooke's grandson, Randle Cooke, gave me permission to use the contents of these journals to produce collages for The Working Gundog Forum.

SLICE OF THE PAST

Reading the journals was a privilege, and it was to prove a fascinating insight into 'when it all began'. I was so enthusiastic about the journals' contents, I wanted others to have the opportunity to see them. As this was not possible, I decided, with the encouragement of Amelia Jessel, to attempt to condense some of the information into the form of a book. I started this lengthy task in 1997, and began by choosing my favourite entries – I never tire of reading them and each time I look I see something else I wish I had included. However, one has to stop somewhere and I hope the choices I have made will give others as much pleasure as they have given me.

THE LIFE OF H. R. COOKE

Mr. H. Reginald Cooke was born in 1859 at Arden House, Ashley, Cheshire. He was educated at Eton, and Trinity College, Cambridge. He whipped in for the Trinity College Beagles, and also represented Cambridge in the high-jump competition against Oxford in 1879.

He established his kennel of Flatcoated Retrievers in 1881, shortly before the death of the late Mr. S. E. Shirley, who was the founder of the breed. HRC was president of the Flatcoated Retriever Association, originally established by Lady Howe, but he resigned in 1936.

Mr. Cooke's favourite recreations were hunting, shooting and fishing – activities he enjoyed frequently at his Shropshire home of Dalicote, Bridgnorth. His now-famous Riverside Kennels were not based at Dalicote, however, but at Nantwich in Cheshire.

In January 1941, Mr. H. Reginald Cooke announced that he would not be exhibiting any of his dogs in the future. The Riverside Kennels had then been in existence for 60 years. He did, however, retain his stud dogs and continued to breed.

THE JOURNALS

All the information presented in this book has been taken from the wonderful journals compiled and belonging to Mr. H. Reginald Cooke. This book attempts to mirror the journals, in that each volume is represented by a chapter in this book.

Each chapter contains the most-prized of the journal's entries for that period. The journals begin in the year 1903, at a time when the Riverside Kennels were already being acclaimed as one of the most outstanding; producing Dual Champions from the start.

The final entry is in 1951, the year that Mr. Cooke died. Between those years, the journals offer an amazingly detailed, thorough, and fascinating glimpse of the Field Trial exhibitor's lifestyle.

1 EXTRACTS FROM VOLUME ONE (1903-1908)

The first volume of H. Reginald Cooke's journals begins with a cutting taken from the 1903 Christmas edition of Illustrated Kennel News. The extract reads:

"The enormous strides taken in the last few years by the Wavy Retriever has been due to the efforts of recent lovers of that useful and ornamental variety of sporting dog. Principal amongst these comes the name of Mr. H. Reginald Cooke, who owns the leading kennel of this variety."

There then follows page upon page of reports about Retriever Trials, which have been cut and meticulously pasted in these journals. These days, the Field Trials are reported with very little detail; usually the winner, placings and judges are listed, with a short report on the Trial if space has been allocated. Obviously, in these modern times, there are so many clubs holding Trials throughout the country that it would be impossible to have a report printed on each trial. However, in the early days, when H. Reginald Cooke was running his dogs, the Trials were reported in great length. Two or three columns of print was not unusual and they have all been cut out and stuck in to these wonderful journals. There are far too many to list, but one hopes to give just a small historic insight into the Trials of yesteryear.

PRIZE MONEY

The prize money is one aspect that jumps out from all these reports. To compare them with the prize money of today is almost a joke, as the winners in 1903 were receiving more than a contestant would win now! If prize money had kept up with inflation there would be some very wealthy Retriever handlers around today.

The Retriever Trials held at East Bergholt in 1903 were held over two days and the reports on these Trials are far too lengthy to include, but the listing of prizes, as follows, makes very interesting reading.

"THE INTERNATIONAL GUNDOG LEAGUE RETRIEVER TRIALS

Nomination stake for Retrievers, Smooth, Wavy or Curlycoated; first prize £35, second prize £17:10s, third prize £10, fourth prize £5. Special prizes: Challenge Cup, kindly presented to the society by Mr. B. J. Warwick, was offered for competition: Challenge Cup (the Bergholt Challenge Cup), kindly presented to the society by Mr. C.C. Eley, was offered for competition: given by Mr. W. Arkwright and Mr. B. J. Warwick, £12 for the best working Retriever or Retrievers at the meeting which has not previously run at Trials, either in one or two prizes at the discretion of the Judges: Given by Mr. G. R. Davies, £3:3s, for the best-looking dog or bitch at the meeting: Given by Mr. G. R. Davies and Mr. F. M. Remnant, £4:4s for the best dog or bitch at the meeting showing the greatest amount of dash combined with steadiness: Given anonymously, £20, to the winner in the stake on these conditions, viz., the winner must be a dog (not bitch) that has won a total of three prizes, not counting brace or team classes, at any two of the following shows, viz., Kennel Club, Edinburgh, Birmingham, Manchester, Crufts and Darlington. No dog can win a special prize without having won either a prize or a Certificate of Merit at these Trials."

The card for this stake was made up of eight Flatcoats, ten Wavycoats, one Roughcoat, and one Curlycoat. Not all of these dogs had records of how they were bred. For example, one of the competitors on the card was listed thus:

"Major Eley's Flatcoated bitch Santanella, sire Ducal, dam unknown: date of birth unknown, breeder unknown."

Santanella went on to win the stake, with Capt. Eley's Wavycoated dog, Sandiway Major, in second place, and Mr. C. C. Eley's Flatcoated dog, Bergholt James, in third place. Mr. A. Aitchison Jnr.'s Flatcoated bitch, Jubilee Moll, came in fourth, with Mr. H. Sawtell's Flatcoated dog, Melksham Prime, in fifth place. The cutting also mentions that:

" Mr. E. G. Buxton's Lexham Bob and Klepper, Melksham Wallace, Lady Ainslie and Melksham Victor had Certificates of Merit.

"Bergholt James won Mr. Eley's challenge cup, Santanella the grand cup of all, Moll and Prime Messrs. Arkwright and Warwick's prize for the best dogs that had not previously competed at Trials, Sandiway Nellie that for the best looking dog or bitch at the meeting, Melksham Wallace that for the dog that showed the greatest amount of dash combined with steadiness, and what may be called the show-bench winner's prize was not awarded.

"Rain was falling when Mr. Arkwright, in pleasant and flattering terms, thanked Mr. Eley for the interest he took in the Trials, and for the kindness in placing his shooting at the disposal of the society. He expressed his gratification, as one of the judges, at the good show of game they had been given in an extraordinarily bad season. In reply, Mr. Eley said his tenantry were to be thanked more than himself, for not only had they preserved the game well, but, when they knew that the Trials were to be held, kept their stock out of the fields as much as possible.

"Hearty cheers were given for the farmers and tenantry. The Hon. Gerald Lascelles was happy in his pleasant remarks, so far as the judges were concerned, and so concluded what was, without the slightest doubt, the most successful meeting for the Trials of Retrievers hitherto held."

COLONEL LEGH'S RETRIEVERS

Following the report on the International Gundog League's Retriever Trials, H. Reginald Cooke then devotes several pages to reports about Lieutenant-Colonel H. Cornwall Legh's Retrievers. He begins with a magazine cutting giving a glowing appraisal of Colonel Legh's contribution to the development of the Flatcoated Retriever breed.

"The reputation of Lieut.-Colonel Cornwall Legh's Flatcoated Retrievers is familiar to every lover of this breed."

HRC then goes on to report the death of Lieut.-Colonel H. Cornwall Legh, in November 1904.

"We are called upon to chronicle the demise

*Above: A group of Flatcoated Retrievers from the High Legh kennels, the property of Lieutenant Colonel H. Cornwall Legh. Pictured from left: Champion Twiddle; High Legh Druid; High Legh Blarney; High Legh Moment; and High Legh Blossom. The photograph was taken in 1904 by Dorcas.
Left: Colonel Cornwall Legh.*

of a prominent figure in the sporting and kennel world. Col. Legh came of old, English stock, his ancestry dating back, in a long illustrious line, to William the Conqueror. He was a great sportsman, High Legh Hall being a miniature museum of trophies of the chase from all parts of the world, supplemented by those of the show ring.

"The fact that over 800 Pointers, Setters and Retrievers have been bred at High Legh during the last quarter of a century, proves in what direction the late Lieut.-Col. Cornwall Legh lay. No member of the Kennel Club was held in higher esteem than Col. Legh, as is testified by his long connection with the club as one of its three Trustees and a Vice-President. Col. Legh's death is an especial blow to the Kennel Club, which can ill afford to lose gentlemen of his high social standing, transparent integrity and honour in all his dealings. He was a gentleman in every sense of the word, and it is to men of the calibre of Col. Legh, whose bona-fides were above suspicion, that the public have pinned their faith, and which has resulted in the Kennel Club having commanded respect and attained its present high and solid position.

"The funeral of the deceased gentleman took place at Rotherne on Thursday, amid the manifestations of sorrow of a large concourse of relatives and friends. Col. Legh leaves a widow but no family."

THE DRAW

As mentioned before, Trials were given a great deal more coverage in the first half of the 20th century. Even the draw for the Trials was given much coverage. Today, the draw is usually held in the confines of the Field Trial Secretary's home, with perhaps one or two witnesses. Imagine if the draws of today were held as the following excerpt – I, as a Field Trial Secretary, would not welcome this amount of extra work!

The International Gundog League's Field Trials at Sherbourne, (near Warwick) in October 1904, had the following coverage on the draw:

"The draw to decide the order of running took place at the Warwick Arms on Monday evening and was well attended, amongst those present being Sir. H. Smith, Col. Cotes, Col. Roberts, Major Harding, Major Eley, Capt. Eley, Capt. Webb, Rev. R. L. Raine, Mr. C. C. Eley, Mr. J. G. Mair-Rumley, Mr. G. R. Davies, Mr. C. Cockburn, Mr. A. T. Williams, Mr. Lister Read, Mr. S. A. Harding, Mr. A. E. Sansom, secretary, and a few others. Quite a number of handlers were waiting in the hall, but the draw took place unknown to them. The entry must be deemed quite satisfactory, the whole of the twenty nominations having been taken up early; however, two of these were absentees, Mr. Gordon Canning's and Mr. H. Sawtell's, the latter not appearing on the card. They were drawn in lots of half-a-dozen, each lot being in the first round together, stationed a certain distance apart, their handlers being allowed to shoot as occasion required. As is usually the case, the Curlycoated retrievers were badly represented, there being but one nomination, Mawdesley Daisy, and there was one Labrador Retriever, Munden Single. However, as already stated, the entry was good and the draw was speedily got through by Mr. Sansom, the secretary. The judges were: Mr. C. S. Cockburn, Mr. G. R. Davies and Mr. G. Teasdale-Buckell, the latter taking the place of Mr. Remnant who was unable to be present owing to a recent family bereavement."

The details put in print were unbelievable – consider the idea of that happening now! Perhaps it would be to the benefit of our massive entries of today, were the draw to take place on the day of the Trial. It would squash the modern habit of entering every Trial, including those known to clash with each other, simply to ensure a run in one. Imagine the chaos caused by making the draw on the day of the Trial under these circumstances!

THE TRIAL IN FULL

All the reports in the scrapbooks are so fascinating that this missive would not be complete without illustrating one in full. The following is taken from the report of the 1904 Trials at Warwick.

"TUESDAY: The meet was arranged for the Tea House, Coplar's Hill, about three miles from Warwick, and a start was made with the first day's work just before ten o'clock, in the presence of a numerous company, including besides those present at the draw, Messrs. Smith-Ryland, Fullerton, Alfrey, Major Maul, Messrs. W. W. Henby, R. H. A. Pritchard, Hon. A. Holland Hibbert, Mr. E. G. Wheeler, Capt. Richards, and a number of ladies. Headkeeper Haines arranged the beats in a capital manner, particularly as the area covered necessitated the same ground being worked over several times. Beautiful weather prevailed throughout the day, though it did not appear that scent was very good. Taking the performance of the competitors as a whole, steadiness was more manifest than really good drive work, but, as a

Volume One (1903-1908)

matter of fact, all the shooting was done in the open, and runners were at a discount until later in the day. None of the competitors were qualified for the special prize of £20, the conditions attached to which are rather impossible.

"The morning's programme consisted of walking up game, the dogs being worked in batches of six, the first down being: Munden Single (Labrador) handled and shot to by the Hon. A. Holland-Hibbert; Sandiway Nellie (Wavy) in the charge of her owner; Beechgrove Regina (Smooth) behind Mr. Lister Read; Bergholt Mary (Flatcoat) with Mr. C. C. Eley; Ben worked by Joyce; and Shotover (Smooth) in the charge of King. The first beat was taken over a hill of rough grass and small fir plantation, which afforded excellent cover. Munden Single was first to distinguish himself, retrieving two pheasants cleverly, and was also steady to both shot and fur; she went out willingly and fast and used her nose to very good purpose. Beechgrove Regina made a good find of a wounded partridge, and retrieved fur very nicely, though she was rather too long in finding her game. A second hare she missed finding and Bergholt Mary was brought across and as her owner took her to very near the spot, she quickly found. At first she seemed disinclined to retrieve, but on persuasion brought puss to hand. Regina had another chance, this time at partridge, which she found nicely; but, just when she was nearing the shooter, she dropped her game, preferring to run in to a hare, which was bowled over in her sight. Hares were plentiful, and she soon had another opportunity, behaving properly. Then Ben got a turn on the right, and did all that was requisite with fur. Mr. Eley took a back shot at a hare, Bergholt Mary was sent in pursuit, and came up with it, but much of the merit was taken out of the performance by the shooter running after her to the end of the field. Shotover had displayed nice steadiness and retrieved very cleanly both fur and feather, but, at length, he ran in and chased badly into the next field, and on his return sat down about fifty yards in front of the line.

"The next section consisted of Swansfield Lorna (Wavy) handled by her owner; Acolyte (Smooth) also with his owner in charge; Black Mystic (Flatcoat) with Alexander; Don of Gerwin (Flatcoat) in the charge of Allen; Klepper (Smooth) worked by Michie; and Pitchford Marshall (Wavy) with Downes. Crossing a ploughed field, Lorna had the first chance and retrieved a hare in nice style quickly and right to hand. Then, Alexander, who worked Black Mystic, accounted for another, and, ordered on, the dog went out fast and by nice questing found, retrieving carefully. Another fell to Mr. Eley's gun, and Acolyte was equally good. Turnips were being worked which afforded nice covert; but partridges were wild, several coveys going away out of reach; then at long range Allen wounded a hare. Don being sent in pursuit, made a capital line and retrieved finely to hand at full gallop. Next Capt. Eley wounded one and Acolyte treated himself to a short chase. Klepper so far had nothing to do, but now retrieved a hare in full view. Pitchford Marshall had a nice opportunity on a pheasant, but he pottered about rather too much, and, when he did find, was rather too long in picking up. A move was then made and a crop of mangolds worked. The sun, being powerful, did not aid the scent. A partridge dropped on the right was entrusted to Kelpie, and he was allowed a considerable time to hunt for it, at times getting too far in front of the line. Several times he appeared to run right over his game, but at length found and bought right to hand. A big covey caused quite a fusillade, but distance helped escape and nothing fell, all the dogs being quite steady. By this time we had reached the limits of the ground to be worked, and a return was made to the starting point to try the ground over again, and Alexander was first to renew the attack, dropping an odd bird which Black Mystic retrieved nicely. Lorna had a pheasant, which she attended to with credit to herself, and, in the corner, two others were dropped. Allen was called up to give Don an opportunity, who very quickly brought both cleverly to hand, negotiating double fences with fine style. One of the best pieces of work so far, for the whereabouts of neither could have been known to him.

"Again we came to root crops when the third group of dogs was brought out and a long shot by Mr. Rome who was handling his own dog Roman Sweep brought down a single bird near the end of the drills, some 150 yards in front. Sweep went out, but though he went very directly to the spot, passed the bird several times and only found it after a prolonged search on being called back to the line. On stubble which had been manured, the scent was very bad, but Mawdesley Daisy, the only one of the Curlycoated variety in the stake, and a puppy rather too young to expect much brilliancy from, was handled by her owner and retrieved a hare fairly well. Almington Merlin worked and shot to by Cooke, made a very quick and clever find of a wounded partridge which he placed into Cooke's hands quite clean and alive. A very big lot of birds were in the next turnip field, but, unfortunately, Daisy got quite out of hand and disturbed many of them. An odd bird fell to Mr. Fullerton's gun, and again Merlin did all that was requisite. Moll in charge of Quinn was taken over the fence in quest of a bird supposed to have dropped, but it could not be found. Then she had a chance of distinguishing herself on a pheasant, which turned out to be dead, and she retrieved it cleverly. Mr. Rylands had been fairly busy with the gun and at length found work for Wallace of Faskally (whom Abbot was working) in the shape of a hare, which was retrieved after being dropped twice. Sweep, on being sent for another, improved on his earlier effort, and was quick about his work. Merlin got two others very quickly and quite clean; but Molly fumbled a bit too much with her next. Some nice overhead shots were provided and Sweep retrieved one bird very tenderly, though he also fumbled it a bit. Wallace also had another nice chance, and behaved well, though at times he seemed rather too anxious. Lucifer, in charge of his owner, got no favourable opportunity.

"This ended the first round and it was announced that Regina, Shotover and Mawdesley Daisy would not be required again. Driving was now resorted to and Munden Single, Sandiway Nellie, Bergholt Mary, Ben, Swansfield Lorna and Acolyte were called up. The first drive produced shots for the three right-handed guns only, but all the dogs were perfectly steady, and at its end, the Labrador Munden Sweep was the only dog called upon to work. He found very well and retrieved tenderly two partridges, which fell in a rough patch before reaching the fence behind which the guns were placed. The second drive resulted in hares, Acolyte being the only dog required to display his qualifications, being taken through onto the next field and put on to one which travelled about 200 yards after being hit; this he made out well, going at a good pace on the line, and retrieved correctly. At the next essay, birds were numerous, but the shooting was not of the best. Again the Labrador found well a wounded bird in the fence. Bergholt Mary was sent for a bird Mr. Eley had dropped, got on to one which Joyce had brought down and played her part well, but Joyce had the satisfaction of seeing his dog Ben retaliate when sent out for the other bird, as he went away stylishly, quested well, and retrieved tenderly to hand. Swansfield Nellie retrieved nicely a single bird on the open field. No other had opportunities. Another move was made, when a partridge was brought down a long way back and Nellie, being utilised, made a capital find and retrieved tenderly to hand. Another bird was marked down in adjoining stubble, and Ben was taken on, but, after trying for ten minutes, failed to find; then Mr. Eley with Bergholt Mary tried with no better result. Munden Single again distinguished himself, this time with a hare and also a partridge, which dropped out of his sight in an adjoining field. Acolyte, having one in the open, which he brought to hand cleanly.

"Klepper, Pitchford Marshall, Black Mystic, Don of Gerwin, Lucifer and Roman Sweep were next brought up. Birds came in packs for

Volume One (1903-1908)

their first drive, Don of Gerwin being sorely tempted by a red leg which dropped close to him and ran about in front of him till the end, to which he was proof. Black Mystic taken to a runner, found and retrieved a dead bird from under a thorn bush in a pit hole, and though given further time failed to find the runner, so Don was tried and he too failed, but after the judges had left Mystic found it in a hole close to the water edge. Lucifer and Sweep each retrieved dead birds in the open tenderly. Then Klepper made a clever find, and again delivered well to hand, and Michie, his handler, came in for a lot of shooting at the wind up, and both he and his dog acquitted themselves well, though he had no chance at a runner like both Pitchford Marshall and Mystic Lad. The former crossed the line of two several times without effect, though he brought a dead bird nicely, and Mystic did not make either of them out for some time; still, when he got on to a hot scent, he worked it out nicely. As darkness was setting in, picking up was decided upon by the dogs indiscriminately, this, the last drive over the hill, where the start was made in the morning, being the most productive of the day. With the exception of the three dogs thrown out, all the others were obedient and worked well to hand.

"WEDNESDAY: An early start had been decided upon for today, half-past eight being the appointed time to meet at the same rendezvous as yesterday, but a change was made to Newton Littleworth. The company, consisting of practically the same as on the previous day, was joined by Lord Ernest Seymour, who was one of the shooters, Major Armstrong, Capt. Cowan, and others. The weather again proved very fine, if anything too warm in the middle of the day for good scent. Game was plentiful enough for trial purposes, but, in the afternoon particularly, the greatest difficulty was experienced in driving it over the guns, though Haines, the keeper, regulated his beaters to the best advantage.

"A commencement was made by driving a plantation of young fir trees, under which was a nice dry covert, the first dogs called being Lucifer and Sweep on the left, Merlin and Don in the centre, and on the right were Klepper and Wallace. Quickly, pheasants were on the wing, but not many suitable shots were provided. Merlin retrieved a rabbit, picking up smartly, and, sent out again, made a good find of a pheasant, which he delivered nicely to hand. Don, sent in to another, which fell behind was very quick in finding, and also brought tenderly to hand. Sweep had two dead birds, rather easily found; still, he performed well. Lucifer persistently quested for another, which was down wind, and he acquitted himself well. Klepper was put on to what was thought to be a strong runner, but turned out to be an easily found dead bird, which he brought to hand. None of the others had an opportunity at this drive. The next heat sent game down wind, but only two pheasants were dropped, which were gathered, one by Klepper nicely, though Michie, who worked him was rather noisy, and the other, a runner, by Wallace. Merlin was also taken to what was thought to be a third, but investigation proved only two had fallen. Wallace had given such satisfaction this time that he was ordered up to make room for the Labrador Munden Single for the next trial at the end of which the very best performance of the meeting was displayed by Don of Gerwin, who, put on to a strong, running cock pheasant, which dropped on a high fence, immediately struck its line which led into a blind ditch full of brambles, which he faced with gusto, and, never leaving the scent, found, and retrieved to hand alone in a very quick time. This was ample, coupled with his previous efforts, to virtually settle matters, so Don was not required further. The next beat was taken through small fir plantations, the shooters walking through the undergrowth. Jubilee Moll took his place after Klepper had found one bird, and Sweep two birds, each of which occupied rather too much time. Moll had the next chance, and retrieved a hen pheasant well. Cook dropped a partridge, a long shot, which was relegated to the Labrador and nicely found and retrieved. The beaters went on, leaving the guns standing for birds breaking back. Moll sent for a rabbit, was quick, but had no questing to do. Another move was necessary; the dogs now required being, Bergholt Mary, Black Mystic, Jubilee Moll, Almington Merlin, Swansfield Lorna and Munden Single. Rather a long wait resulted fruitlessly, all the birds breaking back behind the beaters; but at the next essay, a nice lot of pheasants were put out of a covert of tall trees. Two or three of the much desired runners being the result, one of which proved fatal to the chances of Munden Single, for, though she made the best of her nose and went quickly when she got scent, she simply mashed her bird up. Lorna had just before made an excellent impression by picking up the line of a bird which fell on the grass and had run in to a ditch, quite a nice piece of work which she supplemented by delivering clean and well to hand. Moll had two dead birds, which she retrieved tenderly, but they did not require much finding. Mary had a dead bird right in the open, but she was much too slow on finding and did not pick up well.

"Next we had a partridge drive, Sandiway Nellie and Ben taking the place of Swansfield Lorna and Munden Single, the others being kept at work. Ben was first sent for a dead bird, which he saw, drop, so went straight to the spot and picked up. Wallace brought one through a fence nicely. Merlin was sent a long way back for a bird, which towered, and was quick about his work, bringing it well to hand, a good performance. Another move was made, and the hill, which had proved the best holding place tried, was again requisitioned. Ben on the right, retrieved a dead hare correctly; Munden Single was rather longer in finding a dead partridge than usual; Merlin, taken down a plain grass field, showed very nice questing for partridge, but met with his undoing, most unfortunately, for he came across a rabbit on it's seat, which he put away and chased. Mary was taken a long way forward to a fallen bird, which she missed finding."

"After lunch, Lorna, Acolyte, Lucifer, Moll, Klepper and Marshall were given another turn, but by this time birds had been so much knocked about that it was most difficult to drive them to the guns, and shooters were so keen that several barrels were emptied at the same mark, hence the much desired runners were scarcer than ever. Little of moment resulted from the first drive, but Klepper did not make good use of the opportunity given him, being much too long in finding a partridge on the grass, necessitating his handler taking him close to the spot where it lay. Moving on and along a high fence Downe dropped a partridge, which made for the ditch, and when Marshall was sent for it he displayed much more activity than previously, and was quick in locating it, retrieving to hand cleverly. On the other side Klepper was inclined to run in, stern command stopping him; Moll misunderstood the word of command and occasionally went forward when not intended she should to a bird, which Lucifer was sent for and brought back nicely. Dead birds, which were not now required, was the only result of the next drive from turnips and fallow, but Acolyte was tried for one which fell on a thick fence; he hunted backwards and forwards many times, and only when his owner took him to the exact spot did he hit its scent; then we saw the unusual spectacle of a Retriever mounted on the top of a fence, assisted up by his owner, to get hold of a dead bird, which ought to have been gathered by hand. Wallace took Klepper's place, but he was too long in finding a dead bird in the open, Abbot having to go close to it to help him. Then, after crossing a turnip field in line, we came to the excellent ground where we first started, and it once again proved prolific in more senses than one, for a good running partridge was provided by Downe, and Pitchford Marshall, having the call, quite convinced everybody that he had not previously shown his best form. The very first time he crossed the scent, he hit it, and going on a perfect line, reached his bird near the fence and came back quickly, delivering it well and clean to hand.

"This finished the work and the results were announced as follows:

Volume One (1903-1908)

1. Mr. A. J. William's Don of Gerwin
2. Lord Falconer's and Mr. E. G. Wheler's Swansfield Lorna
3. Col. Cote's Pitchford Marshall
4. Capt. H. Eley's Acolyte
5. Capt. Timson's Lucifer

Certificates of Merit were awarded to the Hon. A. Holland-Hibbert's Munden Single, Mr. C. C. Eley's Bergholt Mary, the Hon. G. H. Lacelle's Nora, the Marquis of Manchester's Ben, Major Eley's nomination Messrs. Cox and Shipton's Black Mystic, Sir. H. Smith's Klepper, Rev. R. Lorimer Rome's Roman Sweep, Major Harding's Almington Merlin, Mr. A. E. Butter's Wallace of Fascally, Mr. A. Aitchison's Jubilee Moll and Capt. Timson's Lucifer.

"Don of Gerwin also took Mr. B. J. Warwick's Challenge Cup, the five-guinea special given by Mr. C. C. Eley, and also four guineas for the dog showing the best dash and steadiness: Acolyte was awarded the Bergholt Challenge Cup; the special prize for the best animal in the stake which had never run before at trials was divided, Swansfield Norma taking £8 and Almington Merlin £4; and the special for the best looking dog or bitch was secured by Black Mystic.

"Before separating soon after at 5 o'clock, Mr. C. C. Eley proposed a vote of thanks to Mr. Smith Ryland for having placed his estate at the service of the club, which was responded to with hearty cheers. Mr. Smith Ryland, in reply, said it had given him pleasure to help the efforts of the Retriever Club, of which he was proud to be a member. The services of the judges were acknowledged by Mr. A. J. Williams proposing thanks to them, to which Mr. G. R. Davies suitably replied. Col. Cotes asked for a vote of thanks to the farmers over whose land they had worked, remarking that every man they employed had been drafted to assist in the sport, to which Mr. H. T. Cattell replied, and so terminated a pleasant and interesting meeting."

I found the whole report completely fascinating, and amusing in parts. What I found most interesting was the awards. Having such a lengthy and informative report (a rare opportunity to view the whole Trial), I noticed that those to whom Certificates of Merit were awarded included: Mystic, who as far as I can make out was first dog down on a runner; Munden Single, who "mashed her bird up!"; Merlin, who chased a rabbit; Klepper, who ran in; and Moll, who moved on another's command. Obviously, in those early days, the Certificate of Merit was awarded regardless of faults. Can we assume that this is going to once again be the norm?

CORRESPONDENCE

Throughout his life, H. Reginald Cooke wrote frequently to magazines such as

Don of Gerwin.

Illustrated Kennel News. The first letter to be displayed in the scrapbooks relates to 1904 Warwickshire Retriever Trials, and was published in Illustrated Kennel News on October 22nd 1904:

"Sir, – In reading the various accounts which have appeared of the Retriever Trials, I notice that, in some instances, the winner Don of Gerwin is described as a crossbred Retriever. That is clearly a mistake, as a reference to the Kennel Club Stud Book will show, at any rate so far as one side of his pedigree is concerned. His dam, Rust, was by Tatt (a dog once in my possession) ex. Belle; Tatt was by Ch. Taut ex Stamford Myrtle, Ch. Taut by Windward ex Rivington Gypsy; Standford Myrtle by Zelstone ex Standford Trace. Don of Gerwin is therefore descended from a direct line of pedigree Retrievers."

HRC's letter seems to have sparked an ongoing debate about the qualities of the dogs entering the Trials, for the following pages of the scrapbooks contain several letters about the matter. Don of Gerwin's owner, Mr. A. T. Williams, replied to HRC's letter as follows:

"Sir, – Referring to Mr. Reginald Cooke's letter in your issue of this date, I may be permitted to say that he is perfectly correct in saying there is no purer-bred Retriever than Don of Gerwin. One report described the dog as being liver and white. There is not a white hair on his body. As to the liver colour, I consider it a most beautiful colour and Don is, to my mind, a very handsome dog. Of course, he is broader in the skull than the modern show bench Retriever; but he is all the better for that, and this may account for his extraordinary nose and brains."

AWARDING MARKS

Having made my own observations regarding the 1904 Retriever Trials, and given my own remarks on the awards (particularly the Certificates of Merit), I was interested to find more pages containing the opinions of others. The following is an excerpt from a letter from Cox and Shipton, published in The Field, October 28th 1904:

"The method of judging the merits of the performers seems to us to be weak and unsatisfactory. The draw, having settled the order in which the dogs were to be put down, it might fairly be assumed that each dog would be given the same chance as his neighbours, so far as such a thing is humanly possible. We doubt, however, that any two dogs were placed on equality in this respect, save in the test for steadiness. At any rate, it seemed to the onlookers (who in this case it must be admitted did not see most of the game, for they were at times rigorously excluded), that certain dogs were unduly favoured; thus, to give specific instances, one dog with a great reputation was made frequent use of, was kept in the stake until almost the last moment, and was then awarded a certificate of merit, when it was apparent to the rankest outsider that he was very deficient in nose, and, as a rule, only found his game by incessant galloping with his head in the air, in the course of which he, sooner or later, stumbled upon it. Another dog was retained in the stake and was given a certificate, when at her first attempt she dropped the game she was sent to retrieve, and at the second her owner was allowed to race in her wake half-way across the field to relieve her of the necessity of bringing to hand the hare she was sent back to seek. A third dog sent to find a dead bird put up a rabbit and chased it, yet he was kept in, was given the only opportunity the last drive afforded of retrieving his reputation and the single bird that fell, and he actually shared the stake. A fourth mouthed a pheasant badly, yet, she was given a certificate of merit; and a fifth failed to find a dead bird that was plainly visible to all beholders, yet, even he was similarly favoured.

"Now it may be argued that many of these are minor short-comings that would be thought nothing of in everyday practice, but when it is borne in mind that it is only by penalising a dog for the mistakes he makes on the day that the winners can ultimately discovered, and the awards given to the most deserving. We have, we hope, justified our view that the weeding out process should be more rigidly applied, and that, too, without fear or favour. As it is, dogs are excluded from the prize list, not because they have failed to do everything they were asked to do, and to do it in a workmanlike manner, but because, partly through ill-luck (which must always be present) and partly through faults in the system adopted, they have not been given a fair chance of demonstrating their capabilities.

"We readily admit that the limited space at the disposal of the committee rendered the task of the judges an exceedingly difficult one, for some of the ground was driven and walked more than a dozen times until the birds absolutely refused to 'face the music:' but without the slightest degree belittling the merits of the venue selected for the trials – the courteous owner of which was kindness personified – we venture to think that the committee of the Retriever Society should experience no difficulty in so improving this year's programme as to secure better results another season."

The correspondence relating to just this one Trial goes on for page after page, the last missive to be printed on the very same subject would appear to be on 10th December 1904, when a short letter, signed 'Rambler', was printed:

"Sir, – At last there seems some practical outcome of all that has been said and written, and, although these Trials have been much discussed in your various issues, I doubt if a tithe of what has actually been said by competitors has found it's way into print. Let us be grateful therefore for one practical suggestion which may lead to a better state of things. Messrs. Cox and Shipton suggest a new society, and, without attempting to discuss details, I would point out that what the Spaniel Club can do by holding Field Trials and supporting shows, surely Retriever exhibitors and breeders may hope to accomplish."

Well, this was obviously not accomplished, as today there is a very definite line between the show-bred Labrador Retriever and the working-bred Labrador Retriever, although it must be said that the working stock produced today retains all the looks of a Labrador and the ones bred purely for showing are so ungainly and interbred that they would find a day's work impossible. The same can be said for the Golden Retriever; the working line produced over many generations bears no similarity to the ones that are seen on the bench. The Flatcoated Retriever, however, is still claimed to be a dual-purpose dog, although there have been only three post-Second-World-War Field Trial Ch. Flatcoats. The society is an international breed society and remains 95 per cent show oriented.

Statistics show that within the society there are but a handful of serious Field Triallers who breed only for work and still manage to retain the looks. It is, though, a thankless task, as for generations the working side was bred out in favour of looks and the Flatcoat ended up as an also-ran. Although the society has run its own Trials for many years and still has an Open qualifying stake, there are never enough qualified dogs to fill the card, and dogs without a Trial award, or just a Certificate of Merit in a Novice Trial, are needed to fill the card.

GUNDOG GOSSIP

Further into the archives of these journals I discovered 'Gundog Gossip', an article which made an interesting point – that although Lieutenant Colonel Cornwall Legh died in 1904, his kennels were not dispersed until 9th June 1905, when, under the heading of 'Gundog Gossip' the following report was printed. Interestingly, the article included a several lines about the sale of High Legh Blarney, who went on to become a very famous dog:

"To return to Friday's sale, there was not much excitement until the Flatcoated Retrievers sent up by the executors of the late Lieut.-Col. Cornwall Legh were reached, but the opening was disappointing, for there was absolutely no bid for Pirate, a seven-year-old son of Buoyant – Mabee, and said to be very steady in the field. The next lot, High Legh Druid, a son of Darenth – Kite, beautifully bred on both sides, went for eight guineas,

Waiting by the park gate before the start.   *Mr. J. R. Davies with Sandiway Witch, which gained second place.*

The Retriever Society's Field Trials at Sutton Scarsdale, near Chesterfield. Clockwise from top left: Waiting by the park gate before the start; Mr. J. R. Davies with Sandiway Witch, who gained second place; The Hon. A. Holland Hibbert's Munden Single, winner of a certificate of merit, after bringing in a hare; Mr. A. T. Williams's Don of Gerwin, the winner in 1904, who gained a certificate of merit this year; Mr. P. Palmer's Swattsfield Truth, winner of a certificate of merit, bringing in a pheasant.

clearly a bargain; and then we reached the tit-bit of the sale, High Legh Blarney, a second-season Retriever by Black Quilt – High Legh Moment. He was put down in beautiful trim and started at 50 guineas, was very quickly run up to 200 guineas, the bidding between the two north-country men, Mr. T. H. Miller and Mr. H. Reginald Cooke, represented by his chief kennel man being very spirited. The latter, however, stayed the longer; in fact, he seemed quite prepared to go on, and, at the price named, he secured what must prove to be a valuable addition to the already strong team at Riverside. Blarney is now in his prime, and, although 200 guineas seems a lot of money to give for a Retriever, Mr. Cooke is not the man to pay more than the real value for a dog. It may be taken for granted that Blarney is worth every farthing of the money, and we congratulate his purchaser and sincerely hope that his pluck will meet with its just reward."

The Retriever Trials in Chesterfield, 1905. Clockwise from top left: Making for fresh ground; The game cart; Some of the spectators; Off for the first drive.

PHOTOGRAPHIC EVIDENCE

The first photographic evidence of Trials appears in Mr. Cooke's journals in 1905. There are obviously many more throughout the scrapbooks, but, as these were the first recorded, I am including them. The Trials were run by The Retriever Society and held at Sutton Scarsdale, near Chesterfield, in October 1905.

HANDLERS AND THEIR DOGS

It becomes apparent, from reading the accompanying text that, in the past, it was even permissible to change handlers for the second day of a stake! This happened at Taunton, in 1906:

"We congratulate Mr. H. Reginald Cooke on the win of his retriever Grouse of Riverside, who qualified by his win at Taunton as a full champion. Ch. Grouse of Riverside has only been exhibited on four occasions, and, it will be remembered by Field Trial followers, that this is the dog that ran so well at the Retriever Trials last October at Sutton Scarsdale, winning fourth. No doubt he would have done even better if Mr. Cooke had not been obliged to leave the meeting on the evening of the first day. This necessitated Grouse of Riverside being handled the next day by a stranger."

SPORTING-DOG SALE

Mr. Cooke kept a close eye on the sale of Retrievers, fully abreast with who owned what. He pasted in numerous cuttings about the sale of Trial dogs, such as this one, which covers the sale of sporting dogs at Aldridge's.

"Breeders, however, must regret having let slip a gamekeeper's Retriever which came out at Richmond (Surrey) Show a fortnight ago, and was allowed to go in the auction class for 66 shillings. The lucky buyer transferred the dog almost immediately for £25 and this week he had the mortification of being beaten for the Kennel Club Championship at Hemel Hempstead by the same Retriever, and of being told that the dog is on offer to a Scottish shooting man at £115."

All in a fortnight!

Ch. Grouse of Riverside, the winner of the 1906 Retriever Trials at Priory Hill, St. Neots. Pictured with his owner Mr. H. Reginald Cooke.

RETRIEVER TRIALS AT ST. NEOTS

These Retriever Society Trials occurred on the 25th and 26th October, 1906, at Priory Hill, St. Neots. Mr. H. Reginald Cooke with Dual Ch. Grouse of Riverside was the winner.

KENNEL CLUB FIELD TRIALS

For many years, Retriever Trials were held mainly by the Retriever Society. The first Retriever Field Trials to be held in connection with the Kennel Club were held at Horstead Hall, Norwich, over three days; 27th, 28th and 29th November, 1906. The Trials was recorded as follows:

"A large house party at Horstead Hall included the Duke of Hamilton, Major R. M. Poor and Lady Flora Poor, Major and Mrs. McLaughlin, Mr. and Mrs. Cator, Captain and Mrs. Cator, the Hon. Mrs. Ailwyn E. Fellows, Mr. John Kerr, Mr. A. W. Maconochie, and Mr. H. Piper, who were present with Lady Birkbeck during the Trials."

This was an All-Aged stake for 20 dogs and bitches, with an entry fee of £5. The first prize was £50, the second prize £30, the third prize £15, with a fourth prize of £5. The judges were Messrs. F. C. Lowe, C. A. Philips and E. G. Wheeler.

Held over three days, the dogs were worked in batches of six, and the card consisted of eight Flatcoat dogs, seven Flatcoat bitches, three Labrador bitches, one Labrador dog, and one Curlycoated dog.

On the first day, the Junior stake was also held. This was for dogs and bitches under two years old on November 27th 1906. The entry fee was £5, with a first prize of £30, a second prize of £15, a third prize of £10, and a fourth prize of £5. In the Junior stakes there were nine competitors; five Flatcoat bitches, two Flatcoat dogs, one Labrador bitch and one Labrador dog.

The reports detailing these Trials are very lengthy, but I have tried to extract some of the more interesting paragraphs:

"The first group having been down for over two hours, the second batch was called for, Jubilee Rival being handled by his owner, Mr. Blagg had the charge of Busy Mite, Downes

Volume One (1903-1908)

worked Pitchford Marshall, Mr. H. Reginald Cooke had Grouse of Riverside, while Mr. Portal and Mr. Harris worked Flapper and Smut of Gerwin respectively. Another drive was tried, this time from roots, the shooters being ranged behind a high hedge. There was now quite a strong wind, and the birds were some time in coming over. The flanks were taken by Mr. Lowe and Mr. Phillips, Mr. Wheler having the middle brace, which were the Labrador Flapper and Pitchford Marshall. The drive was not very prolific, and only one runner was provided, dead birds being retrieved by Busy Mite and Jubilee Rival on the left, but Grouse of Riverside ran in on the extreme right, and after Smut of Gerwin had picked up a dead bird, neither she nor Flapper could track a strong runner, and Pitchford Marshall was put on. He carried the line through the roots and down to the plantation, where he was at fault, and possibly the bird had again taken to the wing. Jubilee Rival also failed to retrieve a runner, which broke back, and ran some distance along the side of the hedgerow. Rival, however, marked his bird at a rabbit hole and he was credited with the points by Mr. Lowe. The corner of the belt that had been visited earlier in the morning was now driven, King, the gamekeeper, having declared that the stops there were open at the earlier drive. The Aylsham road separated the shooters, but none of the pheasants dropped on the turnpike. Jubilee Rival and Busy Mite were on the left, quite close to the wood, and, although the first named missed a runner, he picked up and brought to hand a dead bird; afterwards Busy Mite retrieved the runner which had been left

Below: The Kennel Club Retriever Trials at the Horstead Hall Estate, near Norwich.

Sweep of Glendaruel.

by Rival, and she also brought dead birds to hand. Grouse of Riverside and Smut of Gerwin were light; each retrieved well, Grouse being especially quick in his return, but Smut hunted down two runners, one of which had been left by Mr. Cooke's charge.

"The tests, although not so long as those given the first batch, were considered sufficient, and the next Retrievers were called for."

On the following day:

"The Retrievers first called for were Flapper, Pitchford Marshall – on Mr. Phillips' flank – Sweep of Glendaruel and Black Chaplet (Mr. Lowe), Smut of Gerwin, and Sloe o' Leck (Mr. Wheler), and the game was driven over to the guns from Clamp Wood and a fine field of roots to the left. On the right flank, Sloe o' Leck could not find a hare, which had been bowled over by Mr. Falcon, and both Smut of Gerwin and Shotover were put on the line of strong runners. The last named carried the scent down the field for a considerable distance to the hedge, but the pheasant then took to wing and had to be left. Smut of Gerwin had a long quest after a runner, but she was not successful, although her perseverance was commendable. On the other ground, Pitchford Marshall retrieved a brace of dead pheasants, his task being a light one, but no game was shot to the Labrador Flapper. A covert between Clamp Woods and the roots was then driven, and game came over in large numbers, especially as the edge of the plantation was reached by the beaters. Several runners were provided. Pitchford Marshall, disregarding dead birds, worked out his line both quickly and readily, but the bird was dead when he reached it. His retrieving and delivery to Downes could not have been better. Shotover also had a runner, but the pheasant, a hen, had not gone far and he retrieved it alive. Flapper, however, after picking up a bird which died in the field, was put on the line of two runners, the later one very strong, but after that which had run into covert, he hunted up the second one, which had run for a long distance into an adjoining field.

"A long walk on the Horstead road was taken before the next batch was Trialled, the Retrievers being Flapper, Sweep of Glendaruel, Sloe o' Leck, Pitchford Marshall and Busy Mite. A fine field of roots was walked up the left of the line, which was very long, being flanked by Mr. Maconochie and Mr. H. Jones. Both Busy Mite and Pitchford Marshall brought legged hares to hand alive, neither showing any sign of being hardmouthed, the retrieving of the young bitch in particular being good. Another crippled hare was hunted for nearly 200 yards by Flapper, and nothing could have been better than his style and readiness in bringing the game to hand, while, what was equally creditable, he received no assistance from his handler. Sloe o' Leck picked up a live rabbit during her quest for a strong runner, and she brought it to her handler without pinching, but she did not find the winged bird. Forward, Flapper could not make out the line of a running pheasant and more roots were then walked up, a pheasant which had been dropped from the adjoining ground being picked up both readily and cleanly by Sweep of Glendaruel. Sloe o' Leck was then put on the line of a winged pheasant, which had been noticed running along a newly ploughed drill. Sloe went out at a rare rate, and judged by her action, she was certainly on the line of the bird, but the pheasant got up and could not have been hardly hit judging by the flight. Sweep of Glendaruel also had a runner, but his search was only a short one. Sloe o' Leck was a little headstrong in going to fetch a dead bird without being ordered to do so, and Sweep of Glendaruel made the most of the chance which was offered him in tracking down an especially strong runner through the roots and across cleared ground into covert. All who were up felt his ability to make out the line meant that he could not very well miss the stake. His progress was watched with great interest. Feathering around the spot shown to him by Stewart he quickly struck the line and never raising his head he hunted through the roots and to within a few yards of the fence where the bird could be seen by the shooters, and actually heard calling. Sweep used neither his eyes nor his ears, depending entirely upon his nose, and when he had clearly indicated where the bird had gone he whipped round and ran back to Stewart. One section of the crowd declared that another bird had crossed the line, and that, instead of running heel, as he seemed to do, he had hunted the second pheasant back to the roots; but the judges gave him credit for his very good work.

"Then to luncheon at Stanning Hall Farm, Horstead, and afterwards the judges announced their awards as follows:

1. Mr. Lewis D. Wigan's Sweep of Glendaruel
2. Mr. M. Portal's Flapper
3. Lieut. Col. Cote's Pitchford Marshall
4. Mr. R. R. P. Wearing's Sloe o' Leck.

Busy Mite was Reserve and she was also awarded a Certificate of Merit, other Retrievers awarded Certificates of Merit being, Shotover, Dinham Smut, Royal River, Grouse of Riverside, Black Chaplet and Frenchway Sweep."

I note with interest, once again, that although Sloe o' Leck "went without being ordered to", she was awarded fourth place. Likewise, Grouse of Riverside ran in on the extreme right, Black Chaplet "could not be persuaded to swim the Bure", and Smut of Gerwin "had a long quest after a runner, but she was not successful". Despite these failings, all these dogs were awarded Certificates of Merit.

SCOTTISH FIELD TRIALS ASSOCIATION

The Scottish Field Trials Association held its first Field Trials at Yester-Haddington, East Lothian on 2nd & 3rd October 1907. Again, extensive coverage was given, and, once more, I have attempted to sift out the more interesting paragraphs:

"WEDNESDAY: Everything considered, the entry of twenty-one in the two stakes was good, the non-winners event, in which the entry was restricted to ten, being full, but four nominations were unallotted in the Open stake. It was, however, admitted that the support given to the association was satisfactory, and quite sufficient for a meeting which was intended to finish in two days. No Curlycoated Retriever was amongst those entered, but Mr. Jas Brown sent Longfield Lion, a good looking specimen of the Tweedside Variety, while not only Mr. Maurice Portal --whose Flapper is considered the best of his breed in the country – but the Duchess of Hamilton entered a Labrador Retriever, Dungavel Juno, and Lieut.-Col. Cote's Pitchford Monarch would easily pass for one of the same variety, for he is by Munden Sovereign out of Pitchford Monarch, a Flatcoated bitch.

"The special train left Edinburgh punctually, but the run of twenty miles into Haddingtonshire was a slow one, taking over an hour, and, in consequence, we were late in arriving at Gifford.

"Campbell, the head gamekeeper on the Yester estate, had planned out the ground to be shot over especially well, and in that very important essential he had received great assistance from Mr. C. A. Phillips who has been so closely associated with Spaniel Trials since they were begun on the English side of the border, and, although the shooting on some of the beats was a little loose, there was game, both fur and feather, even in a year when the partridge crop at Yester is the lightest for many seasons. The carefully mapped-out programme of the day was, therefore, fulfilled to the letter, and no Field Trials ever were launched in such favourable conditions.

"The head of the field was now reached, and after Burnside Beaut had retrieved a rabbit, a move was made to fresh ground, Bell's Wood being driven and two sides covered by the shooters. Mr. E. W. H. Blagg flanking the right hand side of the line. The Retrievers

The Scottish Field Trials Association Retriever Trials at Yester-Haddington, East Lothian. 1: Lieutenant. Col. Coles's Pitchford Mart brings in an unshot, young cock pheasant. 2: A line of guns. 3: Sir Arthur Orde waiting for a shot. 4: Over a stone wall to a fresh beat. 5: In the cornfields. 6: Mr. E. Turner's Park Darkie with a partridge. 7: A Tweedside Retriever. 8: The Duchess of Hamilton's Dungavel Juno bringing in a partridge.

making up the first batch of six were recalled and tried for steadiness to the gun. None showed the least trace of unsteadiness and Longfield Lion, when sent in quest of a partridge that had dropped over the railway line, brought it to hand very readily. Dungavel Juno also had her chance, and she brought both a partridge and a pheasant to hand readily, a while before leaving the ground, she also retrieved a big hare which had been stopped on the right flank. Another move was now made to New Hall, a walk of only half a mile, but along a beautiful line of country. The birds were driven from ground on which the stooks were still standing, for the harvest in Haddingtonshire is especially late this

Volume One (1903-1908)

Autumn. Very few birds came over, and the shooters then lined the hedge running at right angles to the road. Several coveys came over, and Dungavel Juno, Sandhoe Juno and Toboggan were given opportunities of retrieving. All worked well, and, as it was now long after one o'clock an adjournment was made to luncheon which was taken at Wood Head Farm.

"A move to another drive bordering the Long Newton road and past the Gifford golf course and rabbit warren brought the shooters to another drive, and the batch of Retrievers was made up as follows: Young Sweep of Glendaruel, Longfield Lion, Dungavel Juno, Burnside Beaut, Pitchford Monarch and Park Darkie. Plenty of birds came over, although the first flight went across the road instead of towards the shooters, and the single bird of the covey, which was in range, could not be stopped. On the right flank Park Darkie retrieved a bird very nicely, but, put on a stale line, which Pitchford Monarch had failed to make out, she had no better luck, although, like Downe's charge, she was very persevering.

"The light was now beginning to fail, and, as a final Trial, the same ground – Meg's Hill – was walked in line the opposite way, the following Retrievers forming the last batch: Keir Juno, Burnside Beaut, Toboggan, Cadzow Nell, Park Darkie, and Sandhoe Juno. Keir Juno and Park Darkie both had dead partridges, and the first named also retrieved a hare very cleverly, while Burnside Beaut worked out the line of a runner, and, after the remainder had retrieved dead birds, it was decided to stop for the day, the judges announcing, that, although they did not intend to have any of the Retrievers in that stake down again, they could not make up their minds as to the winners, and the awards would not be made until the morrow, when the meet was at Yester Mains, a mile and a half from Gifford railway station, at half-past ten o'clock."

"THURSDAY: Musselburgh Races proved to be a powerful counter attraction today, and although several new arrivals from various parts of the border country brought the crowd to nearly the same dimensions as on the first day, neither the Marchioness of Tweeddale nor any members of the Yester house-party put in an appearance.

"The first business of the day on arrival at Yester Mains was the announcement of the awards in the non-winners stake. They were as follows:

1. Mr. Andrew Pearson's Burnside Beaut
2. Mr. Thos Scott's Toboggan
3. Mr. Maurice Portal's Sandhoe Juno
4. Capt. A. Stirling's Keir Juno.

All the remainder were awarded Certificates of Merit.

"The Retrievers in the first batch of the Open stake were: Cadzow Nell (Owner), Keir Ivy (Foster), Keir Juno (MacNaughton), Pitchford Mart (Downes), Busy Magnet (Owner), and Dungavel Juno (Alexander). A fine field of oats in stooks was walked in line, and after a big covey had got up out of range several partridges, which broke back from a second covey, were brought down. Keir Juno did not find the one of which she was sent in quest, but Pitchford Mart retrieved her partridge, and on her right Cadzow Nell first hunted up a runner and brought it to hand alive and then retrieved a dead bird very clearly and readily. A large turnip field was then walked up, and Pitchford Mart was put on the line of a legged hare, but she showed little inclination to hold the line until another hare which was afoot moved on. Then she settled down and brought her hare to hand very quickly. Another, bowled over by Lord Arthur Hay, was retrieved by Keir Ivy, and equally good work of the same character was done by Busy Magnet. Partridges which dropped some way ahead, were gathered by Keir Ivy and her kennel mate Juno, the last named, however, not being so quick a finder as she might have been, but her retrieving was very clean. Nearing the boundary fence, one partridge out of a fairly big covey was killed and dropped on stubble some distance ahead. Busy Magnet gathered it, but only after she

The Retriever Society's Field Trials at Rushmore, Wilts, in 1907. Above left: Mr. W. Atkins's Mona (first prize). Above right: Duchess of Hamilton's Dungavel Juno (second prize). Left: Mr. H. Reginald Cooke's Champion Grouse of Riverside (third prize, plus a special prize awarded for the best-looking dog).

had been encouraged by her owner.

"On higher ground, both Pitchford Mart and Dungavel Juno had easy tasks of it in very thick covert, from which three braces of pheasants got up – and had to be left – before partridges were walked up. Busy Magnet retrieved the only bird which was brought down on the right flank, and Dungavel Juno retrieved a fine hare in capital style, using her nose well and ranging her ground very carefully.

"We had along walk of nearly a mile to another field of turnips at Long Yester before the Retrievers were called upon to do any work. On the right, Park Darkie brought a dead partridge to hand at a gallop, and Sloe o' Leck retrieved a big hare, while further in the covert both Busy Mite and Dungavel Juno made the best use of opportunities which were given to them of proving their aptitude for retrieving. Park Darkie brought a legged hare to hand, carrying it especially well, although she was rather reluctant to give it up, and then Busy Mite and Jordieland Bess did all that was asked of them cleanly and readily, and, after being warned against chasing a hare, Dungavel Juno hunted up a runner, but it had not travelled far. A fine piece of work was then done by Young Sweep of Glendaruel, who took up the line of an especially strong runner, and carried it for some distance through a plantation, holding it until he came up with the bird. His return was smart, and he delivered the partridge to Stewart without the least hesitancy.

"Keir Ivy was not very obedient, and Young Sweep of Glendaruel pinched a hare in its seat – but brought it to hand alive, when on his way to retrieve a dead partridge dropped by Capt. Fyfe-Jamieson. He gathered the bird and was then sent in quest of another, but it had to be left, after quite a long hunt. Busy Magnet then lost all chance of winning she had possessed by failing to pick up a bird and chasing a hare for a considerable distance. This good ground being exhausted, another batch

The Retriever Society's Field Trials at Rushmore, Wilts, in 1907. Top left: The judges: M. Gortal, W. Arkwright, and F. M. Remnant. The other photographs show spectators, guns and handlers at the Trials.

was made up of the following: Sloe o' Leck, Young Sweep of Glendaruel, Busy Mite, Jordieland Bess, Keir Ivy and Cadzow Nell. A field of oats was driven, the shooters lining one of the banks of Gifford Water, a most picturesque spot, the Lammermoor Hills forming a charming background. It was now five o'clock, and the light was already beginning to fail. Several coveys came over and Busy Mite found a brace of birds and a hare, which were on the other side of the burn, while both Sloe o' Leck and Young Sweep of Glendaruel did well on the same ground but neither they nor Cadzow Nell could hit the line of a hare, which seemed to have been stopped in some whins.

"The awards were then made as follows:
1. Capt. A. Stirling's Keir Ivy
2. Mr. R. R. P. Wearing's Sloe o' Leck
3. Equal: Mr. Lewis D. Wigan's, Young Sweep of Glendaruel and Mr. Ernest Turner's Park Darkie.

Certificates of Merit were awarded to Cadzow Nell, Keir Juno, Pitchford Mart, Dungavel Juno, Jordieland Bess and Busy Mite."

DIFFERENT BREEDS

By 1907, the debate surrounding the different qualities of the working and show-bred lines of the different Retriever breeds was raging. It occupies many pages in the first volume of Mr. Cooke's scrapbooks, each one filled with articles and correspondence about the merits of the different breeds of Retriever. One such example of a letter, written by Mr. Cooke himself, was published in The Field, in December 1907, under a regularly appearing column entitled 'Working and Show Retrievers':

"Sir, – Much has been written on this subject of late, and opinions naturally differ among owners of the various breeds of Retrievers. Although holding a most decided opinion myself, I have no wish to enter in to any discussion with the supporters of either

H. R. Cooke's first dog, Spot.

show or working dogs on a subject, which has already been well thrashed out. Far better drop all fancies and come to facts. In order to arrive at actual facts it is interesting to examine the pedigrees of the various Retrievers that have been successful this year at the public field trials. In giving the appended list of these dogs, space will not admit of extended pedigrees, so I have merely given the name of the sire of each of the successful competitors. 'The Stud Book' will supply all further details."

The letter continues and lists all the prizewinners from the Scottish Field Trial Association's Trials, the Retriever Society's Trials and the Kennel Club's Retriever Trials; all of which I have given details of previously, so I felt no need to list them all again.

The letter continues:

Volume One (1903-1908)

"A glance at this list will show at once to what a great extent these winners of Working Trials are bred from the best show-bench dogs of the day, and this is more remarkable when it is to be remembered that all the public field trials are open to every kind of Retriever, no dog being barred, provided that he is a Retriever 'of sorts' and that his owner can secure a nomination.

"Moreover, a perusal of the cards of entry at each of the Field Trials will reveal the fact that (excluding Labradors and Curlycoated dogs), quite four-fifths of the competitors are pure bred Flatcoated Retrievers – some winners themselves on the show bench, and others descended from the best prize-winning sires. Other strains of Flatcoated Retrievers, if they exist, are conspicuous by their absence. Surely, these facts should be somewhat convincing to those who doubt all analogy between a show-bench and working Retriever.

"It may be said, and is said by some, that the best working dogs of today are inferior to the old-fashioned Retrievers. This may be true, but it has yet to be proved, and I would remind all owners who possess the descendants of the old-fashioned breed that the public Field Trials are open to all comers; and that there is nothing to prevent them from competing with, and defeating, if good enough, the present race of 'working-cum-show-bench' Retrievers. From experience, I can assure them that these Trials are conducted with the utmost fairness and impartiality, and that the greatest pains are taken by the judges to sort out the best dogs, whatever the breeding may be.

"I am unable to comment on the pedigrees of the Labrador Retrievers who have done a good share of winning at the Field Trials this year, as I have had no experience of this breed, but nothing would surprise me less than to find that they are as full of 'blue blood' as their Flatcoated brethren.
H. REGINALD COOKE"

Other letters, concerned with the same subject matter and appearing in the same magazine column, read as follows:

"Sir, – I have read your Kennel Notes and the correspondence with interest, especially as

The Retriever Trials of 1907. Above: H. R. Cooke and Grouse moving away to low-lying land. Right: Mr. Maurice Portal and Flapper, winner of the All-aged Stake at the Retriever Trials.

31

I have owned Flatcoated show-bred dogs of Darenth and other blood, and also some Labrador Retrievers; but if Mr. H. R. Cooke is correct in his contention, how is it that his kennel and other large kennels of show-bench dogs of the Flat or Curlycoated breed, do not produce endless Field Trial winners? It should be a certainty for them with the blue blood of generations behind them to help them in their work and the extra qualifications they have from show-bench training. It is, of course, possible to have a show-bench dog and a worker, but I would say that 90 per cent of the show-bred dogs would prove moderate performers in Field Trials, and I think I underestimate it. Why should it be otherwise? We breed from show dogs for looks, and looks alone, and with the eternal hope that the offspring may be a show dog. If fate decrees that it does not have the necessary looks then it is probably sold out, and then gets more chance of a sporting education and may do well in the field or at Trials. Its brother, who perchance has show looks, may be broken to a limited extent (if we have the means and opportunities), but is not broken and used for sport alone, because shows intervene, and our show dogs coat must shine and must not be ragged or torn from brambles and thorns (supposing always the dog would face them). The dog is not allowed to go in the water much or it would spoil his coat if the show was near. Perhaps the dog becomes a Champion in time, and, as such, is looked up to and is used by breeders. From a working point this dog has not had the proverbial 'dogs chance' of even developing the natural instincts he may have in him; he does not know what perseverance is or what pluck is in facing icy cold water or thick brambles, or half the elementary things the true sporting dog knows, and when this is carried on for a few generations we get what we so often see now, and what is after all only what we might expect.

"Another thing that shakes ones show-bench belief is that many Flatcoated bitches of ancient lineage have been put to Labrador dogs. Why? Is it that show-bench breeding has dwarfed their dash and stamina? Is it that the show-bench type fails to satisfy the shooting man and that he is forced to fall back on the non-show Labrador for help?
MAURICE PORTAL"

"Sir, – The correspondence which has arisen in 'The Field' appears to have developed into a discussion as to the merits of different breeds of Retrievers. I am not in a position to judge whether or not your correspondents who state that Labradors are more hard-mouthed than other breeds are correct. If they are, then it is the strongest argument yet produced against making them a show breed. If they are kept as a useful sporting dog, any hard-mouthed ones will be put down, and they will trouble us no more, but if they become a show breed you may have a hard-mouthed Champion of dog shows, and as such bred off by the unfortunate ignorant man, who has no chance of knowing otherwise.
OBSERVER"

These letters led Mr. Cooke to respond with another letter of his own"

"Sir, – I quite expected that my recent letter in your columns would call forth some criticism, and I have read the replies of your correspondents with much interest. My last letter was a simple statement of facts and I studiously avoided any expression of my own opinion, which might be liable to misconstruction. I think the mistake nearly everyone makes in discussing this subject is to go to extremes and draw too hard and fast line between the show-bred dog and the working dog. In many cases they are one and the same animal. But supposing they are not, and the show-bench dog lacks working qualities, and the working dog show-bench qualification, is it beyond the bounds of possibility that the two may not be brought together?

"My answer to this is emphatically no, and this is what many others beside myself have been trying to accomplish for many years.

Surely, if such a dog can be produced he gives much greater pleasure to a gentleman and far more profit to a keeper than the yellow-eyed, bandy-legged, cow-hocked, bad-coated 'miseries' that we used to see formerly!

"One thing I candidly admit in connection with the modern Flatcoated Retriever, i.e. that he is greatly in need of an outcross, although it is really wonderful how he has stood so much in breeding. The late Mr. Shirley some years ago bought a dog called Plough Chain, which he renamed Rightaway, and wrote me at the time that he had at last discovered an outcross, but he was doomed to disappointment, for he soon found that this dog's pedigree ran back in the third or fourth generation to the original strain. I myself have had similar experiences, and the present race of Retrievers has 'caught on' to such an extent that it is almost impossible to find a dog unrelated to them in any kennel.

If I may be pardoned for one illusion to my own kennel, I would like to mention that I bought such dogs as Minuet, Wimpole Peter, Worsley Bess, Rocket of Riverside, and Sandy of Riverside from gamekeepers who had bred them, and their late owners will, I know, bear me out in the assertion that they were all good working Retrievers. I think some of your correspondents would be rather surprised if they saw the scores of letters I received from all parts of the British Isles testifying to the working qualities of the modern Flatcoated Retrievers – this, too, from men who have no interest whatever in exhibiting. As long as members of this strain continue to win at public Field Trials, they must have my vote. When they are defeated I may alter my opinion, but not before.

"One word as to Labradors. I see one of your correspondents says that he has heard that 75 per cent of these dogs are hard in the mouth. I am unable to substantiate this, but I do know that on two large estates in Shropshire, no less than nine Labradors have been destroyed during the last two years on account of this failing.

H. REGINALD COOKE"

Mr. Cooke's letter seems to have called forth more replies, such as these:

"Sir,- I quite expected that Mr. Cooke's letter would have silenced those who assert that a handsome dog cannot be a good worker. I have bred Flatcoated Retrievers for several years, and, like many others, prefer to shoot over a good-looking one. I do not possess in my kennel a dog that is not a good worker, and all of them over 18 months have won prizes on the bench at the leading shows. As regards Mr. Cooke's kennel, one only has to notice the number of nominations he applies for at the various Trials to be convinced that he has plenty of first-class workers in his possession, and I should have thought that this alone would have borne out his statements. Surely, the results of the Field Trials this year, as Mr. Cooke has pointed out, prove, beyond any shadow of doubt, that dogs can be first-rate workers as well as capable of winning prizes in the best company. One has only to attend the annual sales at Aldridge's and compare the price paid for a handsome dog with good character to that paid for an indifferent-looking dog with a similar character to show that the combined qualities are still in great demand, and very rightly so. If we are to do away with shows, what is to happen to looks? Surely the object of showing dogs is to preserve their good points, to allow breeders the chance of seeing what dogs are best for their requirements and of finding out where these dogs are. In my opinion, the type of Flatcoated Retriever is much superior and better than it was ten years ago, and this has been brought about solely by the encouragement given by show committees. Your correspondent who states that show dogs are faulty in the legs can hardly have attended many of the leading shows of late. If critics would confine their attention to the Curlycoated variety, and leave the Flatcoated breed alone, there might be reason for their statements, but the last named have undoubtedly proved that they can combine the qualities of show and work.

ERNEST TURNER"

"Sir, – Mr. Cooke's letter in your issue of 22nd December only strengthens my previous arguments. If Flatcoated Retrievers are badly in want of fresh blood, what is the reason? Simply that they have been bred for the last twenty or thirty years with one sole object, namely show type. The same thing applies to nearly all breeds of dogs that the Kennel Club has taken up. I will not defend Labradors with regard to some strains having a tendency to hardness of mouth, but does Mr. Cooke think that dog shows will remedy this fault? If he does, I can assure him that he is grossly mistaken. No. Let the Labrador, with all his faults, remain in the hands of men who will use him for work only.
LABRADOR"

"Sir, – The controversy which began as the advisability of showing Labradors has widened into the very important question whether dog shows have been harmful to the sporting instincts of dogs. Speaking generally, I think most sportsmen will agree that they have, not excluding the Peterborough Hound show. But are we prepared to exclude sporting dogs from our shows? Everyone likes to have a good-looking dog, provided he is good at his work, and no one worthy of the name of a sportsman would think of breeding from a dog merely because he has won a prize at a show, without knowing whether he was any good at his work. The whole question is a difficult and important one, and I hope your columns will remain open to further correspondence on the subject. I had the rather thankless honour of judging the Labradors at the recent Kennel Club show, and I found it very difficult to hit upon a type of show dog. I endeavoured to give the prizes to well-coupled, comparatively short-legged active dogs, with intelligent heads as that is the type I have seen working the best in the quick, untiring manner peculiar to Labradors; I had no show type to guide me as far as I have been able to see, so that now seems to be the time to cease showing Labradors if it has to be done.
CHARLES. T. PART"

By February of the following year, 1908, the debate was still ongoing, as can be seen from letters published in The Field at the time:

"While being delighted to see the Labrador Flapper, an easy winner of the only stake in which he ran, for his owner, Mr. Maurice Portal, was judging at the Rushmore meeting, and was shooting when he might have run his fine worker in Scotland. We were no less pleased when, at the same meeting, Longshaw Bruce, a blue-blooded Flatcoated dog, bred, broken and handled by Ashton, a working gamekeeper, spread-eagled the field, to use a simile which will be well understood, in the junior stake.

"Flapper gained his win by the clever way he winded a bird which had dropped on the banks of the River Bure opposite the shooters, and nothing better than the way he took to the water, quartered his ground, and, making the best use of his nose, gathered his bird, and then returned across the river to his owner, had been seen at any of the Trials. He not only covered himself with glory, but he gave his breed a big lift, and Labradors are certain to be more common at next season's trials than has yet been the case.

"Flapper, it may be added, has won bench honours in a district where Labradors have been more popular than either Flat, or Curlycoated Retrievers for many years. He was, however, broken and worked before he was shown, and, broadly it is the failure of quite two thirds of the breeders of Flatcoated Retrievers to adopt the same method which has brought about opposition to shows, and both dogs and men which are associated with them, from those who keep Retrievers only for work.

"Mr. H. Reginald Cooke, Mr. C. C. Eley, Mr. E. W. Blagg, Mr. Ernest Turner, Mr. Lewis Wigan, Lieut.-Col. Cotes, and many other men have supported the Trials by entering Retrievers of the bluest blood, Mr. Cooke, indeed, winning the £20 which has been offered anonymously for some years to the winner of the Open stake at the Gundog

League meeting, providing he (a bitch being ineligible) had won three first prizes at the five leading shows, with Grouse of Riverside, one of the most handsome dogs of the day. If men of the stamp of those which are mentioned, break their Flatcoated Retrievers first and show them afterwards, it is not unreasonable to suggest that the Labrador men might do the same.

"Mr. Holland-Hibbert's warning about the selection of the judges being borne in mind. That shows can ruin dogs is not sound argument; it is the appointment of unqualified men as judges which has done so much to spoil the working characters of some of our best sporting varieties. That the establishment of shows was for the good of the dog can be proved by a visit to the Agricultural Hall next week, or Manchester next month."

MR. COOKE'S RETRIEVERS

After HRC's written opinions on the merits of the working and show-bred Retriever, it is interesting to examine the dogs produced as a result of his own breeding programmes. This excerpt, taken from an article titled 'A Visit to Mr. H. R. Cooke's Retriever Kennels at Nantwich, Cheshire', and published in the January 1908 edition of The Field, does just that:

"Mr. Reginald Cooke is one of those exhibitors who do not make mistakes. Obviously, if one wishes to win prizes at shows, one must find out the taste of the judge and supply them with their particular fancies. This needs a large kennel, for there is no general and absolute agreement between show judges of what exactly a Retriever should be like, although most of them probably subscribe to the idea that he should pretty near be like Mr. Cooke's High Legh Blarney, for this dog has won all before him since Mr. Cooke became his purchaser after the death of Lieut.-Col. Cornwall Legh, who bred him. For a long time the last-named breeder, along with Mr. Farquharson of

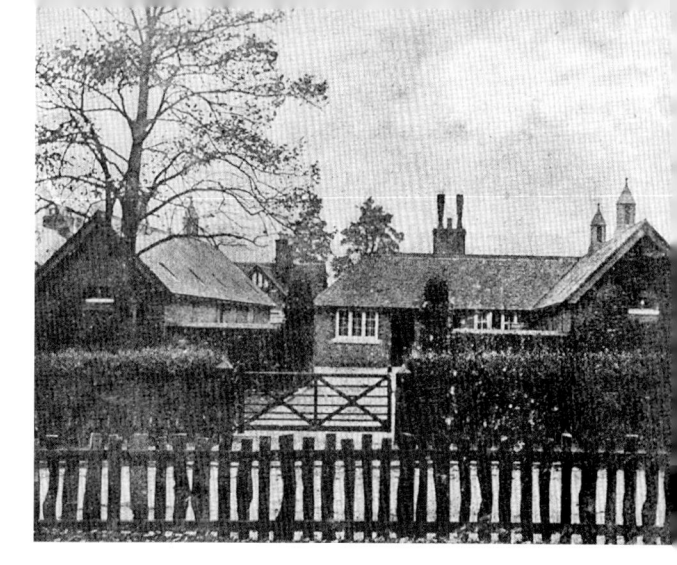

Top: Mr. Cooke's stables and kennels at Nantwich. Above: Jimmy Galway's Terriers, a photo given to him by Henry Cooke.

Dorset and Mr. Shirley of Ettington Park, between them had the best of the show successes. Mr. Cooke now supplies the place of all three for from the show judge's point of view no one has ever had the same exhibition superiority of kennel as Mr. Cooke has now. He has not, however, succeeded in breeding many of his winners, but at very high prices buys such dogs as are sure to make names for themselves. One of his first bold purchases was Wimpole Peter, a dog that made the record sale price up to that time, but holds no record for these later times for High Legh Blarney cost about twice as much. Mr. Cooke has won with teams so often that the Challenge Cups meant to be for perpetual competition are now finding permanent resting sites in seclusion at Riverside, near Nantwich. At the last Crystal Palace show, for instance, Mr. Cooke's team was invincible in the ring, I believe for the fourth time in competition for a particular cup; and the Birmingham authorities took the wiser course of asking Mr. Cooke to judge, which made the prizes much more open for competition than they ever can be when this collector of the fancies of all the judges dominates the ring with his numbers. As a matter of fact, large kennels are not in the interests of the breed. The late Mr. Shirley kept an enormous kennel, perhaps sixty, and without having work for six. Even if the majority were broken, this implies that they were never wise with experience, and there is little doubt that it is far better to breed from hard-worked dogs in the interests, not only of constitutions, but also of the brains, that, by the help of the nose, recover difficult, wounded game.

"Mr. Cooke's stud dogs have been rather successful in producing winners at Field Trials. His Wimpole Peter was the sire of Pitchford Marshall, an excellent dog. But such successes as these must be expected when the dam's side has been bred for work in the same sporting family for three-quarters of a century, as was the case here. Those who look at the matter broadly, say that as long as show dogs monopolise the majority of the stud fees, as they have in the past, it is no great credit for their offspring to win, since there are no others bred to run against them. High Legh Blarney has also sired a puppy winner at Retriever Trials, this one having been bred and broken by a gamekeeper of the Duke of Rutland, and naturally from a mother kept entirely for work. It is a great pity that the conditions of the Trials debar Slip Retrievers, because what breeders want to know about stud dogs is not their breaking, which can be applied by any good man, but their natural qualities, which can be created by no breaker but have to be bred in the bone. The bright particular star of Mr. Cooke's kennel is Grouse of Riverside, which has taken first prizes at principal shows, and has also won first at the Retriever Society's Trials for Retrievers, when there was very bad scent, and every dog in the stake that had runners to find, lost some of them, and Grouse was no exception.

"Mr. Cooke is a past president of the Retriever Society, and has a difficult task in his attempt to combine show and Field Trial winning in the same animals. The principal difficulty consists in the fact that show judges generally prefer a type that is neither active in mind or body. On the other hand, Field Trials are influencing the production of, and the admiration for, dogs that are both. Of course, in the end, the confidence of sportsmen will be given to the small and active sorts. There will be six public Retriever Trials this year, and, of course, the more there are the greater will be the insistence for Field Trial winning types and blood in Retrievers."

MORE SALES
Almost at the end of volume one, Mr. Cooke has pasted in more cuttings regarding sales of well-known dogs. Of particular interest is the article dated July 3rd 1908, which, as before, is titled 'A Sale of Sporting Dogs at Aldridge's'. Included in this sale were some of Mr. Cooke's dogs, and the bidding was as follows:

"The keenest bidding of the afternoon was seen when Mr. H. Reginald Cooke's Retrievers were reached, and there was a bona-fide bid of 260 guineas for Rocket of Riverside, a Kennel Club Champion, and a good dog in the field, but his owner did not allow him to go at that price, which is one of the highest ever offered for a Retriever at a public sale. Sandy of Riverside, however, was sold for 25 guineas, and an offer of 164 guineas for Kelpie was accepted, while Seldom, a son of High Legh Blarney, seemed to be cheap at 26 guineas. A good-looking bitch, Blossom of Riverside, brought in 25 guineas, and the remainder changed hands at prices ranging from 5 guineas to 15 guineas."

The last entry in Volume one regards a small publication written by Mr. H. Reginald Cooke, called Short Notes on Choosing and

Left: Cheshire, Shropshire and North Wales Retriever Trials at Brogyntyn, Oswestry, October 1910. Pictured are Mr. Goode and Kestrel.
Above: Mr. Cooke's Retrievers on the benches.

Breaking a Retriever. He had obviously sent a copy of the article to various newspapers and magazines, who all obliged by printing a review of the booklet in their respective publications. The one I have chosen was published in Illustrated Kennel News in 1908:

"Mr. H. Reginald Cooke, the doyen of the Flatcoated Retriever, possessing, as he does, the most powerful kennel of the variety ever got together in the United Kingdom, has sent us a little booklet he has just published entitled Short Notes on Choosing and Breaking a Retriever. In his letter to us Mr. Cooke states that he wrote the 'notes' in the first instance solely for the guide of 'walkers' of his own puppies; but the information and hints on the bringing up and breaking of young Retrievers have proved so practical and successful that he has often been asked to give them a wider circulation, and has, at length, consented. Mr. Cooke does not claim exclusive knowledge of the art of breaking the Retriever – far from it – nor that his work is a complete treatise on the subject, as stated in the preface, in which he says:

"My object is to produce a small guide to those who find pleasure in this most delightful occupation, by condensing into a handy form the generally accepted rules and adding thereto some valuable hints I have, from time to time, received by the close observation of methods adopted by a few (alas, how few there are!), excellent handlers, both amateur and professional."

"We can confidently recommend the work to all owners of sporting Retrievers, and even Spaniels required to do Retrievers' work, as a most practical and rational little work, the proceeds of the sale, we are pleased to note, are to be handed over to the R.S.P.C. to Children. The price of Short Notes is one shilling, and the Publishers are Messrs. William Neill and Sons, Mornington Street, Manchester."

I am very fortunate to have a signed copy of Short notes on Choosing and Breaking a Retriever. It did, however, cost rather more than one shilling! It was a very welcome surprise present from my husband, who saw it advertised in a sale of antique books!

2 EXTRACTS FROM VOLUME TWO (1908-1911)

We begin the second journal with a report of the second Scottish Field Trial, held at Knockbrex over three days in October 1908.

KNOCKBREX, 1908

There were three stakes; Open, Non-Winners, and the Gamekeeper's stakes. The card for the Open stake consisted of fifteen dogs, and was made up of seven Flatcoated bitches, six Flatcoated dogs and two Labrador bitches. The Non-Winners stake comprised one Flatcoated bitch, seven Flatcoated dogs and two Labrador bitches. The Gamekeepers Stake was made up of six Flatcoated dogs and one Flatcoated bitch. This stake was restricted to bona-fide gamekeepers only.

The Trials were described at great length, in much the same style as the earlier entries contained in the scrapbooks. However, from October 1908 onwards, a new dimension appears in the Field Trial reports. An extended pedigree of the winner is given, as can be seen in this, the final paragraph describing the proceedings of the Open stake:

"An adjournment was made for luncheon very late, for it was after half past two o'clock. On our way, Lubra of Glendaruel was sent in search of a dead partridge, which had dropped in a water course, and she brought it to hand in capital style. After luncheon the awards in the Open stake were made as follows:-

1. Lieut.-Col. Cote's Pitchford Monarch (Flatcoat dog)
2. Mr. Lewis D. Wigan's Sweep of Glendaruel (Flatcoat dog)
3. Mr. Ernest Turner's Park Darkie (Flatcoat bitch)
4. Mr. T. Scott's Toboggan (Flatcoat dog)
5. Mr. R. R. P. Wearing's Sloe o' Leck (Flatcoat bitch).

Busy Mite was Reserve, and Certificates of Merit were awarded to Highland Daer (Flatcoat dog), Sam of Dalblair (Flatcoat dog) and Denne Jetsam (Labrador bitch).

The extended pedigree of the winner is as follows:

PITCHFORD MONARCH	Munden Sovereign (Labrador)	Unknown	
		Unknown	
	Pitchford Mermaid	Monk	Not recorded in K.C. Books.
		Pitchford Mina	Not recorded in K.C. Books.

Pedigree of Pitchford Monarch.

The last paragraph for the Non-Winner's stake reads as follows:

"After the weeding out of the Retrievers in the Non-Winners stake on Wednesday, there was not much to be done on the following day, and only a small crowd saw the meeting out, the bulk of the work being done on the Chapelton side of Knockbrex. The judges awarded the prizes as follows:

1. Mr. W. M'Call's Highland Daer (Flatcoat dog)
2. Mr. T. Scot's Lambton Park Carlo (Flatcoat dog)
3. Mr. W. C. Alexander's Sam of Dalblair (Flatcoat dog)
4. Col. Malcolm's Poltalloch Drake (Flatcoat dog).

Logan Lorna (Labrador bitch) was Reserve, and a Certificate of Merit was awarded to Faskally Sam (Flatcoat dog).

The extended pedigree of the winner is as follows:-

HIGHLAND DAER	Sam	Sailor	Not recorded in K.O. Books
		Nell	Not recorded in K.O. Books
	Dess	Bruce	Not recorded in K.C. Books
		Jess	Not recorded in K.O. Books

The extended pedigree of Highland Daer.

The Gamekeeper's stake was written up very briefly, with only a list of the results, as follows:

"The winners in the stake for dogs owned by bona-fide gamekeepers were:-
1. Mr. T. Scott's Toboggan (Flatcoat dog)
2. Mr. W. M'Call's Highland Daer (Flatcoat dog)
3. Mr. W. C. Alexander's Sam of Dalblair (Flatcoat dog)

Wakeful (Flatcoat bitch) was Reserve, and Cadzow Comit (Flatcoat dog) and Carscallen Chief (Flatcoat dog) were awarded Certificates of Merit.

The extended pedigree of the winner is appended:

TOBOGGAN	Howdene Darkie	Darwin	Darenth Handeford Trace
		Howdene Meg	Young Shot Lady Grace
	Bertha	Bob	Not recorded in K.C. Books
		Ruth	Not recorded in K.C. Books

The extended pedigree of Toboggan.

Although three different stakes are mentioned, I note that the Gamekeepers stake must be run in conjunction with the other stakes but with a separate list of awards to be given in addition to those already won. For example: Toboggan, who won the Gamekeeper's stake, was also fourth in the Open stake; Highland Daer, who was second in the Gamekeeper's stake, also won the Non-Winners stake; and Sam of Dalblair was third in the Gamekeeper's stake, third in the Non-Winners stake and was awarded a Certificate of Merit in the Open stake. How could he run in the Open stake and the Non-Winners at the same time? Whichever way the event was run, Sam of Dalblair obviously had a good three days, with awards in all three stakes!

TRIBUTE TO HRC

In December 1908, the following article appeared in The Field:

"Probably the largest breeder and most successful exhibitor of Flatcoated Retrievers, to wit, Mr. H. Reginald Cooke, has drawn more attention to the extremity to which many other breeders have gone in their attempts to produce long narrow heads. Every practical shooter knows that if a dog is expected to be good in the field he must possess a skull large enough to contain an average amount of brains, hence it is that this eminent authority taboos such as are either too Houndy or too much like a Borzoi in head. That his contention is right will be readily admitted by all practical shooting men."

THE RETRIEVER TRIALS DEBATE
Following the debate about Retriever head shapes, a great deal of correspondence headed 'Retriever Trials and their Conditions' appears in the journals. The instigating letter reads as follows:

"Sir, – In reviewing the work of the Retrievers at the three Open meetings this season, I feel sure even a very casual observer must have been struck by the uncertainties of the game. A dog that did not even get into the money at one place succeeded in carrying off the chief prize at another, and so on. Now, surely this is not as it should be, for a really good Retriever ought to be able to run through all the chief stakes in one year; but in the very variable conditions with which the competitors have to contend and the still more variable ideals of the men who so kindly act as judges, this is at present impossible. What is now needed is a scale of points for judges to go by. At present we have one set awarding prizes to dogs and another condemning them for the same things which the others thought so highly of. Too much attention is paid to whether or not a dog gets a runner without ever taking into account such a thing as a time allowance. For instance, take the case of a dog who has the good luck to be put on the line of a runner two or three minutes after the bird falls. He gets it all right, and is alluded to the sky. Now take the other side. A dog has to sit still until the end of a drive perhaps for three quarters of an hour, and then he is asked to get a runner which was seen to fall at the beginning of the drive. If he fails, which is more than likely, he is blamed, and if by any chance he finds the runner, he gets no more credit than the other competitor. Retrievers often fail on a bird that has been long down for various reasons, and a dog sometimes has tried far harder on an unsuccessful quest than his more fortunate rival, whose runner had not got the chance to get so far away because of wire netting or some other obstacle.

"The instinct of a Retriever teaches him to hunt for the gun, and therefore no dog will do his best when he is called into the line and asked to do something unless he has been in touch with the shooting. The failure of so many really good dogs at the water test at Horstead the other day will be fresh in the memory of most of us. Had these same dogs been on the bank of that river and the handlers shooting the birds for their own dogs, we would have seen something very different. Then if a dog will not cross the river for game killed by his handler the remedy is obvious. There is also the case of the dog who is lucky to have a nice line to hunt in the open. He may do it well; but take the other side. Again there is a runner in covert; the start and the finish are all that can be seen. Does the latter get as much credit as the former? I doubt it. This is now the third year of the Kennel Club trials, and I consider the work as a whole the poorest of the series, simply because there was too much standing still and not enough walking in line.

"The most sporting meeting that has ever been held, and the one at which you could really find out what dogs were capable of, and that under the strongest temptation, was the Scottish meeting on the Knockbrex estate in October. The organisation there was perfect, and such covert and such variety of tests I have never seen south of the border. Owners and handlers making excuses for their dogs, that they do not allow them to carry this, that, or the other thing is all nonsense. No dog has any business to be at a Field Trial unless he will carry anything he is told to do. If he deliberately chases and brings back something which is not in the game list he ought to pay the penalty. That puppies should not carry fur is another of the cries we hear a good deal of nowadays, I would humbly suggest that in future we each keep a dog for every different kind of game we shoot – one for partridges, another for pheasants, and so on, and label each one accordingly.

"Why – oh! why – do we not conduct Retriever Trials the same way that we would an ordinary day's shooting at home? For instance, if I have a bird down I do not stop all my friends from shooting until I gather it. Oh dear no! I send my dog for it if it is a runner, and he goes on and gets it, paying no attention to the shooting. Of course heaps of dead birds falling are rather confusing for any dog on a bare field at the end of a wood, but why do the judges not cast their two dogs about to the fall of the runners is more than I can understand, for that is what we keep men and dogs doing at all the big shoots. The dog's individual chances of distinguishing himself would be greater and the competitor's chances more nearly equal.

"In at least one of our Retriever societies there is a rule which says appearance must be taken into consideration. I am afraid this is a rule much more honoured in the breach than in the observance. Now, if Retriever Trials are to do a tithe of the good they were first intended to do, sooner or later this rule must be enforced because we are now supposed to look to the winners at these meetings for our future sires and dams, and if we weigh them in the balance and find them wanting we shall not be getting very much forward. Labradors have been very much in evidence lately, but I do not think it will be permanent; in fact, from what I know of the breed it will not, because as we become more uniform in our ideas of what constitutes a really first-class Retriever they will gradually recede to the dark corner whence they came, and the premier position will be occupied by an improved breed on real working lines, which can still be bred from Flatcoated parents by a judicious blending of the best working blood.
READY, AYE READY!!"

There were many replies to this letter – to repeat all of them is impossible (not to mention repetitive). I give you one:

"Sir, – Your correspondent Ready, Aye Ready, writing about Retriever Trials, is amazed at what he calls the uncertainties of the game, laying stress on the fact that a dog which did not "get into the money" at one trial succeeded in carrying off the chief prize at another. The particular case he refers to is easily explained, inasmuch as the dog was, either worked by different handlers at the two Trials, or, had been away from the handler for some months before the first Trial – I forget which. But, apart from this particular case, is it so very strange that a dog should do well one day and not on another? Dogs are not machines! and there are scores of reasons which may alter a dog's behaviour, none more so than condition (bitches especially), whether he is called out first or has to remain for hours waiting his turn; also, I am certain dogs are apt to behave worse at the Trials than at home, owing to the over-anxiety of the handlers. If Ready, Aye Ready had ever judged at these Trials he would have learnt that nearly every one of his criticisms is wide of the mark, and merely the outcome of listening to the wisdom of the spectators or the grumbling of the disappointed handlers.

"I have had the pleasure of judging at one Trial. There were three judges, and we each had every dog before us – some more than once – making careful notes of their performances (the condition of the performance vary so considerably that awarding points as suggested is impossible), it was then comparatively easy by a comparison of our notebooks to select the winners. But of course, in Retriever Trials, as in all other competitions, there must be an element of luck. Take the pursuit of a runner, the particular soil, the time of day, whether a blood trail, whether the dog has seen the bird fall, whether the handler has successfully marked the bird, and scores of small points known to dog workers. Doubtless, those responsible for the Trials are willing to receive suggestions for their improvement; the Trials are carried out by sportsmen and dog lovers with the one object of awarding merit where merit is due to dog and handler; the judges are men of experience in dog training and dog

Horstead Hall.

work, and all such talk as Ready, Aye Ready reports as to the game each dog should or should not carry, has no weight with the judges, but is again merely the talk of the spectators, among whom is always to be found the man 'who once had an old dog that never by any chance missed a runner, and who had never seen a single dog at the trials do anything at all'. Your correspondent makes a suggestion that each judge should work his two dogs, so to speak, independently; that would be the best plan if the Trial ground was very extensive, but would end in dire confusion in existing circumstances. We are very grateful to those sportsmen who kindly give us the ground for the Trials, and I hardly think we can ask for two beats instead of one."

"I am sorry Labradors do not "fill the eye" of Ready, Aye Ready. There is always a certain prejudice against anything new, but I wonder why he thinks that because a breed has been much in evidence lately "that they will gradually recede to the dark corner whence they came". I am hardly able to understand this picturesque allusion, but I cordially agree with him (particularly when one remembers the comparatively limited choice), that Labradors will continue to hold the remarkable position they occupy today – that out of an entry of eight for the Championship Trials no less than five should be pure bred, and a sixth a half-bred Labrador. Having owned a kennel of the variety for twenty-five years I have no fear of your correspondent's "dark corner". In fact, so long as Labrador owners will breed for work and not only for looks, I am bold enough to hope that the breed will hold its own against any other.

A. HOLLAND-HIBBERT"

THE FIRST RETRIEVER CHAMPIONSHIP

Now we come to a historical report on the very first Retriever Championship, and I shall, because of its importance, give the report in its entirety. The report is published with the heading 'The Retriever Field Trial Championship at Little Green, Havant, January 9th 1909.'

"The Championship Sweepstakes for

Opposite Page: The Champion Retriever Trial at Little Green, near Havant. 1: Sir Algenon Ledger, one of the guns. 2: The Duke and Duchess of Hamilton with their competing dogs. 3: The winner, The Duchess of Hamilton's Dungavel Phoebe, retrieving. 4: The guns on Stripe's Hill. 5: At Blinker's Copse. 6: The competing dogs. 7: Mr. B. J. Warwick, one of the judges, on whose estate the Trial was held, pointing out the next field of operations to the Duchess of Hamilton. 8: Lord Vivian with his candidate for honours. 9: Mr. A. H. Horman's Thora, second prize. 10: The duchess of Hamilton's Dungavel Phoebe, by Flapper and Dungavel Juno, the winner. This was a competition limited to first and second prize winners at Retriever Trials this shooting season, and the result was a decisive victory for the Duchess of Hamilton's youngster, Dungavel Phoebe.

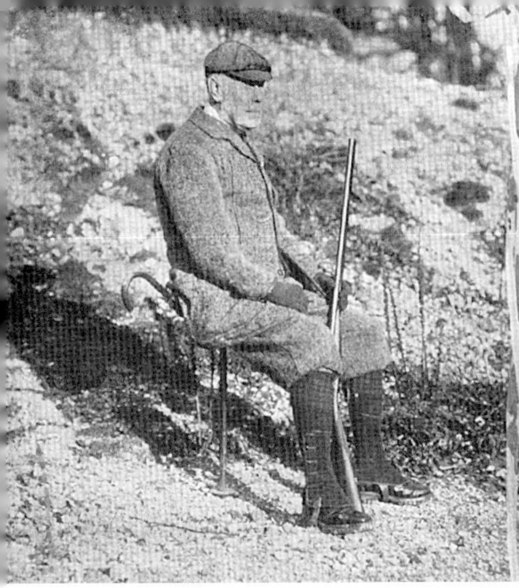

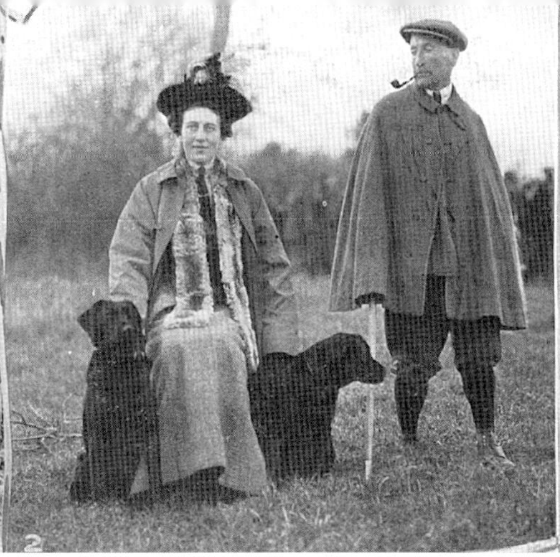

2

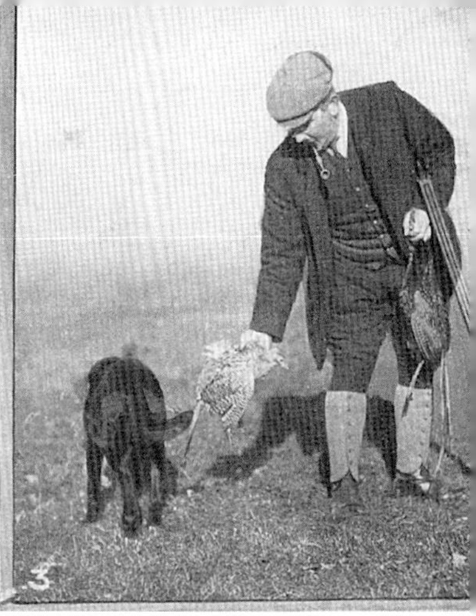

3

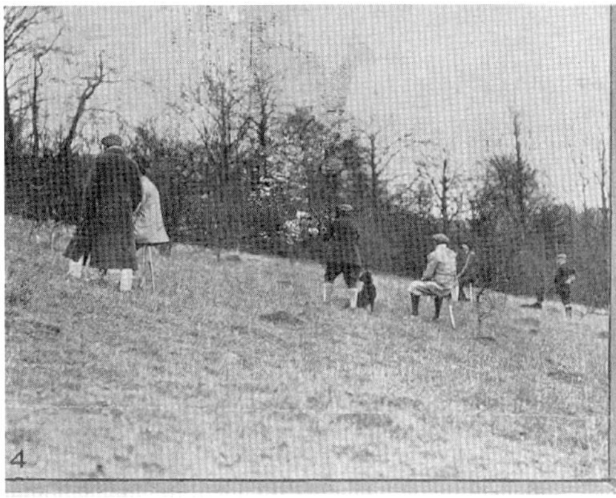

4

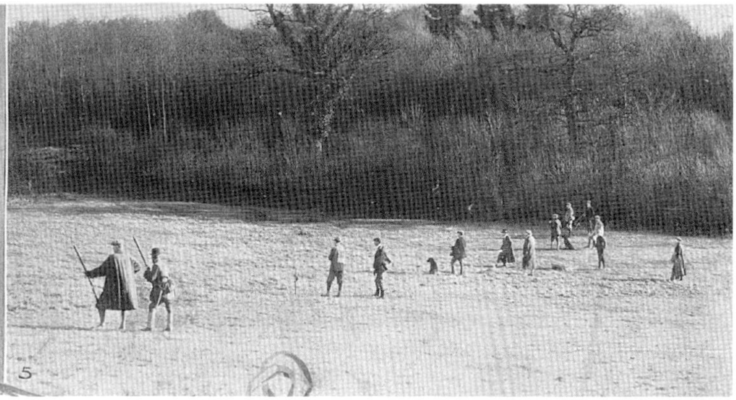

5

4 5

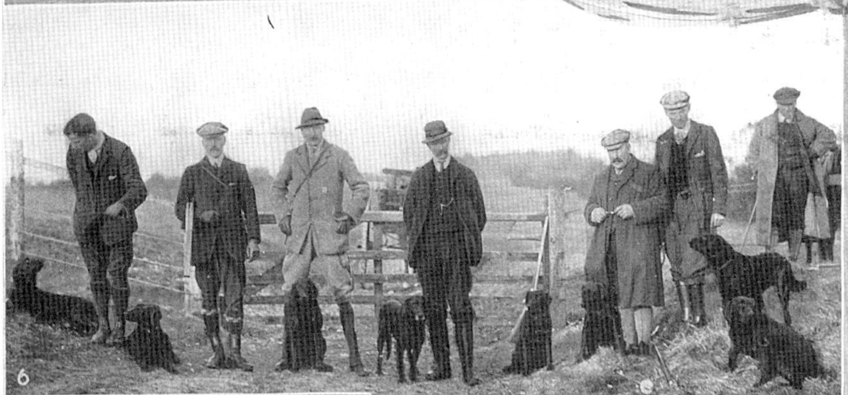

6

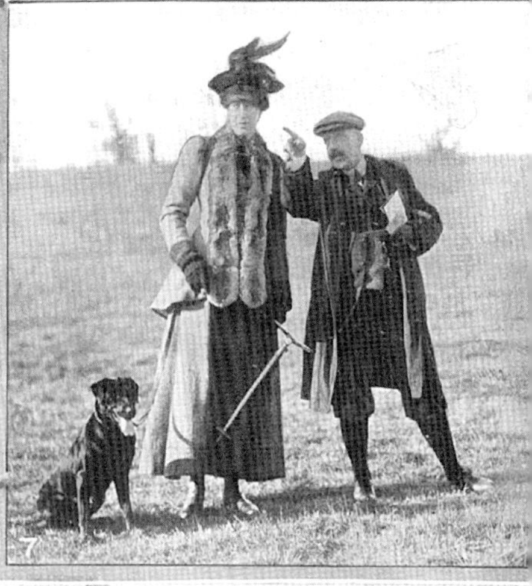

7

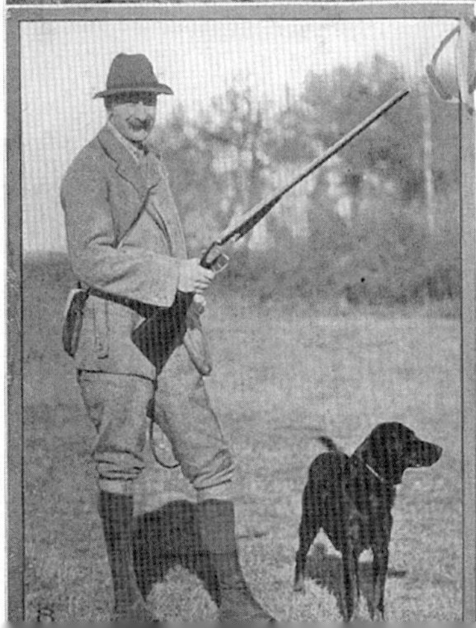

8

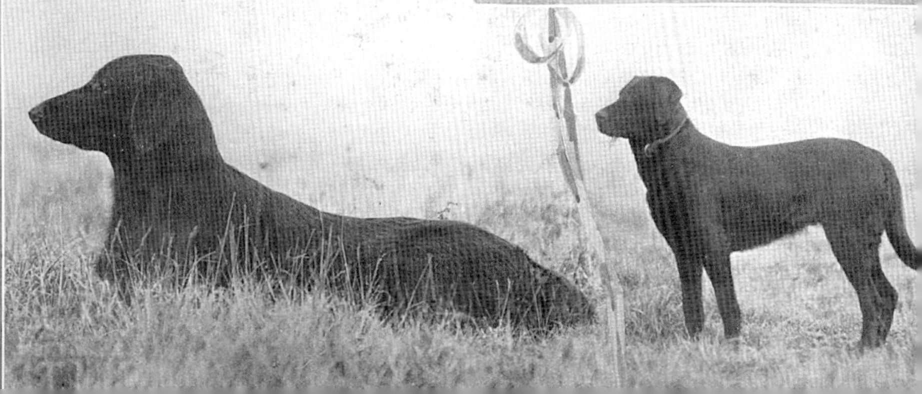

The eight dogs in the sweepstakes of the Little Green Trials.

Retrievers, promoted by Mr. F. W. Remnant, the president of the Retriever Society, and a few other enthusiasts, was run off on Mr. B. J. Warwick's shooting at Little Green, Compton, near Petersfield, on Saturday in last week. Headquarters were at the Bear Hotel, Havant, and the draw was made there on Friday evening. Mr. Remnant presided, and amongst those present were Mr. Warwick, Sir Algernon W. Legard, Mr. S. Smale, Mr. G. H. Evans, Mr. A. H. Horsman, Mr. C. C. Eley, Mr. Maurice Portal, and Mr. Peter Clutterbuck. As only eight dogs were entered, the draw to decide the order in which they should run did not occupy many minutes, and the order was given to meet at Fernbeds, Compton, nine miles from headquarters, at half past nine o'clock on the morrow.

"The card was as follows: Championship for Retrievers that have won a first or second at any Field Trial (puppy or junior stakes excepted), held by a recognised society during the season 1908: first prize £28, second £8, third £4, a silver medal to the winner of the first prize, presented by the Retriever Society of the International Gundog League; a 5-guinea Cup presented by Mr. Portal for the best Labrador if in the first three; a 5-guinea Cup presented by Mr. Warwick for the best Flatcoated Retriever if in the first three.

"Mr. G. May's black Labrador dog Shallow Flapper, by Flapper – Steller; breeder/owner; born March 18th 1907.

"Viscount Ridley's black Labrador dog Blagdon Shot, by Rover – Jet, breeder Mr. T. Finlay; born May 19th 1903.

"Duchess of Hamilton and Brandon's black Labrador dog Dungavel Juno, by Ben – Gyp, breeder Mr. J. Gordon, born February 8th 1905.

"Col. C. J. Cotes's black Smooth dog, Pitchford Monarch, by Munden Sovereign – Mermaid; breeder/owner, born 1905.

"Lord Vivian's black Labrador dog, Scamp of Glynn, date of birth, pedigree and breeder unknown.

"Mr. E. W. Blagg's black Flatcoated bitch Busy Mite, by Wimpole Peter – Stylish Queen, breeder/owner, born August 31st 1904.

"Mr. A. H. Horsman's black Flatcoated bitch Thora, by Black Charm – Belwardine Byna, breeders Messrs. Cox and Shipton; born July 24th 1905.

"Duchess of Hamilton and Brandon's black Labrador bitch, Dungavel Phoebe, by Flapper – Dungavel Juno, breeder/owner, born April 4th 1907.

Volume Two (1908-1911)

"The outlook was by no means bright overnight, but there could have been no better day for Field Trials than Saturday, and, though the pools on the roadside were noted to have a coating of ice as we were driving out to the meet, the sun came out shortly after the first batch had been put down, and, for the remainder of the day, the weather was more suggestive of that associated with the spring Field Trials than with a meeting winding up the winter series. The attendance was very large, the wonder being where all the people came from, for the meeting was not a public one; but several shooting men in the district had house parties. In addition to those who have been mentioned as being at the draw, there were present the Duke and Duchess of Hamilton and Brandon, Lieut. Col. C. J. Cotes, Major T. B. Phillips, the Rev. Ernest Sanderson, Mr. Vernon Stokes, Mrs. Curtis, Capt. R. Poore, Mr. C. J. G. Hulkes, Mr. P. Poore, Mr. E. W. H. Blagg and Lord Vivien. The judges were Mr. C. C. Eley, Mr. Portal and Mr. Warwick, and, though the last named received invaluable assistance from his Compton and Marden head Gamekeepers, Bolton and Atkins – who arranged the drives – he was here, there, and everywhere, and, excepting for half an hour in the afternoon, when, as a fact, the result might have been announced, there was not the least drag, and a better managed meeting could not be imagined.

"The fact that the Duchess of Hamilton's younger competitor Phoebe quite spread-eagled the field helped the judges beyond a doubt, and, all the circumstances considered, the entry of eight was quite enough for a meeting in January – a time of year rather too late for Field Trials, and if the stake is to be continued there must be a rearrangement of dates another season.

"As Shallow Flapper had not reached the ground at the time appointed to start, it was decided to try the whole of the remaining Retrievers in one batch, Alexander being perfectly willing to have his two charges down at the same time. Birds were driven off broken ground to the shooters in line at the foot of Apple Down and we had not long to wait for partridges to come over on the left of the line. Mr. Portal on the extreme right, took Thora (Hall) and Busy Mite (owner); Scamp of Glynn (owner), Dungavel Juno and Phoebe (Alexander) were in the middle with Mr. Warwick; while Mr. Eley had Pitchford Monarch (Downes) and Blagdon Shot (Davidson) on the left. The shooters were Sir Algernon Legard, Capt. Phipps Hornby, Mr. M. W. Christy, Mr. G. H. Evans, Mr. F. M. Remnant, Mr. W. F. Chamberlayne and Major Williams. The only partridges down were in the middle of the line, and after Dungavel Juno had brought birds to hand, which fell close in, and required very little finding, Phoebe was put on the line of a partridge which had run some distance and dropped in the hedgerow. Alexander's charge went straight to the fall and using her nose well, she roded her runner and brought it to hand in very pretty style. Her delivery was quick and she worked entirely unaided.

"A move over the top of the downs to Stripes Hill on the other side was then made, and Phoebe being taken up, the batch was reduced to the usual number, six. Mr. Warwick now took Busy Mite and Thora on the right of the line; Mr. Portal had the Labrador Scamp of Glynn and Dungavel Juno in the middle, while Pitchford Monarch and Blagdon Shot were again on the left, with Mr. Eley. Hares came through the wood, and, being stopped, they were retrieved in capital style by Juno and Scamp of Glynn, while Busy Mite, on the right, brought a cock pheasant to hand; Juno was then sent in quest of a dead partridge which had dropped some distance behind the shooters. She hunted well and was again very quick in her return. A hen pheasant was retrieved by Scamp of Glynn, and Thora, after a good hunt, brought a dead partridge to hand from thick covert. On the left side of the line Blagdon Shot brought a dead partridge to hand and Pitchford Monarch had a dead partridge and then a dead hare, his retrieving being both clean and ready.

"As Shallow Flapper (owner) had now arrived, a new batch was made up, Mr. Portal taking the newcomer and Blagdon Shot; Mr. Warwick watched the working of Pitchford Monarch, Dungavel Juno and Phoebe; while Mr. Eley had Busy Mite, Thora and Scamp of Glynn. Not many birds came over, and after Blagdon Shot had retrieved a dead pheasant in really good style Pitchford Monarch was set the task of finding a dead partridge of which he could not have seen the fall for it had been stopped by a shooter in the middle of the line. Thora did not find a hare of which she was sent in quest, though it had run some distance on the road, but Monarch scored by finding his bird in capital style, and, sent in search of a towered bird which had dropped in thick covert some distance behind the shooters, Shallow Flapper was successful, his search being persevering, while his retrieving was quick. There was now a long walk to the Blinkards, a small covert from which pheasants were driven, but only the first four Retrievers on the card were tried. They were Shallow Flapper, Blagdon Shot, Dungavel Juno and Pitchford Monarch. The last-named jumped a fence with a big hen pheasant in his mouth very well and brought it to hand, while Dungavel Juno, after retrieving a dead bird which lay in the open, was taken to the wood in quest of a strong runner. Scamp of Glynn had already carried the line for at least a hundred yards, and had put a rabbit afoot without taking the least notice of it, but Juno would not own the line at all. and she was therefore taken up. Another batch was now made up, Mr. Warwick taking Shallow Flapper and Pitchford Monarch in the wood, Mr. Eley had Thora and Busy Mite in the ride, while Scamp of Glynn, Blagdon Shot and Dungavel Phoebe were in the open with Mr. Portal. There was no game in the wood, but Phoebe was given a long hunt for a hen pheasant which had dropped in covert and then run for some distance; she was persevering, and retrieved her bird in capital style. On the other side of the wood Shallow Flapper, Pitchford Monarch and Blagdon Shot were provided with easy tasks in picking up, and each did his work well. A long walk back to Stripes Hill was now called, and covert at the foot was driven to the shooters on the side of the hill. Dungavel Phoebe brought a live hare to hand, her carrying being especially good, and Thora and Blagdon Shot were set the task of finding birds which had dropped in the open outside a narrow strip of covert connecting two parts of the wood. Each found the pheasant, though the quest in each case was long, and then Thora had a runner after a hunt on open ground.

"Then to luncheon, over which very little time was spent, for it was two o'clock, and the light was beginning to fail. Afterwards a move was made to North Marden, a batch of retrievers being made up of Shallow Flapper, Blagdon Shot, Busy Mite, Thora and Dungavel Phoebe. The beaters were over half an hour in getting round and the first Retriever sent was Thora. She brought a partridge through the fence off the high road, and then Phoebe had quite as easy a task in picking up a partridge which had dropped in the open; but Busy Mite, though hunting her ground well, could not hit the line of a strong runner. Thora had more partridges which dropped close in, and Shallow Flapper had quite as easy a task; then Dungavel Phoebe, put on the line of the bird which had been missed by Busy Mite, put her nose to the ground at once, hunted a few yards, and found what seemed to be the runner, though

The Duchess of Hamilton and Brandon's Labrador, Dungavel Phoebe (progeny of Flapper and Dungavel Juno).

some of the spectators declared that Busy Mite was dead on the line of quite a different one, and a stronger bird, when she was called up. A pigeon, which had been dropped in the road by Major Williams, and then crept into the hedge, was retrieved alive by Phoebe.

"The awards were then made as follows:
1. Duchess of Hamilton's, Dungavel Phoebe (Labrador)
2. Mr. A. H. Horsman's, Thora (Flatcoat)
3. Mr. G. May's, Shallow Flapper (Labrador)

Phoebe was also awarded Mr. Portal's Cup, offered for the best Labrador, and also the Silver Medal of the International Gundog League; while Mr. Warwick's Cup naturally went to Mr. Horsman's good Flatcoated bitch.

"The extended pedigree of the winner is as follows:

"The card was run through by a little after four o'clock, and headquarters were reached in time to enable the bulk of the visitors to catch the early evening train to London."

DUNGAVEL PHOEBE	Flapper	Stag	Jock / Squib
		Betsy	Ben / Sah
	Dungavel Juno	Ben	Unknown / Unknown
		Gyp	Munden Sentry / Munden Jet

The extended pedigree of Dungavel Phoebe.

TRIAL PREREQUISITES

In the January 1909 edition of Sporting Dogs, the following article appeared:

"Mr. H. Reginald Cooke's ideas on Flatcoated Retrievers for show or work are always worth listening to or reading, and there is no more interesting contribution to the current issue of the Kennel Gazette than the article under his name. Regarding the Field Trials, he thinks the chief difficulty is in obtaining for all the dogs an equal chance, and this is almost impossible, for one dog may have an excellent opportunity of distinguishing himself on a running bird, while another equally good dog may work all through a stake without having a really good chance of showing of what he is capable. He does not begrudge the Labradors their triumph, but in discussing the Championship stake he considers that all Retrievers eligible to compete in so important event should have "won their spurs" at the open meetings, and not have been made eligible on the strength of having won at county or district trials. Mr. Cooke adds his plea to the one we made some weeks ago that the Kennel Club Trials should be held a month or six weeks earlier than the end of November, for it is admitted that the best Trials for Retrievers are in roots which are not always available in that month, and a really strong running bird in good roots will try a dog more effectually than picking up a dozen birds in the open. Advice to breeders finishes a most instructive contribution. He cautions them against going to extremes. "For instance", he remarks, "in the case of heads, some people seem to think that a long head must necessarily be a narrow head. On the contrary, there is no reason why a dog should not possess a head of nice length, with room for brains as well, but the narrow, Borzoi type of head in a Retriever is much to be deprecated. Then I think, more attention should be given to neck and shoulders. Though much improvement has been made, one still sees too many dogs with short necks and straight shoulders. On the other hand a most wonderful improvement has been made in such points as eyes, ears, legs, feet, styles, sterns, and no doubt that as time goes on we shall arrive nearer to perfection in this breed." Breeders of retrievers certainly have every encouragement, and after a record Field Trial season it is pleasing to hear that the gamekeepers trials in Shropshire which were inaugurated have been kept going, a well-managed and successful little meeting being run off on the Duke of Sutherland's estate at Lilleshall, Shropshire, last Saturday."

From the same publication, in March 1909:

"Shooting men will be interested in the decision of the International Gundog League to accept the invitation of Mr. H. Reginald Cooke, a past president of the Retriever Society, and the owner of the finest kennel of the Flatcoated variety in the Kingdom, to decide next season's Trials on his ground at Davenport, near Bridgnorth, Salop. The district has not been visited before, but all who know it must admit that a better choice could not have been made. The shooting is quite close to the village of Worfield, and only three and a half miles from Brignorth on the Severn Valley Railway, and eleven miles from Wolverhampton from whence all parts of the country can be reached – London being only two and a half hours run. The country is undulating; while the soil, being of a sandy and dry nature, is favourable for game, though the last two seasons have been bad for partridges. That, however, is not an uncommon complaint, and as the meeting has been definitely fixed for Thursday 7th October, and the following day – a week earlier than usual – there is every prospect of conditions being of the best.

"Mr. Cooke's ground is mostly arable, intersected by small coverts, and, as the River Worfe flows through the shooting, it is to be hoped that some tests of retrieving from water may be possible. The calendar for next season, by the way, is being made up much earlier than usual, and Mr. C. E. Wright, the Hon. Secretary of the Trials of Irish Water Spaniels, which are to be held near Mildenhall on October 22nd and the following day, intimates that a committee meeting of his club is arranged for Tuesday, at which the working of the Trials will be discussed, and the arrangements decided on. He will be pleased to receive suggestions at Kingsley Cottage, Yately, Hants.

"Mr. H. Reginald Cooke, a past president of the Retriever Society and the owner of the finest kennel of the Flatcoated variety in existence, invited the International Gundog League to decide the trials fixed for Thursday 7th October and the following day on his ground at Davenport, and intimation that the invitation had been accepted was given in The Field as long since as the last Saturday in May. Davenport is three and a half miles from Brignorth and eleven from Wolverhampton, a main road, one of the best in the Midlands, running between the two towns. Headquarters will be at the Crown and Raven Hotel, Bridgnorth, but the railway journey from London and the south is considerably shorter to Wolverhampton, with of course, a fine service on both the London and North-Western and Great Western railway lines, but the Severn Valley line to Bridgnorth will land passengers close to Headquarters. There is a motor omnibus service between Wolverhampton and Bridgnorth, but it will not be of much use in connection with the trials, for progress is slow and dogs are not carried. Intending visitors, however, will be interested in knowing that Messrs. Barnett and Co. (The Garage, Salop Street, Wolverhampton) are prepared to run motor cars from Wolverhampton to the meet at Davenport and back each day at a reasonable charge from 15s. to 30s. according to the quality of the car. Arrangements for single seats at from 5s. to 7s.6d. for the double journey can also be made, but early application to Messrs. Barnett is advisable."

JUDGING

There follows a great deal of correspondence about judging. Many letters were published on the matter, which consequently found their

Date.	Meeting.	Trial ground.	Railway station.	Dist. miles.
Oct. 1	Herts County	Sarratt	Chorley Wood	2½
" 1 & 2	Northumberland County	Wooperton	Wooler	5½
" 2	Cheshire and N. Wales	Hawarden	Hawarden	1
" 7 & 8	International Gundog League	Davenport	Bridgnorth	3½
" 19	Eastern Counties	Plumstead	Whitlingham Junction (Norwich)	2
" 26-28	Kennel Club	Gaddesden	Boxmoor	4
Nov. 2	Western Counties and South Wales	Sherborne	Bourton-on-the Water	3
" 4	Horsham and District	Denne Park	Horsham	1
" 4	Essex County	Stisted	Braintree	2½
" 10-12	Scottish Field Trials Association	Hamilton	Hamilton	1

Schedule of the forthcoming-season's Trial events.

way in to the pages of H. Reginald Cooke's journals, all during August 1909. I chose two of the letters, published under the heading of 'Retriever Trials and their Conditions'. H. Reginald Cooke also published Short notes on Judging. Sadly, this one is not in my possession, but I was privileged to see it and to be given a photocopy of the entire 'little book'.

"Sir, – It is frequently the custom at Retriever Trials for judges to ask the shooters not to shoot when a dog is working. No doubt it is considered unfair for some dogs to work under fire with birds falling when others may not be subjected to the same ordeal, and there is much to be said in favour of the point of view.

The question which arises is: Should not the dog that is thoroughly trained and prepared for such an occasion be allowed to show how well he can behave in circumstances which may be trying, but occur every day in the shooting field? It is the opinion of the writer that the highest standard of training should be looked for at Open Trials, and that partially broken animals should not be catered for. The opinions of Retriever men on this subject would be of interest.
A PROSPECTIVE JUDGE"

"Sir, – Though it is true that no power is directly assigned to a judge to say where shooting shall or shall not take place, it may be assumed that it is desired that a judge shall do his best to ensure as equal a Trial as possible to every dog. I have acted on this assumption on many occasions and have asked the guns not to shoot when a dog under my observation is at work. It is true that it is desired to approximate Trials as nearly as can be to actual shooting, but A Prospective Judge must remember that if, in ordinary shooting, someone drops a bird a few yards from his dog when out, and he leaves his line and retrieves, it does not much matter to anybody, but if his dog did this in a Trial, he might be penalised by some judges for running in to shot.

Many a good dog can be stopped by a word at this stage, but the real point is, that it is impossible at a Trial to be sure that every dog when on a runner or when looking for his bird shall have birds dropped all round him, and therefore I have long ago made up my own mind that the fairest thing is to ask guns not to shoot, and I have in nearly every case found Retriever men, who break their own dogs, agree with my action.
A JUDGE"

CHAMPION GROUSE OF RIVERSIDE

Grouse of Riverside had a very impressive list of awards both in Field Trials and on the

Mr. H. R. Cooke and Grouse (the winner).

bench. On the show bench he won no less than five Open classes, four Limit classes, one Novice class and four Brace classes. In the field, Ch. Grouse of Riverside was made a Dual Champion after winning two more Open stake Trials during the 1909 Trailling season.

Davenport House.

In 1905, at the International Gundog League's Open stake at Sutton Scarsdale, he was awarded fourth place. In 1906, he took first place at the International Gundog League's Open stake at Priory Hill, St. Neots. In 1907, at the International Gundog League's Open Stake at Rushmore, Wiltshire, he was awarded third place. Likewise, in 1908, at the International Gundog League's Open stake at Six Mile Bottom, Cambridgeshire, Grouse was awarded third place, while he took first place at the 1909 Cheshire and North Wales Retriever Society's Open stake at Hawarden, Cheshire. Also in 1909, Grouse won the International Gundog League's Open stake on his own ground at Davenport, giving him Dual Champion status.

The Retriever Trials held in October 1909 under the auspices of the International Gundog League's Open stakes, were hosted by H. Reginald Cooke himself, on his grounds at Davenport. The following events took place on October 8th 1909:

"There were 18 dogs on the card for this nomination Open stake and was made up by 8 Labrador dogs, 2 Labrador bitches, the remaining 8 being of the Flatcoated variety but listed as 4 Smooth dogs, 3 Smooth bitches and 1 Wavy bitch. Prizes were: first prize £55, second prize £25, third prize £10, fourth prize £5. Special prizes: Challenge Cup kindly presented to the society by Mr. B. J. Warwick, The Bergholt Challenge Cup kindly presented to the society by Mr. C. C. Eley. Given by Mr. G. R. Davies and Mr. F. M. Remnant, £4:4s. for the best dog or bitch at the meeting showing in his or her work the greatest amount of dash combined with steadiness. Given by Mr. E. G. Wheler £5 for the handler (or handlers) who, in the opinion of the judges, shall have worked his dog in the most efficient manner during the Trials.

"The meet on the first day was at Davenport, the woods at Bath Bank, near to the house, being first driven, but not many pheasants were found there, though both Drake of Pudleston (Atkins) and Busy Mite (owner), did all that was asked of them, the last named retrieving two birds shot to her, and one which had been missed by Dungavel Thor (Alexander). A move was made to roots at Allscott, and after a Retriever on the far right of the line had picked up a hare, Dungavel Thor and Besthorpe Reine (owner) retrieved pheasants perfectly, while on adjoining ground, Drake of Pudleston hunted well for a runner, and though aided by the wind he did not waste any time in going out and returning with his bird. On the left flank Park Darkie (owner), retrieved another pheasant in capital style, while Rimside Flapper (Parmley) and Busy Mite, picked up a hare and a pheasant respectively. The style of each was good.

"Another batch was now made up of Bergholt Thomas (Pockney), Pitchford Monarch (Turrill), Raitt's Jet (Humphrey), Katya (Vaughan), Sarratt (owner), and Besford Coquette (owner). Mr. Arkwright had Thomas and Monarch on the right of the line. Jet and Katya worked under Mr. Hulkes in the middle, and Mr. Marchant watched the work of Sarratt and Coquette on the left. Turnips were walked up, the crowd being kept on the road, and after Jet had missed a bird which had dropped close in Katya met with no better luck, and she was called up. Walking on, a partridge was dropped in the middle of the line, and, though Pitchford Monarch was

Volume Two (1908-1911)

very patient in his quest, he was not successful, and Bergholt Thomas was called. Pockney's charge was successful, for, going straight to the fall, he returned with the bird and delivered it to hand. Besford Coquette was then given a chance, and, going out quickly, she returned with her partridge, her retrieving being capital. More roots were now walked up, and partridges were soon flushed, two big covey's getting up less than thirty yards from the hedge. Sarratt had an easy task on the extreme left, but Coquette had a longer hunt for another partridge which was down; again her retrieving was very quick. In the middle of the line Katya failed to find a partridge which was down in mangolds, but Sarratt was more lucky on the left, and another batch was then called.

"The Retrievers making up the group were Grouse of Riverside (owner) and Munden Sculler (Ashby), which worked under Mr. Arkwright; Soarer (Buckell) and Winhaston Rufus (Sutton), taken in the middle by Mr. Hulkes; and Sandhoe Frost (Alexander) and Scamp of Glynn (owner), whose work was watched by Mr. Marchant. Sandhoe Frost had a long hunt for a partridge which had dropped close in, and near the hedge Munden Sculler picked up a hen pheasant which had dropped out of sight and for which the Retriever had to hunt. On the right Grouse of Riverside had a runner in the wood and brought it to hand very cleanly, while on the left Frost retrieved a partridge which had dropped on stubble. Scamp of Glynn , Frost and Wenhaston Rufus all failed to find a partridge which had dropped behind the shooters, and on new ground – roots – Rufus, though down while shooting was going on, was in no way disturbed, and brought his bird to hand very readily. Neither Soarer nor Rufus, however, could hit the line of a bird which seemed to have dropped in potatoes, but Sculler picked up a brace of partridges which were down in mangolds; and on the left of the line Scamp of Glynn retrieved a big hare in perfect style, but on being put on the line of a runner which went across stubble and through the hedge to grass land at a great speed he did not use his nose as he might have done, and had to be called up. Rufus while apparently hitting the line of the bird. Sandhoe Frost and Soarer also failed to locate the same runner, and an adjournment was made to Davenport for luncheon, Mr. Cooke entertaining all the visitors to the Trials.

"Afterwards, the first batch of six Retrievers were recalled and roots walked up. Mr. Arkwright took Dungavel Thor and Busy Mite on the right, Park Darkic and Besthorpe Reine were in the middle of the line under Mr. Hulkes, while Mr. Marchant had Rimside Flapper and Drake of Pudleston on the left flank. Besthorpe Reine did not retrieve a pheasant at all well, but on more roots several partridges were down, Park Darkie picking up a brace very cleanly; while Busy Mite and Dungavel Thor also had birds on the right. On the left Rimside Flapper and Drake of Pudleston did equally good work. Rain now began to fall, but scent improved, and, in roots, Besthorpe Reine and Drake of Pudleston had easy tasks in picking up birds which had dropped close in. Other Retrievers were now called for, and the first one to be given the chance of retrieving was Raitt's Jet; she went out very quickly, and having marked her bird, brought it to hand at a gallop. On the left flank of the line Bergholt Thomas also did well, his picking up being all that could be wished for. In the middle of the line Sarratt retrieved a dead bird very cleanly, but Coquette was unlucky with a bird which was wrongly marked by the shooters. Bergholt Thomas, however, did all that was asked of him, and Coquette then made amends by picking up a dead partridge, which had dropped close in to the shooters. Pitchford Monarch had a more difficult task on the left, but after a long and patient quest he was successful, and he brought his partridge cleanly to hand. A high-flying pheasant in the middle of the line provided one of the shooters with a fine shot, and on the bird being down Sarratt brought it to hand, marking the fall and being very quick, while Bergholt Thomas was called on to hunt for a partridge that had dropped on the other side of the hedge. Again his quest was successful, and after a move for some distance the Retrievers forming the third group were called, and a line quite 300 yards long formed in a mixed field of turnips, mangolds and potatoes. A lot of birds were put up, and on the left bordering the road Grouse of Riverside retrieved a hare very well, though he was a long time in picking it up; his delivery however was very clean. Munden Sculler, Sandhoe Frost, and Wenhaston Rufus also did all that was asked of them, but Soarer failed to pick up her bird, and it was left for Rufus.

"The light was now beginning to fail, but the Retrievers were kept down, and after Grouse of Riverside had retrieved a pheasant in perfect style Munden Sculler and Sandhoe Frost each picked up a partridge and retrieved it in capital style. Sculler then had a runner and Soarer did all that was asked of her on the far right of the line. Scamp of Glynn then had his chance, and he made the most of it, his retrieving being very clean, and Grouse of Riverside also had another bird; while as a wind-up Sculler retrieved a partridge which had dropped close in. There was now a bad light, and the judges decided to stop work for the day, it being announced that the meet on the morrow would be at the cross-roads, Hermitage Hill, near Bridgnorth, at half-past nine o'clock.

"On Friday, there was a great improvement in the weather compared with that of the day before. Heavy rain had fallen during the night, and the day opened fine, and with the exception of one or two short showers it remained so during the rest of the day. A continuation of the Trials was made at about 9.45am when Park Darkie and Sarratt were placed in charge of Mr. Arkwright, Rimside Flapper and Drake of Pudleston by Mr. Hulkes, and Dungavel Thor and Busy Mite by Mr. Marchant. A start was made in turnips, which were walked, when on some partridges being shot, Dungavel Thor failed to find a strong runner, and Busy Mite was sent in search of the same bird, but she also failed to find it. Park Darkie retrieved a dead bird, then, passing into seeds, Sarratt was sent to gather a wounded pheasant; after working the hedge he found his game and brought it cleanly to hand. Passing into more seeds, a rabbit jumped up close to Thor, when he was perfectly steady; then into turnips. Busy Mite retrieved a dead bird quickly to hand, a hen pheasant was down, and Thor picked it up aright, and on the extreme right Sarratt was sent after a brace of partridges, and Mite again delivered up a live pheasant tenderly. Sarratt, again sent to retrieve, had to give it up, and Darkie, sent after the same wounded partridge did no better. Thor was next sent in quest of a runner which fell in the roots, and, using his nose well, he got on to the line of his game and brought it to hand. Mite retrieved one dead bird and then went on the line of another that had been wounded, but it had been gone too long. Drake of Pudleston tried on the same, bird worked his ground well, and during his search, a pheasant rose, to which he was steady, but did not find the partridge. Rimside Flapper had a dead bird, and Thor retrieved a rabbit, then Mite was longer than she ought to have been in finding a leveret. There was evidently very little scent about this time, Grouse of Riverside and Munden Sculler were taken in hand by Mr. Arkwright, and Raitt's Jet and Bergholt Thomas by Mr. Marchant. The two last named each retrieved a pheasant cleanly to hand, and Drake had another. Going on, Grouse of Riverside and Sculler both retrieved birds but did not bring them to hand quite cleverly. Bergholt Thomas put on a runner, was not successful, and Raitt's Jet was given a Trial. Sculler then found very well a bird that had dropped in the next field by the hedge, but Rimside Flapper took too long in finding a wounded pheasant that had moved a few yards from where it fell. Grouse got a partridge creditably that had fallen. Park Darkie and Dungavel Thor took the place of Rimside Flapper and Bergholt Thomas.

"Starting again in mustard, a partridge was bowled over and Grouse found and retrieved it quickly and Sculler did the same. Then into roots. A brace of hares left their forms and Grouse sent in pursuit of one, quickly came

The International Gundog League Retriever Trials held at H. Reginald Cooke's ground, Davenport, on the 7th and 8th October 1909. 1: Entering Davenport grounds. 2: Coming up to lunch. 3: Shooting over turnips. 4: Off to a fresh beat. 5: The guns climbing a fence. 6: The judge, Mr. G. J. Gladdish-Hulkes. examining bird just retrieved by Besthorpe Reine. 7: Mr. H. Reginald Cooke with his Ch. Grouse of Riverside winner. 8: Ch. Grouse of Riverside. 9: Watching the trials.

back with it. Sculler sent after the other that was wounded, ran the line nicely, and after a run to get it, came back at a gallop, but Dungavel Thor on the right was amusing himself by chasing a low-flying pheasant out of the field. Then in more mangolds Grouse picked up a dead bird and Drake had another and followed it up by gathering a pheasant, which, however, he did not bring quite to hand. Sculler sent for a pheasant, had some difficulty in finding it, as it had run, but he did so eventually, and brought it tenderly to hand, and Drake retrieved a pheasant uncommonly well, another pheasant falling to the lot of Grouse, who was very quick in returning.

"An adjournment was now made for luncheon, at the conclusion of which a covert was drawn adjacent to a stream with a view to trying the dogs in water. The dogs reserved for this competition were Grouse of Riverside, Drake of Pudleston, Busy Mite, Raitt's Jet, Park Darkie and Munden Sculler. Three or four pheasants fell, the result of the first drive, and Busy Mite, Park Darkie and Sculler each faced the water all right and retrieved a bird; Park Darkie getting a pheasant that had run in at the bank of the stream. Then a short walk brought us to a nice field of roots, and Raitt's Jet was sent to find a partridge that had fallen dead, and Sculler had a pheasant; then Park Darkie went to find a runner, but failed to get it, and finished up by chasing some birds for a short distance. Raitt's Jet, sent after the same bird, was also at fault. Drake got a dead pheasant very smartly.

"The prizes were then awarded as follows:
1. Mr. H. Reginald Cooke's Grouse of Riverside
2. Mr. C. Brewster Macpherson's Raitt's Jet
3. Mr. Ernest Turner's Park Darkie
4. Mr. G. E. Wright's Drake of Pudleston

Munden Sculler was Reserve, and Certificates of Merit were awarded to Rimside Flapper, Busy Mite, Dungavel Thor, Bergholt Thomas and Sarratt. Mr. Cooke's Retriever was also awarded the Warwick Challenge Cup and the special prize offered by Mr. G. Reynolds Davies and Mr. F. M. Remnant for the best dog or bitch at the meeting showing in his or her work the greatest amount of dash combined with steadiness, while Drake of Pudleston won the junior special prize and Messrs. Turner and Atkins divided the handler's prize offered by Mr. E. G. Wheeler."

The ascendancy of Grouse of Riverside was the subject of several letters and articles following the Davenport Trials, as can be seen in the following article, taken from The Field in 1909.

"The form shown by Mr. H. Reginald Cooke's Flatcoated Retriever Grouse of Riverside at both the Cheshire and North Wales and International meetings must cause regret among the thick and thin supporters of the variety first bred by the late Mr. S. E. Shirley, and perfected by shooting men of the stamp of Mr. L. Allen Shuter, Mr. Harding Cox, Mr. G. Reynolds Davies and the late Col. Cornwall Legh, and the owner of the Hawarden and Davenport winner that there is no likelihood of a Championship stake for Retrievers being promoted at the end of the season. The meeting arranged by Mr. F. M. Remnant and run off over Mr. B. J. Warwick's Compton shooting last January was a success in every way, though the conditions were not all favourable, and the stewards could not but feel pleased at the end of the day that just sufficient game had been found to enable all the Retrievers entered to be thoroughly tried. A stake of the same character arranged for this season at the end of the Field Trials could not fail to be successful, for the bulk of the meetings, with the exception of the district gathering at Horsham, are being held weeks earlier than has been known before, and with October only fairly aired nearly half the long list has been got through. There are men, however, who argue that no Championship meeting is necessary, and that owners really anxious to secure such honours for their retrievers should support each of the three Open stakes. That argument, however, is not quite sound, for each is a nomination stake, and no owner can command success at the ballot. Mr. Cooke, indeed, is among other staunch supporters of the Kennel Club meeting who were unable to secure and original nomination, and till the draw is made at Grafton Street on Monday week he cannot be certain whether or not he will be afforded an opportunity of running Grouse by being allotted a returned nomination. Flapper's Field Trial days are over, but the Duchess of Hamilton and Brandon may run Dungavel Phoebe, the winner at Compton last season, and the competition between the Labradors and the Flatcoated variety, begun at Wooperton on the first day of the present month will certainly be continued at Gaddesden, for there is a strong Northumberland entry and with Flapper not available, a determined effort is to be made to win Kennel Club honours with one of his stock. Mr. Portal's Retriever has been in great demand by breeders, for in the three seasons he has been at public service he has sired 406 puppies, a remarkable record. In the shooting field he is a useful as he ever was, and is as certain in his quest of a runner as he always has been at public Trials. All the same a good many men would go a long distance to see a match between him and Grouse of Riverside, his victor at St. Neots in 1906 for Mr. Cooke's Retriever is now in perfect form, and at Hawarden and Davenport, he never missed gathering one single bird or hare that he was sent for in the three days."

LABRADOR V FLATCOATED RETRIEVERS

Throughout the journals there is much correspondence, page upon page, under the heading 'Retrievers – Labradors v Flatcoated'. It would be possible to create a book on these letters alone, some of which are amusing, others highly detrimental, and some stating valid points which are still echoed today. I will from time to time insert some of this 'banter' and will start with an excerpt from a letter from Mr. E. G. Wheeler. As this letter is a full three columns long, some of which is very repetitive, I have selected one paragraph only:

"The Labradors are the undoubted favourites of the hour. This, no doubt, is largely because of the brilliant successes of Mr. Maurice Portal's perfectly broken and handled Flapper. Their very popularity, however, justly lays them open to criticism, and I venture to think that, with all their brilliancy, the breed has serious inherent faults. These, no doubt, may be bred out in time, but at present there is much room for improvement. Labradors differ somewhat widely from other breeds in their method of working. Very obedient, with any amount of dash, they impress one at first as being vastly superior to their Flatcoated or Curly confreres. Their style, diligence, and obedience is a pleasure to see; but closer acquaintance causes one to discount these virtues to a very considerable extent. There can be no question that there is among them a common tendency to hardness of mouth, though there already seems to be an improvement in this respect. The fault that is perhaps most striking is the frequent failure to recover game that is apparently most carefully and diligently sought for. The explanation seems to be want of nose, and by this I mean not only the actual power of smell, but the capacity of making the most of it. I consider a dog fails in nose if he does not habitually take every advantage of the wind, and does not carry his nose well down when roding out a line. I have frequently seen Labradors fail to gather a dead bird after hunting most diligently over and over the spot where it fell, only to see a beater pick it up as he comes along. Many a slow, pottering, Smoothcoated Retriever would have gone straight to the place, picked up the bird, and brought it back, possibly at a walk, without wasting a quarter of the time. Again, when on runners, few Labradors seem to have an idea of how to use their nose to advantage. Up wind and down wind seem alike to them. They rarely follow a line for any distance, and in the open do not appear to carry their noses as close to the

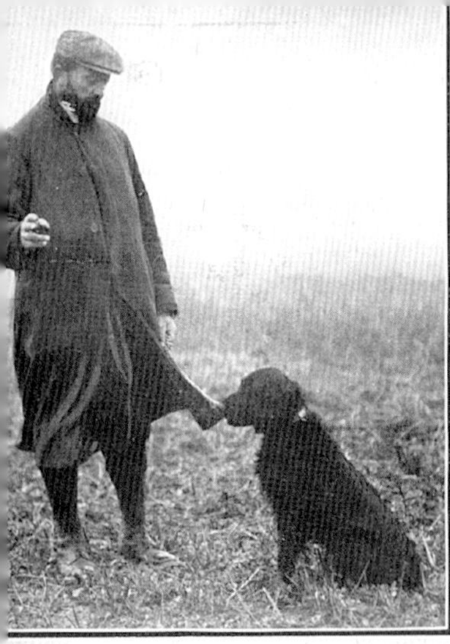
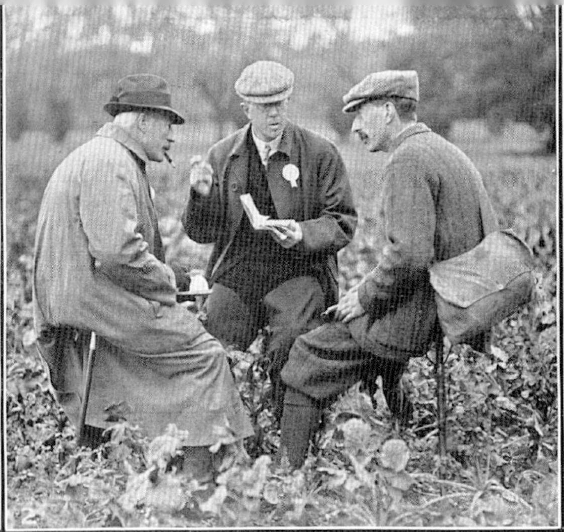
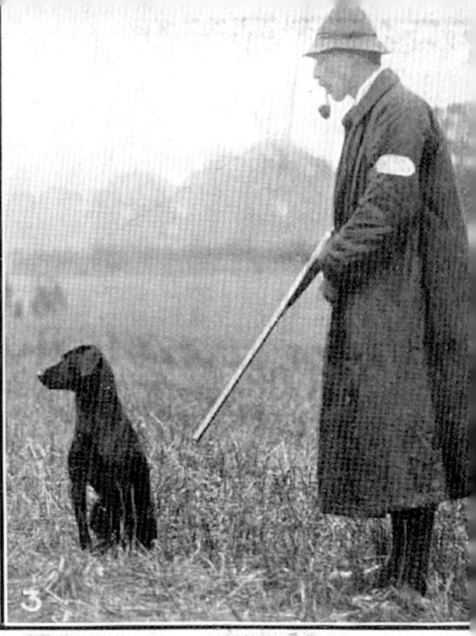
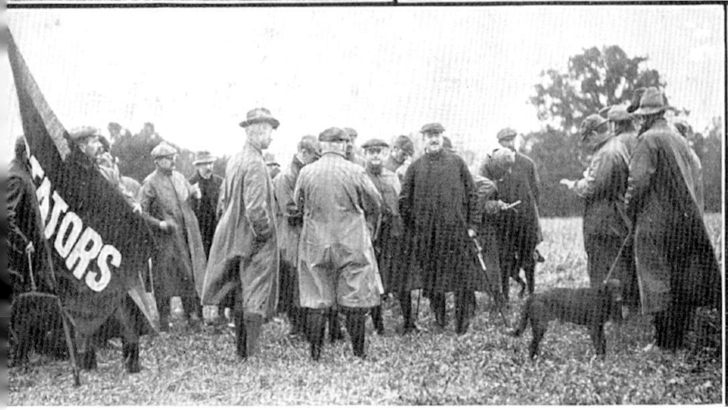
TATORS
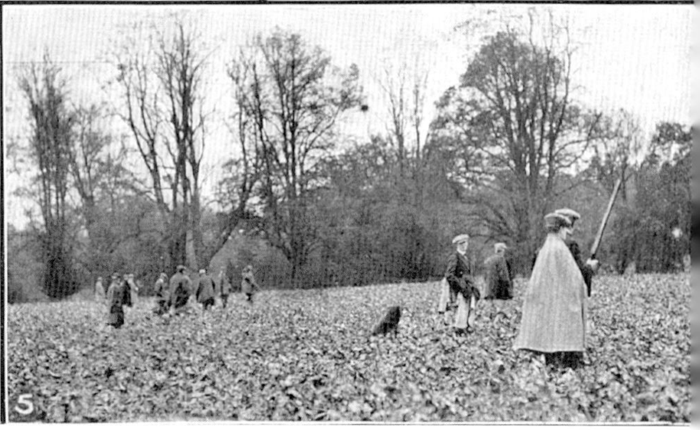
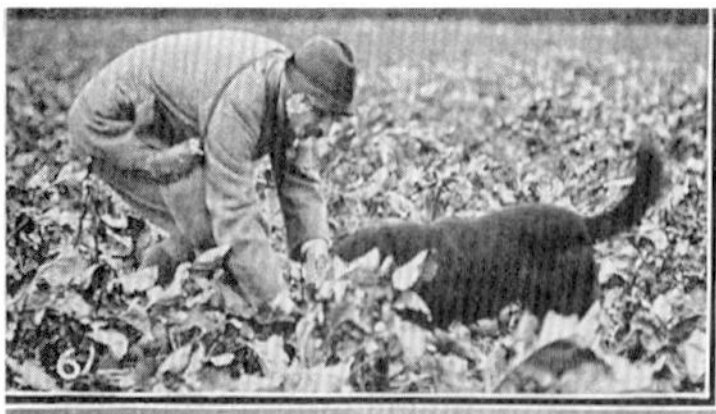
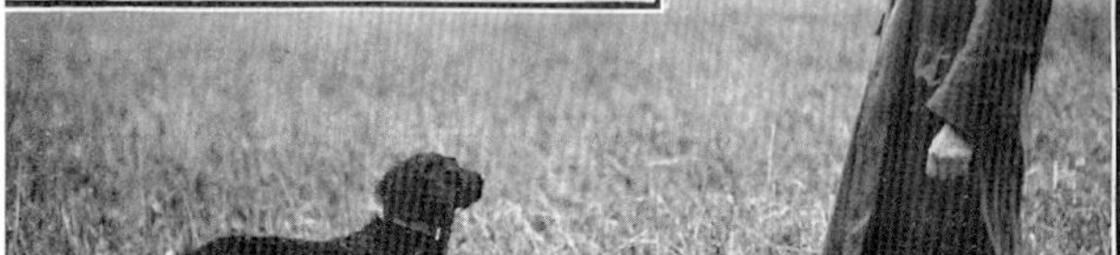
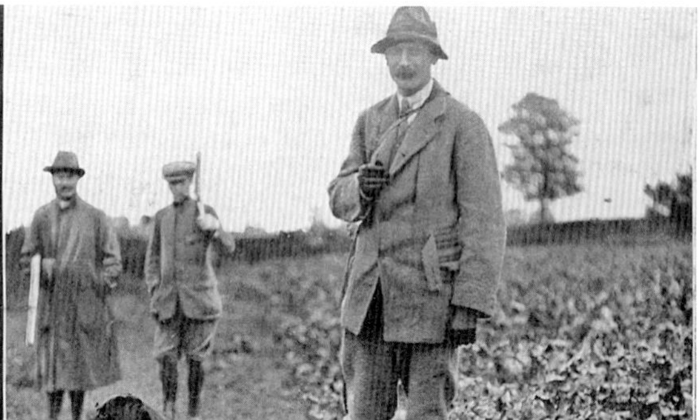
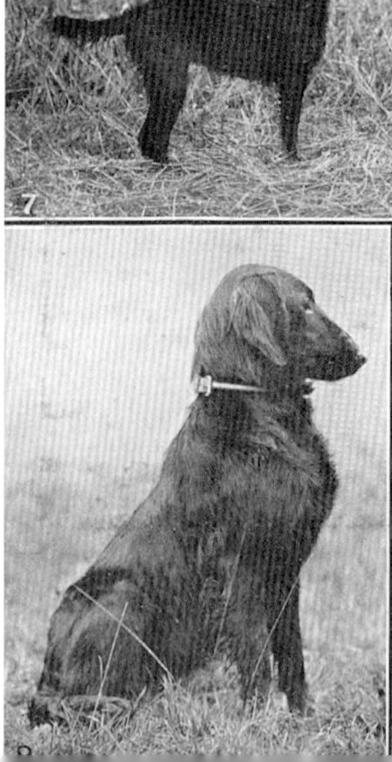
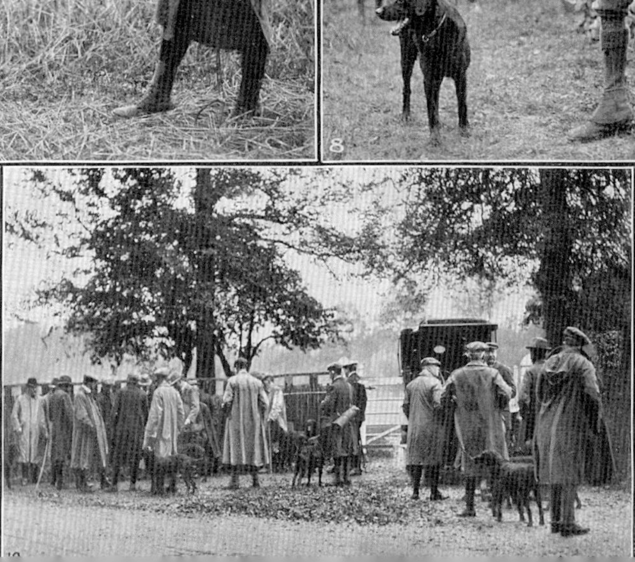
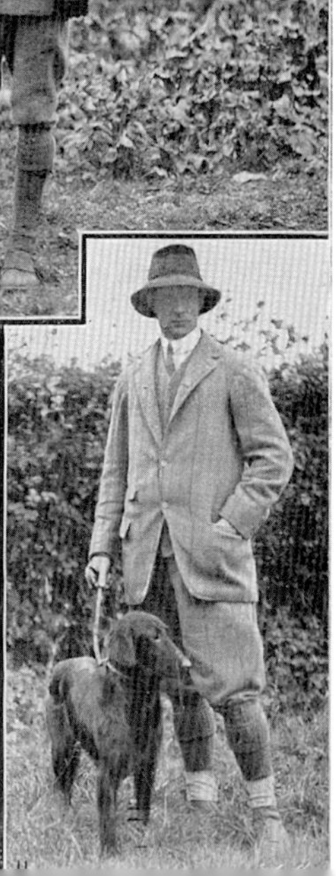

Volume Two (1908-1911)

Opposite Page: The Kennel Club Retriever Trials at Gaddesden, Herts, on October 23rd and 24th 1909. 1: Mr. Richard Sharpe with his Shadden Lass. 2: A conference of judges – Capt. H. Eley, Mr. C. C. Eley, and Mr. C. Eversfield (reading from left to right). 3: Mr. Butler with Peter of Faskally. 4: Mr. E. W. Jacquet (Secretary of Kennel Club) reading out the names of the winners. 5: The guns among the mangels. 6: Scamp of Glynn and Lord Vivian. 7: Mr. E. Blagg with his Busy Mite, second in All-aged Stakes. 8: Lord Vivian with Scamp of Glynn (pedigree, breeder and date of birth unknown), winner of All-aged Stakes. 9: Duchess of Shipton, winner of Junior Stakes. 10: The meet at the gamekeeper's lodge on Mr. John Kerr's estate. 11: Mr. E. Turner with his Duchess of Shipton.

ground as the other breeds. The result is that many runners are recovered by luck rather than honest work and then only after considerable time has been spent and much ground disturbed. In a word, such dogs are flashy, and not thorough. A habit, and one that seems typical of the breed, is to come to a stiff point, stand for some seconds, and then to dash in hard enough to bruise the game, even if they carry it tenderly afterwards.
E. G. WHELER"

This controversy is recorded in the journals from November 1909. It continues for some time, and numerous letters seem to have been sent in as a response to Mr. Wheler's original letter. I have selected the following:

"Sir, –Mr. Wheler's letter is full of interest. From my own observation of the two breeds, I think the following are their good points:
"LABRADORS
1. Quicker to retrieve and go out
2. Hardier: stand exposure or heat better
3. The short coat does not pick up mud or wet
4. The better dog for certain work, such as picking up after grouse or partridge drive, or stand at covert shoot
5. Excellent companion to owner, but essentially a one man's dog.
6. Good nose and mouth as a rule, but inclined often to use eyes too much and cast forward if scent weak, instead of puzzling it out – at times with great success, but it is a fault to my mind.
"FLATCOATED
1. Excellent mouth as a rule
2. In style, slow, inclined to potter
3. Nose good
4. Inclined to be slack on a hot day in heather
5. Very friendly and affectionate with master and everyone else
6. Not keen on thick fences as a rule, though some keeper's dogs are excellent at it.

"Given a good scent, I notice the Labrador easily beats the Flatcoated and has birds quicker. Given a bad scent, the Flatcoated will equal the Labrador, and probably beat him. I refer to the rank and file of both breeds throughout.
M."

"Sir, – I have read Mr. Wheler's letter in this week's The Field with great interest. There are two points where I must differ with him. I take it he advocates crossing the Flatcoated Retriever with the Labrador. I daresay the Flatcoated would benefit by this cross, but I cannot see any benefit to the Labrador. I have a list before me of forty-one Labradors that between them have won about eighty prizes at Field Trials this year and last, including special prizes and Certificates of Merit. Can this be improved on?

"The other point is that he says as a breed the Labradors are inclined to be hard in the mouth. I have never yet known a judge at Trials to give even a Certificate of Merit to any hard-mouthed dog, and if forty-one Labradors can win prizes in two years at Trials out of the limited number of dogs that run at those meetings I do not think much can be said against them on this point.

The Scottish Retriever Trials at Hamilton Park, Lanarkshire, November 1909. 1: The Duke of Hamilton, with dogs, handlers, etc., at Chatelherault. 2: Captain Stirling's Keir Ivy, by Castlemilk de Wet-Keir Juno, winner of Open Stakes. 3. Guns and dogs in Avondale Glen. 4: Colonel le Marchant and Messrs. Elliot's Southwell Abbot (third in Open stakes) bringing pheasant to hand. 5: Crossing the bridge to the duck drive. 6: The Duke of Hamilton. 7: The judges: Messrs. L. D. Wigan, C. B. Macpherson, and E. G. Wheller. 8: Southwell Abbot bringing a duck from the water. 9: The duck drive at Chatelherault.

Volume Two (1908-1911)

"Again, if Mr. Wheler had seen the runners got by Dungavel Juno and Katya at the Western Counties Trials this year, I do not think he would say they fail on runners. Mr. Wheler admits that he is prejudiced in favour of the Flatcoated Retriever, so I must admit to the same on the other side, as at the present moment I have about thirty-five Labradors.
T. B. PHILLIPS."

"Sir, – In a recent issue of your paper, Mr. Wheler asked for a discussion on the relative merits of Labrador and Flatcoated Retrievers "by those who, as judges or otherwise, had good opportunities of comparing them." I have had many such opportunities, and I do not think a better summing up of the comparative merits of the two breeds could be made than that given by M in your issue last week; but I should like to give one more good point to the Labradors, and that is their power of marking.

"I admit the fact that, with the results of the Field Trials the last word has not been spoken, for I have hardly ever been at a Field Trial without meeting the man who bores you to distraction by relating how "that he once owned an old dog of no particular breed that would have just shown these Trial dogs something; he never missed a runner by any chance, and would mark not only his owners dead birds, but every bird in the drive!" But, so far as it goes, I have compiled the results of all the Field Trials this year.

As a Labrador man it would be unkind to make more than a passing remark to last years Trials, when the Labradors practically "swept the board"; but this year, the prizes are more evenly distributed, and therefore I can give them:

PRIZES WON	
LABRADOR	FLATCOATED
Total Entries	
72	64
Firsts	
5	3
Seconds	
5	4
Thirds	
5	3
Fourths	
1	3
Fifths	
1	0
Reserves	
7	1

I have taken no account of special prizes, because the conditions are not identical.

"Considering how vastly the Flatcoats outnumber the Labradors throughout the country, considering, too, for what a comparatively short time the Labradors have been popular among sportsmen. I maintain that the above record is a good testimony for the superlative merits of the Labrador. But then I am prejudiced, for I have kept Labradors for twenty five years. I am certain of one thing – that Retrievers of all sorts sadly lack nose. Compare the nose of the best Retriever with that of an ordinary Setter or Pointer; the Retriever will not be in it, and I confess I often feel inclined to try the experiment of a mixture of Labrador, Setter,

The valley of the Goyt, Buxton.

Goode and Kestrel at the Gaddesden Trials of 1910.

and Foxhound blood – perseverance, nose and dash."
A. HOLLAND-HIBBERT."

Mr. Holland-Hibbert's letter was followed by an editorial note, which reads:

"Mr. Holland-Hibbert has underestimated the wins of Flatcoated Retrievers, their record of first prizes during the past season being as follows: Beechgrove Jet (Sarratt), Grouse of Riverside (Hawarden and Davenport), Duchess of Shipton (Gaddesden), Keir Ivy and Avoch Jock (Hamilton) – Ed."

TRIAL CONDITIONS
In January 1910, there begins a new debating issue under the heading 'Retriever Trials and their Conditions', much of which is fascinating to read because some of the same arguments still apply today. I found the following letter from H. Reginald Cooke with regards to nominations for Trials particularly interesting, as this was probably the beginning of the present system. This letter was published in the January 1910 edition of The Field.

"Sir, – Anyone who has followed the course of these Field Trials since their inception must be struck by their increasing popularity. This is hardly a matter for surprise, for it cannot be doubted that a great deal of improvement in the working Retriever has resulted there from. Speaking generally, all the Trials are conducted on excellent lines, but there is one point in their management which I cannot help thinking requires amendment. I refer to the return of nominations, which are not required by the original allotted. As matters now stand, an owner of a dog who has been fortunate in securing an original nomination can, without incurring a penalty, or in some cases only a very small one, return his nomination to the secretary of his society within a few hours of the first day of the Field Trial meeting. The result is that the secretary has to telegraph hurriedly to applicants who are next entered to nominations, only to find that they are unable to take them at such short notice. For example, take the recent trials of the Retriever Society held at Davenport. When the ballot for nominations was made in London, there were forty-seven applicants for the twenty nominations comprising the stake. On the day of the Trials only eighteen dogs arrived to contest the stake – i.e. two short of the full number, and this frequently occurs.

"This seems both unsatisfactory and unnecessary, for doubtless, many owners would have been glad of these nominations if they had earlier notice that they would be available. I would therefore respectfully suggest to the committees of the various Field Trial meetings that they might insert a rule in their codes to this effect: "Every allottee of a nomination not intending to use the same must give notice to that effect to the secretary of the society at least three weeks before the first day of the Trials. Failure to comply with this will render such holder of a nomination liable to a fine of £10, but this fine may be remitted at the discretion of the committee in cases where it is proved to them that the default was beyond the control of the holder of the nomination." The last clause would cover cases of accident, or if the Retriever entered for the Trials should become sexually amiss. I do not think there would be any hardship in this. Every owner surely knows three weeks before the trials if he intends to use his nomination or not, and by relinquishing it at that time he would give another man a chance of giving his dog that amount of regular work which every handler knows is necessary before a dog can be wound

up to his best form. I have discussed this matter with several owners of Field Trial Retrievers, and there seems to be a general impression that something should be done to remedy the present defect.
H. REGINALD COOKE."

RETRIEVER RUMOURS
Spasmodically within the journals, there are show reports, usually under the heading of 'Retriever Rumours'.

JANUARY 1910

"Mr. H. Reginald Cooke's Flatcoated Retriever bitch, Blossom of Riverside, became a full Champion by her win at Crufts Show. She is a really good bitch and a credit to her sire, Ch. Rocket of Riverside. She has always run a close race with her kennel companion, Ch. Bianca, who became a full Champion at the recent show at Birmingham – not a bad record for two bitches."

"Mr. H. Reginald Cooke's Flatcoated Retriever bitch Bianca, by her win at Birmingham last week, became a full Champion. Bianca is one of the best Flatcoated Retrievers ever seen. Her three Challenge prizes were won off the reel at Darlington, Crystal Palace and Birmingham. She is excellent in her work, and Mr. Cooke hopes to run her in Field Trials next season."

"Not much has been heard of the argument that because a dog has won prizes in the show ring he cannot possibly be a success in the Field since the win of two Field Trials within a week by Mr. H. Reginald Cooke's Flatcoated Retriever Grouse of Riverside last season, while the best reply to the statement that, though a proved worker Grouse has never sired a puppy of any use in the Field is that up to the time of his success at Bridgnorth he had not been used at stud by his owner."

MORE GUNDOG GOSSIP
In October 1910, The Field published the following article under the heading of 'Gundog Gossip':

"The triumph of Mr. H. Reginald Cooke's young Flatcoated dog, Kestrel of Riverside, at the Kennel Club's Retriever Trials this week, must do much to silence the criticism against dogs of the show type and their owners, and it will be interesting to read the explanation given by the man who made so bitter an attack on Grouse of Riverside after his win at Davenport last season – a meeting not visited by that individual, it may be added. The basis of his argument – if it can be given that name – was that Grouse of Riverside had never sired any tried workers; but the falsity of that line was shown when Mr. Cooke explained that his Davenport winner had only been given one chance of perpetuating his good name, and that chance he took himself for his owner had no wish to place him at public service. Kestrel is one of the produce of that little escapade, and, after winning the highest honours in the ring at Newport and Market Drayton, he has now proved his value in the Field, and in an unmistakable way, for he fairly romped through the Junior Stake at Gaddesden. That his Field Trial career will be a brilliant one is

Left: H. Reginald Cooke judging Flatcoated Retrievers at a Manchester show.

Right: Vincent, H. R. Cooke's son, with Grouse.

almost certain. He was broken by Goode, who handled him uncommonly well."

"Mr. Reginald Cooke has been fortunate in breeding one of the finest Flatcoated Retrievers that has ever been brought before the public from a sporting point of view. This young dog, Kestrel of Riverside, out for the first time, won at the Retriever Trials held by the Kennel Club at Gaddesden in Hertfordshire. He ran again in the All-Aged stake the next day but was unplaced; but two days following, he ran again at the Northern Field Trials when he was awarded the first prize. At the International Gundog meeting at Davenport he was awarded a Certificate of Merit. This young dog is sired by Dual Champion Grouse of Riverside, that won more Field Trials last season than any other Retriever has done in its whole lifetime"

TRIAL PHOTOGRAPHS

At this stage, I am going to include some of the wonderful photographs of these early Trials, all of which are reported on at great length. Rather than risk being overly repetitive by including yet more reports, I have decided to let the photographs speak for themselves. They are not to be missed! Do look at the ladies attire; I particularly love the photograph of the Duchess of Hamilton with Dungavel Phoebe, taken at the Scottish Retriever Trials near Perth in 1910. Another favourite is the

Below: Mr. E. W. H. Blagg's Busy Shem retrieving a runner. 5: Walking a field of roots. 6: Working in a turnip field. 7: Mr. H. R. Cooke's Kestrel of Riverside, winner Junior Stakes.

Above & Below: The Retriever Society's Field Trials at Davenport, in October 1910. 1: Mr. B. J. Warwick's Wenhasten Richard, third prize and Arkwright prize for best natural qualities. 2: The judges, Messrs. P. Clutterbuck, C. C. Eley, and M. Portal. 3: The Duchess of Hamilton's Dungavel Juno, second prize. 4: Captain J. H. Duttin's Sherborne Togi, winner. 5: Waiting for the driven birds to fly over the water. 6: Major Phillips's Labrador Katya retrieving in water. 7: Spectators crossing a brook. 8: Dungavel Juno retrieving a pheasant. 9: Mr. E. W. H. Blagg's Busy Mite retrieving. 10: The guns crossing the water.

Above & Below: The Scottish Retriever Trials near Perth, November 1910. 1: Mr. Archibald Butter's Peter of Faskally, by Waterdale Gamester-Nell, winner of Scottish Field Trial Open Stake (the only Retriever which has ever won two Open Stakes in one season). 2: Mrs. Archibald Butter's Dun of Faskally, third in the Non-winners' Stakes. 3: The meet at the crossroads. 4: On the hillside. 5: The Marquis of Tullibardine, one of the guns, and owner of the property worked over. 6: Giving guns their positions. 7: Mr. K. M'Douall's Logan Lorna, second in Non-winners' Stakes. 8. The Duchess of Hamilton with Dungavel Phoebe. 9: The Duchess of Hamilton's Dungavel Juno, third in Open Stakes.

Above: The Retriever Society's Trials at Davenport, in October 1910.

photograph of the judges at the Retriever Society's Trials at Davenport, on October 11th and 12th October 1910, as well as the picture of the guns crossing the water at the same event.

GWERNYFED TRIALS

The second Retriever Championship of 1910 was held at Gwernyfed in Breconshire, during November. On reading the reports of this championship, once again I was amazed to see there were only nine entries for the stake. The stake was open to winners of first or second prizes at any recognised Retriever meeting held in 1910.

"The Championship meeting for Retrievers under the rules of the International Gundog League was held at Gwernyfed, Mr. A. Glen-Kidston's shooting near Three Cocks, Breconshire, on Thursday and Friday (yesterday), the entry of nine, however, being disappointing, and at the last moment the qualification was extended to admit the winners of either first or second prizes at any recognised Field Trial meeting held this season. It was originally intended to confine the stake to the actual winners, but for various reasons owners withdrew likely candidates, and in the circumstances the entry of nine was satisfactory, especially as the winner of each of the three open meetings was nominated. The draw was made at The Hotel, Three Cocks, on Wednesday evening, Major Phillips intimating that the meet on the first day would be near Gwernyfed, less than a mile from Three Cocks Junction."

A lengthy report follows, but I have chosen to insert another report from Illustrated Kennel News, which I felt had some slightly more constructive views.

"Though it was disappointing to find neither the Flatcoated Retriever Kestrel of Riverside, nor the red dog Rust, with which Mr. F. Straker won the chief event on the Northumberland card, included in this week's entry at Gwernyfed, Major Phillips and those associated with him in the establishment of a Retriever Championship had no great cause to be dissatisfied with an entry of nine. The winners of the three Open stakes at Gaddesden, Davenport and Strathord, together with the best Retrievers seen out at the district meetings at Sarratt, Newent and Woolverstone, and the junior winner at the Scottish fixture, were entered; but it was not altogether satisfactory to find that the entry was made up to its full strength by two alterations in the conditions governing the competition. Had the original idea of the promoters been adhered to there would only have been seven entries, for neither Kaal nor Logan Lorna had actually won even a Junior, Puppy or Non-Winners stake, though both had been placed, and each was certainly worthy of a further Trial in a Championship contest. That the conditions of the stake must be altered before it can be considered really representative is freely admitted, and for next season it would be no bad idea to reserve three or even four days, if necessary, for the Trial, and make the conditions identical with those which have governed the International Championship for Pointers and Setters at Shrewsbury for considerably more than twenty years. That event always draws a wonderfully good entry, and it is open to "single Pointers and Setters that have won first and second prizes (not in a Brace stake) at any Field Trial in the world; all ages." The point is that winners in any year are eligible to compete, and the stake is kept open till all others at the meeting have been decided in order to qualify Pointers and Setters whose owners may like to give them the chance of gaining Championship honours which are never questioned. Occasionally 'a light of other days' appears, and wins, while before the quarantine order put a stop to international visits, the best of the French and Belgian kennels were frequently sent on to Shrewsbury to compete against the British cracks. Retriever Trials, of course, are not known on the continent, but were the conditions of a stake, which is certain to be run for two more seasons, to be amended on the lines suggested, far more interest would be taken in the competition, and by allowing sufficient time for Trials, an entry which might be considered unwieldy could be dealt with. The stake is too sporting an event to be belittled in any way, and we are not alone in hoping the promoters will see their way to make future contests for Mr. Glen-Kidston's handsome cup tests for the real Championship."

CORRESPONDENCE

A letter appeared in The Field on October 15th 1910 which caused an enormous response, it is impossible to include all the replies to this letter but I will give you the letter and a selection of the many, many that followed:

"Sir, – As your readers are aware, a great difficulty which confronts judges is the question of giving all competing dogs an equal chance. I have a letter before me, which has induced me to address you. It is from a gamekeeper, a straightforward and right sort, not a grumbler, not of the 'disappointed exhibitor' order. It is in effect a strict assertion that at certain Trials he was never given a chance, that his dog – which I know to be a very good and clever one – was practically idle all day, while others were getting all the work to do. And I am sorry to say that he asserts and honestly believes that -no gamekeeper has a chance amongst gentlemen's dogs - and he adds, "all the other keepers, and even the beaters, said to me the judges had evidently no use for me in that show". Now, we unfortunate judges know very well that, as conditions now are, it is impossible to give every dog an equal chance, and I am sure many of those with whom I have judged will agree that a stake has too often been awarded to a dog, mainly on account of some exceptional bit of work where conditions and luck suited him, while the judges have felt all the time that various others in the stake might have done the thing as well, or even better, if they had been given the same chance. I know the judges who acted on the occasion in question, and I know that my friend is wrong. I feel sure that he is blaming the individuals when the system is at fault. I have only to instance the win of a bona-fide gamekeeper with his own dog at the Scottish Trials last year to show the fallacy of my informant's statement, and I aver, without hesitation, that all judges whom I know, if they allow themselves to have any leanings at all, have, in their hearts, a decidedly warm corner for the keeper working his own dog.

"However, it is, none the less, most unfortunate and deeply to be regretted that it should be possible for a good sportsman to go home from his outing at a Trial believing, however wrongly, that he has failed to get the justice to which he was entitled. I venture to trouble you with the foregoing statement to lead up to this question. Can we do nothing to ensure a more equal chance to all competing dogs? A very old frequenter of trials, a shrewd and capable judge and well known to most of your readers, has several times suggested to me that at a certain stage of the Trial pinioned cock pheasants might be introduced on the scene, and three of these liberated in roots for, say, each of the last six dogs left in, under, as nearly as may be, identical conditions of ground and scent, each dog having thus, the chance of three good runners. There is much to be said in favour of some such plan, or it might perhaps be done for every dog left in after the first round. I do not mean that the dog which acquitted himself best at this should necessarily win, but such a Trial would, at all events, greatly assist the judges in finding the best dog, and would tend to increase the confidence of handlers in the merit of the decisions. Will others, by expressing their views assist in solving this very difficult question?
A FIELD TRIAL JUDGE."

Some replies!

"Sir, – I cannot let pass a letter signed A

Some of the Riverside Retrievers. Top left: Stor Briar. Top right: Champion Jimmy. Above: Seldom Seen. Above right: Champion Rocket. Right: Champion Bianca.

Field Trial Judge in your issue of October 15th. without remarking on it. I cannot see why the beginning of his letter was introduced at all, as the writer says it is not true, as he knows the judges and his informant was wrong. The part, however, which I take exception to – and which to my mind proves A Field Trial Judge as well as the Shrewd and Capable Judge to be absolutely wrong, and doubly wrong because it shows that they can never have really done much work with Retrievers – it is when it is "suggested that at a certain stage of the trials pinioned cock pheasants might be used in roots". How could anyone seriously suggest such a thing? Any man who has ever worked his dog knows that it is the blood scent which the dog is wanted to take up, and which the good dog will hold, no matter how many pheasants are running about in the roots or clover or whatever cover the bird falls in and runs in. Could anything be more ridiculous than to suggest that pinioned cock pheasants should be turned down. I wonder if A Field Trial Judge's dog would be able to distinguish between the scent of the pinioned bird and another bird not wounded? Why, it is the very thing, which, in my opinion, stamps a dog as a good one – or, rather gives him a good point – if he sticks to the blood scent through a lot of game which

has not been wounded. It is a pity A Field Trial Judge could not have seen his way to signing his name to his letter. I venture to think there are few who handle their own dogs who will agree with his views, and, I hope, very few judges who would be "greatly assisted by it".
CHRISTOPHER HESELTINE."

"Sir, – I agree entirely with Colonel Heseltine's remarks as to the futility of putting down pinioned pheasants in roots as a Trial for retrievers. The main point is, as he says, the ability of a dog to distinguish between the blood scent and that of unwounded game. I should like to know how such a test could have been carried out while in some of the fields of roots I walked through last week while judging the Eastern Counties Trials, which were so full of game of all kinds as to severely try the nose and steadiness of every dog sent out, even though assisted by the blood scent. I am afraid none of these artificial tests will be found of any practical use, and Field Triallers, like everyone else, must submit to the 'luck of the game', even though it does sometimes appear to treat some individuals rather harshly.
R. CLAUDE CANE."

"Sir, – May I ask of those of your readers who may be, as I hope, thinking of helping us with useful suggestions not to discard the idea of pinioned runners solely on account of a letter in last week's The Field signed Christopher Heseltine? There is a very simple, and, indeed obvious plan – harmless to the bird – of securing the blood trail, which I have employed with success during some thirty years of Retriever breaking. At how many Trials have I assisted to judge where we have arrived at a virtual impasse, where every dog continued to pick up and return the 'unresisting dead' with equal facility, where piteous entreaties were passed on to the guns to try all kinds of fancy shooting, and then how often have I wished that I might be permitted to clear things up by performing some of my old tricks in the runner line!
A FIELD TRIAL JUDGE."

"Sir, – As a competitor at Trials, I do not agree to the suggestion of pinioned birds as a final test for Retrievers. In the first place, it is artificial; secondly, useless, unless the wing is made to bleed, when it is cruel; thirdly, it would tend to encourage the training of dogs to run scent of unwounded birds, which is not what is wanted, and lastly, it would tend to bring Trials to a low level. If people desire to reduce tests for Retrievers down to a species of Bloodhound Trials, it can be done by a man dragging a freshly killed bird on a string at the end of a 10ft stick, and the judges can see if the dog runs the man's scent (which he probably will not if a stranger) or that of the bird; but I confess if that form of Trial is ever adopted I shall cease to attempt to compete, and I fancy many others will do the same.

"Naturally, judges want runners, and as the type of dog run is so much improved, runners are more needed than ever, but pray do not provide artificial ones! No.4 shot and a fair range often help matters. As to the remarks that keeper's dogs do not get a chance, or that one breed is more favoured than another, I do not think it is worth thinking about for a moment. I am certain that judges of Trials consider dog work done only, and ownership or breed is immaterial to them. If the standard of keeper's dogs is to be gauged by that seen at the Scottish Trials only last week, any judge has the heartfelt sympathy of
ONE WHO RUNS RETRIEVERS."

"Sir, – Lieut. Col. Heseltine when criticising the letter of A Field Trial Judge appears to assume that the capacity shown by some dogs of sticking to a line in spite of cross scents is entirely due to the game being wounded, and that his blood scent theory is an accepted fact; and he tells us that every man who handles his own dog knows it. I have seen it stated that the hounds used in France for hunting deer

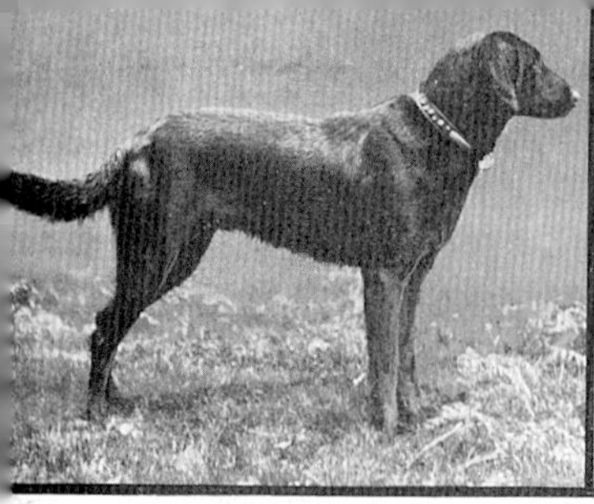

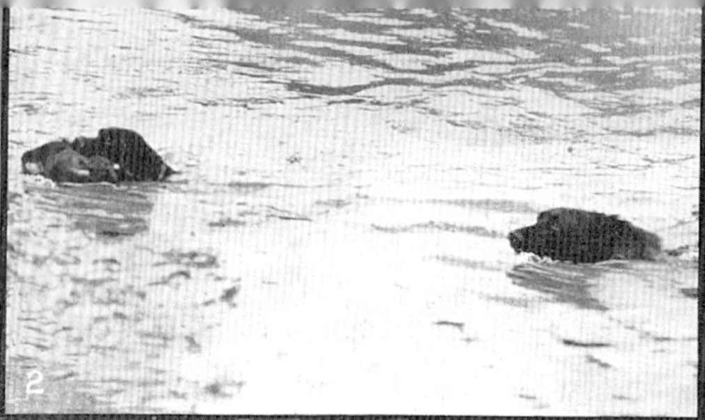
2

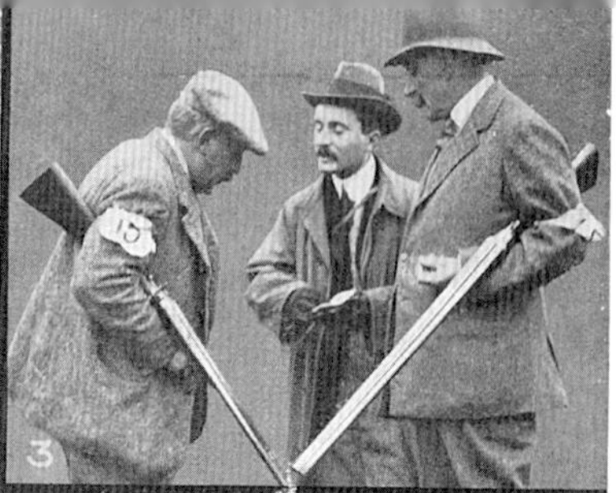
3

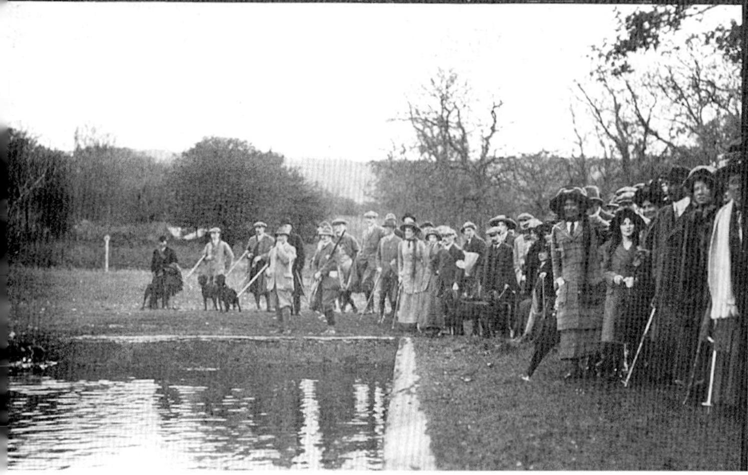

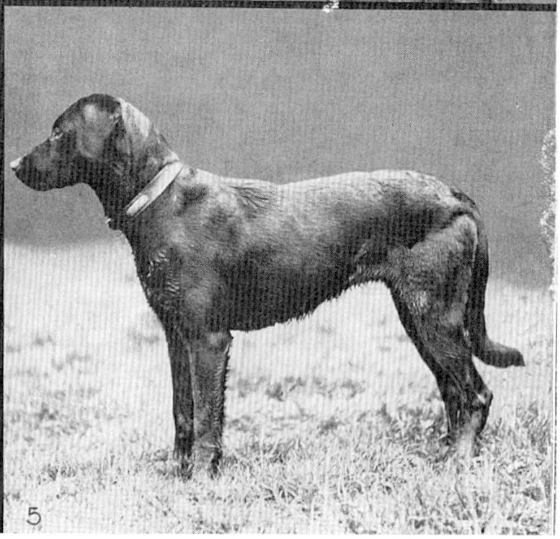
5

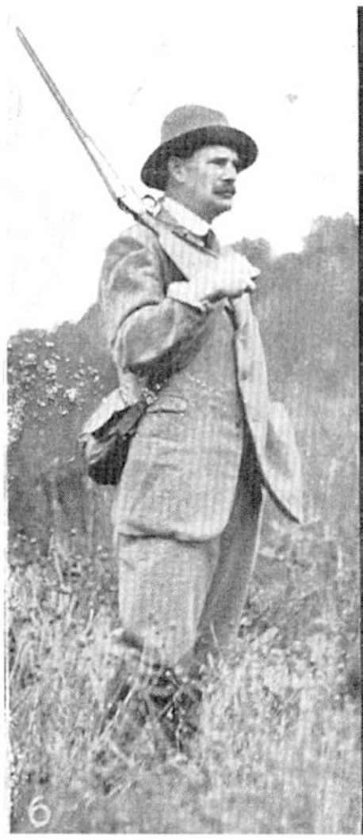
6

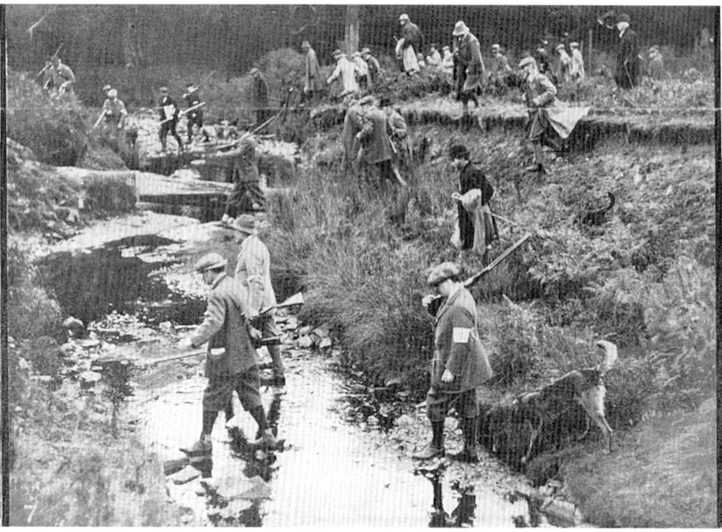
7

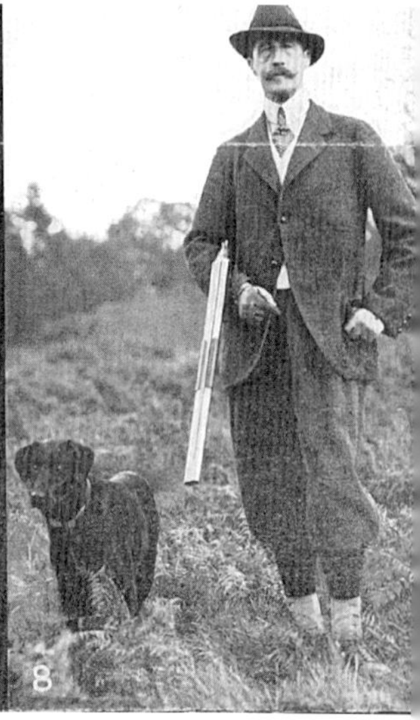
8

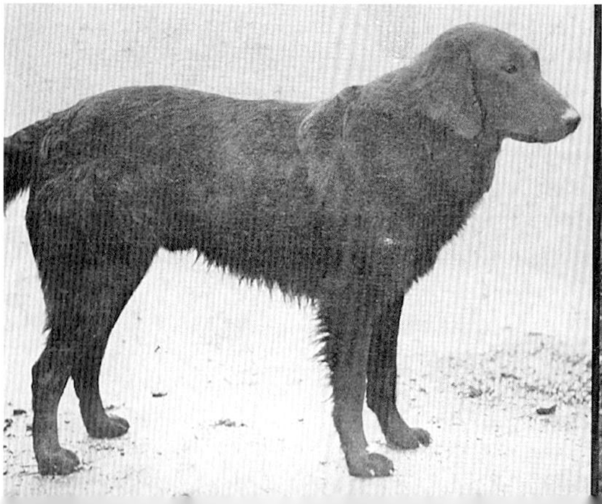

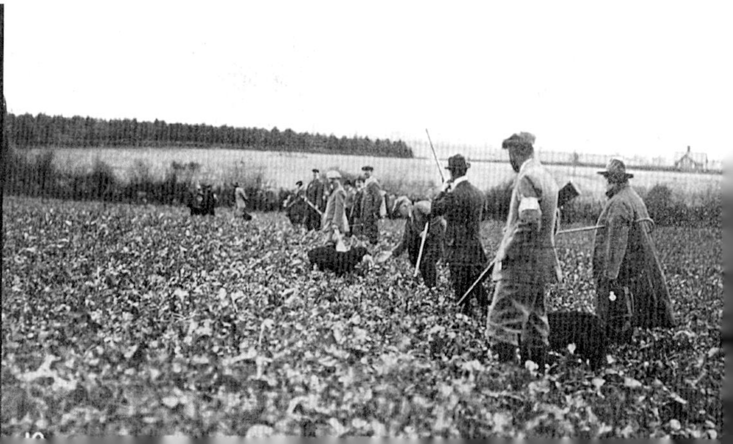

Volume Two (1908-1911)

Opposite Page: The Retriever Society's Trials at Gwern-y-fed, Breconshire, November 1911. 1: Capt. Glen-Kidston's Juniper, winner of first prize. 2: The Duchess of Hamilton's Dungavel Phoebe retrieving a duck from the water. 3: Alexander, the Duchess of Hamilton's handler, talking to Mr. L Tabourier, Vice-President of the French Retriever Society, and to the Hon. A. Holland-Hibbert. 4: Spectators watching the dogs at work in the water. 5: Mr. M. Portal's Sandhoe Flora. 6: Capt. Glen-Kidston (owner of winner), on whose ground the trials were held. 7: The guns crossing a brook. 8: Lord Chesterfield with Logan Lambert. 9: Mr. L. D. Wigan's Rab of Glendaruel, winner of second prize. 10: Alexander with Dungavel Phoebe.

Right: The Kennel Club Retriever Trials at Eamont, Lowther Castle, Penrith. 1: Moving off. 2: A general view of the meet by Eamont River. 3: Shooting over Hackthorpe High Covert. 4: Pheasant shooting, with Lord Lonsdale judging the retrieving, by the river Shapbeck at Bessiegill. 5: Dungavel Jet, the winner of the All-aged Stakes, retrieving to her owner, Mrs. Butters. 6: Crossing the Eamont on the way to lunch. 7: Major T. B. Phillips's Kaal retrieving to hand. 8: The bugler with Lord Lonsdale to give signal to beaters and guns. 9: The meet by Eamont river.

The History Of Retrievers

Some winners at Crufts Dog Show at Islington. 1: The Rt. Hon. L. Harcourt's Golden Retriever Culham Flame, two firsts. 2: Dalmations on the bench. 3: Mrs. Horner's Pointer Ch. Lunesdale Wagg, first and Champion (winner of 34 championships). 4: Mr. H. Cooke's Retriever, Kestrel of Riverside, two firsts (winner of two Field Trials this season).

possess this quality to an extraordinary degree, and that owing to its lack in our Foxhounds the French huntsman will not use our Hounds, yet in this case, the quarry is not wounded. Bloodhounds, again, can in a greater or less degree stick to their original trail in spite of the presence of cross scents, yet there is no blood scent here. Personally, though I claim to be a man who has regularly worked his own dogs, I have little faith in the blood scent theory, and I fancy that a dog which possesses this capacity of sticking to his line and not changing to other lines (which are almost certainly either slightly fresher or slightly staler, and probably vary according to the exhaustion or freshness of the game) would carry the line of a pinioned bird through as many cross scents as though it were wounded. Even if it is not so, there seems no reason why pinioned birds should not be of great use if turned down in roots that had already been walked through earlier in the day; it might assist in equalising the opportunities of the dogs, even though it were not a very severe test. COCKER."

CRUFTS DOG SHOW 1911

The Crufts show of 1911 was recorded in H. Reginald Cooke's journals in the form of a pasted-in cutting describing the show.

"The awarding of the chief special prizes attracted a large crowd to the Agricultural Hall, Islington, yesterday. Competition for all

The Crufts Show of 1911, held at the Agricultural Hall, London. Retrievers were judged by Mr. Theo. Marples.

of them was confined to dogs owned by subscribers to the promoting society, the result being that many fine exhibits were prohibited from competing.

"Mr. A. E. Way's Roughcoated Fox Terrier Collarbone of Notts, was awarded the challenge cup for the exhibit shown in best condition. The bowl previously known as the Sporting International Bowl, for the best animal in the Pointer, Setter, Retriever, Spaniel, or Beagle classes, was won by Jimmy of Riverside, a Flatcoated Retriever shown by Mr. H. Reginald Cooke, of Nantwich. The Reserve was Mallwyd Markham, an English setter, shown by Mr. T. Steadman. A similar bowl previously known as the Non-Sporting International Bowl for the best animal in the St. Bernard, Newfoundland, Old English Sheepdog, Bulldog, Dalmatian, Chow-Chow or Poodle Brentwood Hero, an Old English Sheepdog, exhibited by Mrs. S. Charter, of Brentwood, the Reserve being Foo Chan a Chow shown and owned by Miss Lawton, of Barkomby Rectory, near Crewe."

"Mr. H. Reginald Cooke was naturally proud of the wins of his youngster, Kestrel of Riverside at the Agricultural Hall, and with Jimmy out of the way he must have won the Championship, though Cherry Boy wanted reckoning with. Kestrel's merit, of course, lay in his being able to do so well in the ring after his fine performances at the Kennel Club, and Shropshire, Cheshire and North Wales Trials last season, and the owner of the famous Riverside Kennel may be pardoned the pride which is only natural after all which has been said "in another place" about the uselessness of the show and the show-bred Retriever. Kestrel is a nailer in both the ring and the field; his appearance next season will be looked for with interest, especially as Goode thinks he has cured him of the irritating habit of whining which he had contracted, and which certainly interfered with his work. Another Field Trial item gleaned at the show was that it is unlikely the Cheshire, North Wales, and Shropshire Society will trouble about Spaniel Trials next season, for two projected meetings have fallen through. Such a decision, however, will be rough on Mr. H. W. Carlton and Mr. Eliot-Scott, who, between them, could surely guarantee to fill a stake.

The winner of Crufts 1911, Kestrel of Riverside. Photograph courtesy of 'Sport and General'.

3 EXTRACTS FROM VOLUME THREE (1911-1916)

The third journal begins with 15 columns of letters, the subject under debate this time being puppy stakes at Field Trials. Having read through the first two pages, and then being somewhat at a loss to know which letters to use as examples, I was amused to find Ready, Aye Ready, once again most definitely not lost for words. As we have already 'met' him, my decision was made for me. The letters are not dated individually but H. Reginald Cooke added footnotes, in this case labelled "Correspondence Re Field Trials – November 1911 to January 1912."

CORRESPONDENCE RE FIELD TRIALS

"Sir, – Every year now, when the Retriever Trial season is on, there is a more or less luxuriant crop of letters on the subject. This year the complaint is about puppies getting spoilt, while the pros and cons of the pinioned bird question have also been discussed. To take these questions in their order, speaking as a practical trainer, for the life of me I cannot see what harm can possibly come to the breed through having stakes for youngsters. If two or three go to the bad, why should the many be made to suffer for the sins of the few? The good old Spartan treatment is the thing for the unfit. Knock them on the head and breed from the dogs and bitches that can and do keep their heads through all the turmoil of a Retriever Trial. There is not much puppy about a dog of eighteen or twenty months, and a dog of that age ought to be able to go anywhere and do anything. Dogs under eighteen months should not be allowed to run, as nominations are so difficult to get, and in my opinion, they only monopolise the place of better dogs. As regards steadiness in puppies, that should be insisted on, because, if properly trained, a young dog should never be anything else; his retrieving and delivery ought also to be perfect, because if you do not get a speedy return and clean delivery in the puppy, you will never get it in the old dog. The things to overlook in the youngster are, first, the art of hunting on, and for the wind; secondly, not hunting out far enough from his handler, or perhaps the reverse. Then he may, if a really sharp one, get out the wrong way, and be difficult to lift in the right direction. Age and experience will cure these faults. There is nothing like plenty of practice for teaching a dog the length a gun can kill.

"The trying part of a Retriever Trial, for both handlers and their dogs, be they young or old, is very aptly put in the letter of Mr. Portal. I would, however, add the long weary wait in the firing line, when someone else's dog is having a hunt for something. If this is repeated, and it often is, and you have a really excitable dog, either young or old at your heel, you will soon discover that you have something that wants watching. Good marking I always consider a sine qua non in a dog I am shooting over at home. I am not so sure, however, that the best markers are the best Trial dogs. Your dog may have marked a bird that you did not see, and the judge tells you to send for a bird neither you, nor your dog saw. What happens then? The general reader must understand that at present the judges do not want to see a man's dog doing well. No, what they are chiefly looking for is a fault that they can put you out on, and so get down to a short list.

"If I might be allowed to offer a suggestion, I think an age limit should be put on puppies, say, over eighteen and under twenty-four months old. I would also confine Open stakes to dogs over two years old. Personally, I should like to see an Open stake confined to dogs that had actually won a prize, and perhaps the go-ahead Scottish Field Trial Association will take up this question, as it already provides a non-winners stake. Scottish people are generally reckoned to be pushing and up to date – so statistics prove, at all events. It is popularly supposed that when the North Pole is discovered there will be a Scotsman on the top of it with a bottle of Whiskey in his hand: but I am sorry to say that I am ashamed of Scotland (patriot as I am) for having introduced the use of pinioned birds at Retriever Trials. Oh, shades of my ancestors, where are all the Retriever trainers that the south of Scotland used to produce, that they should now degenerate into a pack of auld wives? The south of Scotland was one of the original homes of the present or modern retriever, and the men who broke and trained these dogs to the highest state of perfection thirty years since discarded all artificial aids to the end they had in view. Then why, oh, why, ye members of the Gamekeepers' Association, did you set back the hands of the clock? It is almost enough to make the ghosts of your Fathers come back and wreak vengeance on you. Plenty of real runners can be provided if you go about it in the right way. Any sceptic can be convinced if he will only pay a visit to Capt. Glen-Kidston's place at Three Cocks. That very good sportsman has learnt how to provide runners, and also how to conduct a Retriever Trial. Any dog can be taught to run the line of a bird that has been handled, but that dog may be a very poor Retriever. The true Retriever has to learn to know the difference between a bird that has been wounded with the gun and one that has not. A little blood from a paint brush is going from the sublime to the ludicrous. What is really wanted in a Retriever is to get things his handler cannot, and if this qualification was more often borne in mind the difficulty of making the awards at trials would to a great extent disappear.

"I must say that I have very great diffidence in mentioning another aspect of this great Retriever question that this season has been very noticeable. It is, however, a delicate question. No man living knows better than I do the amount of trouble and worry, not to speak of the expense incurred by an owner or lease of a shoot which he may have placed at the disposal of one or other of the societies promoting Retriever Trials. All honour be to them, and long may they continue to do so. It is not my intention to enlarge further on this in the meantime, but rather to draw attention to the extraordinary number of dogs this year which have won Trials on the home ground. I will not give a list; the subject is too delicate. The reader can easily find the number himself. I would just mention in passing, that this is not confined to Retrievers, but includes Spaniels. Far be it from me to impute a willing bias on the judges part; still, there the thing is. Probably the judges are the guests of the owner, and they are all jolly fellows, good sportsmen, and there may be an unconscious leaning towards the dog of a most entertaining host. Who can tell? It is so difficult. There may be nothing in all this; it may be the purest accident that so many dogs have done well at home, but so they might. If there is a tricky place out of which to get a bird the dog at home can be practised there. Then he does not have the fatigue of a long railway journey, and so on. The essence of the whole thing can be put in a very few word. All important stakes should be contested on neutral ground.

READY, AYE READY"

The heading was, as I stated previously,

'Puppy Stakes at Field Trials.' Ready, Aye Ready has obviously been 'holding back' for some months on the numerous topics that he managed to cram into his letter. One cannot help wondering who he was, although it is, perhaps, as well that we do not know! I confess, the comments on the Scots made the hair on the back of my neck bristle – he must have upset an awful lot of people in those days, perhaps the reason for his anonymity. As far as I can see, there was only one reply to that letter, or at least there was only one in the journal.

"Sir, – As one who has probably run and handled as many, if not more, young dogs than anyone else at Retriever Trials since they were inaugurated by the International Gundog League in 1900, may I be allowed to say that I have reluctantly come to the conclusion that it is a mistake to run a young dog in an Open stake. In three cases, in one of which the young dog won the Bergholt Cup, my dogs were never any use afterwards, though in another instance, at the Brandon meeting in 1902, Wenhaston Rajah, whom I took in hand only five weeks before the meeting, won the prize for the best puppy and was third in the Open stake. This was an exceptional instance, and one I cannot hope to repeat.

"I would like to point out to Ready, Aye Ready that the International Gundog League, the premier Retriever society, limits the age of puppies to eighteen months. The less said in reference to the last paragraph of his letter the better, as no one who attended these meetings, and knows the difficult task the judges have to perform, will approve of the insinuations of partiality. It reads like the writing of a disappointed competitor. In conclusion, I trust it will never be my misfortune, when acting as a judge, to be called on to try the dogs on pinioned birds, as I should absolutely refuse to have anything to do with it. Leaving aside the question of cruelty, I do not consider the test a desirable one.
F. M. REMNANT."

YELLOW RETRIEVERS

The next Subject, dated February 1912, is the first reference in the journals to yellow Retrievers; Marjoribanks and Ilchester being very famous names. The following was taken from The Field in February 1912.

"The Marjoribanks and Ilchester yellow Retrievers and trackers: An Old Breed Under a New Name.

"Colonel W. Le Poer Trench, of St. Huberts, Gerrards Cross, is responsible for the inclusion in Crufts catalogue of a class for what he claims to be the yellow or Russian Retriever, so highly valued in the Tweedmouth and Ilchester families for close on fifty years. The Hon. Lewis Harcourt, Mr. Brewster Macpherson, Mr. Isaac Sharpe, Mr. Jas Brown (Knockbrex), Mr. D. Macdonald (Ingestre), and other shooting men are known to be admirers of the breed, and it will be interesting to notice how Colonel Trench's invitation to breeders generally to support the class is received. The variety was originally introduced into this country shortly after the Crimean War by that well-known lover of gundogs, Mr. Dudley Marjoribanks, (subsequently created Lord Tweedmouth). He saw them in a circus at Brighton in the year 1858, where they were shown by their Russian owner. They were such splendid creatures that Mr. Marjoribanks determined to possess himself of them, and he bought the lot, transferring them to his deer forest in Invernesshire. There they were found to possess the required qualification of retrieving and tracking.

"They were so much valued that the family kept the breed to itself, the only kennels allowed to breed being those of Lord Tweedmouth and of his nephew, the late Lord of Ilchester. Bitches were never given away, and the favoured few upon whom dogs were bestowed appreciated them fully as The Marjoribanks breed of the yellow Russian Retriever.

"The result of this system of inbreeding was

A group of Marjoribanks and Ilchester Yellow Retrievers, bred at St. Huberts, Gerrard's Cross.

that about the year 1880 the variety was found to have much deteriorated physically and to have become soft. Finding this tendency, Lord Tweedmouth sent to Russia, in Europe, to endeavour to get fresh blood, but failed, the report being "breed unknown". It would appear from information subsequently obtained that the breed did not come from Russia, in Europe, but from a distant and wild part of Russia, in Asia, quite out of the track of ordinary travellers. Had it been otherwise, no doubt the variety would have been largely imported for use in civilised and sporting countries. Finding himself unable to fortify the breed by new blood from it's native country Lord Tweedmouth was obliged to approve of a cross being effected with a bloodhound. This answered for a time, but as a result the purity of the original breed became practically lost. About the year 1882 Colonel Le Poer Trench became the owner of a good specimen dog bred by Lord Ilchester. This dog he found to possess such excellent qualities that he desired to reproduce the breed, but, being aware that bitches were not given away, he sent pictures of Sandy to various parts of Russia in the hope of being able to buy one, but his efforts were attended by the same result as those of Lord Tweedmouth.

"One day in 1884, however, Lord Tweedmouth introduced himself in Hyde Park to Colonel Trench. It came about in this way: Colonel Trench, who lived in London at that time, always had his dog with him, and one day when crossing Hyde Park he was addressed by a gentleman, who said "I beg your pardon Sir, but is that your yellow retriever?" Colonel Trench replied in the

Colonel W. Le Poer Trench's Czar.

Colonel W. Le Poer Trench's Sandy.

affirmative, when his Lordship curtly remarked, "my breed!" Mutual introductions and conversations followed. It was then that Colonel Trench was given the information above quoted concerning the breed, its deterioration, and the various efforts made to resuscitate it. The photograph is that of Colonel Trench's original dog Sandy, bred by Lord Ilchester. This dog was carefully scrutinised by Lord Tweedmouth, and was declared by him to be a typical specimen of the breed as acquired by him.

"One peculiarity about these dogs is worth mentioning. They are as perfect companions in the house as they are sporting dogs in the field. They are excellent water dogs, but are not handicapped by the strong smell generally noticed in dark-coloured Retrievers after immersion in water. The following is an interesting illustration of the double qualification of the Marjoribanks and Ilchester Retrievers. On a night in November 1886, Sandy was present at an entertainment given in a London house at which Mademoiselle Sarah Bernhardt assisted. That lady was quite captivated by the dog, and he was literally worshipped by her and other visitors. Next morning this same dog accompanied his master to a shooting party at Swateleys, in Middlesex, where he was to be seen forcing his way swimming through the ice to fetch birds off an island in the lake. His Lordship, after their interview, gave Colonel Trench a bitch, the produce of the cross above referred to. He bred from it, being allowed by Lord Ilchester the services of his best dog, at that time still pure and of a sandy or cream colour. In the result the Bloodhound cross prevailed, and the whole of the puppies were of a darkish red and heavy headed. Colonel Trench gave the whole of this litter away, and fears that by doing so he unintentionally, but largely, assisted in the disappearance of the true type. He was unable to breed further from the bitch himself, as she was poisoned by a gang of poachers which owed his keeper a grudge. The specimens produced by this cross, no doubt possess many of the good points of their progenitors, but, not being pure, can never be properly classed as a breed, and must continue to deteriorate.

"Since then, Colonel Trench has been casting about to try and find pure specimens. He has ascertained from where the breed originally came, though he has not yet had time to carry out his intention of going there to try and obtain fresh blood. In the meantime, however, he has, by following up the enquiries among gilies and kennel men, succeeded in getting a dog which is the produce of parents existing before the cross was made. After a further long delay he succeeded in obtaining a bitch, but, as she was an albino, he hesitated about using her. However, he at last tried the experiment with marked success. The bitch is beautifully shaped, and evidently free from any cross, and none of her progeny has inherited her albino peculiarity. There are probably still some dogs in the country free from the bloodhound cross. If there are, it is hoped that their owners will join in this effort to resuscitate the pure-breed and keep it pure. This Russian breed is totally distinct from the breed of yellow Retrievers, of which The Earl of Lonsdale has so fine a kennel. His dogs are Labradors, which are unsurpassed as Retrievers. The same may be said of similar dogs to be found in certain parts of Northumberland."

CURLYCOATED RETRIEVERS

Following from this history of yellow-coloured Retrievers, an article about Curlycoated Retrievers appears in the scrapbooks. I have chosen to include the whole of an article published in the August 1912 edition of Fry's Magazine. It is entitled 'The Choice of a Retriever,' and it is written by Mr. Stanley Duncan, known simply by the description of 'wildfowler' in brackets after his name (The wildfowlers' Association of Great Britain and Ireland was formed in 1908 by the late Stanley Duncan. The Association is now the present-day British Association for Shooting and Conservation).

Left: A modern Curlycoated Retriever. Right: Captain Phipps Hornby's Erleigh Sandy, retrieving a partridge.

"That the Retriever is the most popular gundog of today is a fact which goes beyond dispute. Modern methods of shooting have demanded more use for him, and yearly he is coming further to the front. The varieties of our Retrievers are Curlycoated, Flatcoated, and Labrador. The colour of all these varieties or breeds is generally black, but brown, yellow, or golden specimens are to be met with. There are good and bad workers to be found in all the breeds, and after careful observation I have come to the conclusion that given a pup possessing average faculties, everything depends upon the manner in which it is broken and handled for its future success as a gun dog.

"The Curlycoated Retriever is probably a few years older a breed than the Flatcoated, and, although it has a strong club to foster and look after its interests, there appears to be no doubt that it will never gain the popularity its Flatcoated relative has done. About the middle of the last century ushered in the Retriever as a British production. The Curlycoated breed was undoubtedly the result of judiciously crossing the Labrador or Lesser Newfoundland with the Irish Water Spaniel, and possibly using the French, or, to be more correct, German, Poodle as an outcross. That Poodles were originally water spaniels or water dogs we have ample proof, and that many show poodles of today inherit sporting abilities is a fact we have repeatedly seen exemplified.

"The Flatcoated Retriever traces its descent from the Labrador and a cross with the setter. Wavycoated Retrievers as pure-breeds are now dogs of the past, the early part of the present century closing their career. The pure Labrador Retrievers of the present time are descendants of animals imported into this country in the early part of last century. Although kept pure and used essentially for work by a few notable kennels, it is only in recent years that the breed has become popular. More weight in most specimens of the breed is thought to be wanting, and this, coupled with the fact that fresh blood is very much needed, is a lamentable situation with such a fine animal as the Labrador. Marking these unfortunate circumstances, we are confronted by the unaccountable evidence that crosses between the Labrador and the present day Flatcoat result in the progeny being constitutionally weak and altogether physically

A brace of puppies by Champion High Legh Blarney.

below either of its parents.

"This state of things in survivors extends also to stamina and, consequently, working abilities, which are important features so well stamped in the well-bred Retriever of any breed. The Flatcoated Retriever is beyond all dispute the breed of today. In him we have beauty, strength and ability second to none, and considering the enormous numbers of him bred and reared annually for work alone, I need have no hesitation in saying he is the Retriever which has come to stay. Of him it is quite an easy matter to secure good looking and excellent working specimens at reasonable prices – a matter not possible with either the Curlycoat or the Labrador. These circumstances will naturally induce to propagate his popularity for some time to come. As it is beyond the limits of this short discourse to describe technically all our Retrievers, I confine further details to the Flatcoat – the Retriever of Retrievers.

"Before confining my remarks to one variety, it would be well to express that the comparative merits of the breeds are no more variable in one than in another. I suffice to say, as I have previously hinted, that there are good dogs to be found of all varieties – and bad ones – Heaven knows there are plenty. Of the suitability of the varieties for work as Retrievers, I maintain no argument. The Curlycoat, with its tight, astrakhan curled coat, the Labrador with its dense, shorthaired pelt, and the Flat with its heavy jacket, are all admirable dogs for retrieving work both on land and water. To theorise advantages of one variety over another and argue, for instance, that the Labrador is more suited, due to special features in the texture of his coat, for rough cold work, than other breeds, is not only erroneous but misleading. It must occur to all reasonable thinking persons that present-day Retrievers would not be what they are had they not admirably suited the purposes for which they have so long been bred and entered to.

"The modern shooting man is ever anxious to possess dogs not only of exceptional abilities as workers, but also typical representatives of their breed. This natural desire must have alone been responsible with our forefathers for the fine type of Pointers and Setters of the decade prior to dog shows. Since the institution of dog shows, type has been very much regarded in all breeds of sporting dogs. The utility of dog shows in the past has served well to frame type, but much could be said against shows with regard to the establishment of useful sporting dogs. Nowadays matters stand differently, for the Kennel Club has made a rule that no pointer, setter, sporting Spaniel or Retriever can obtain the title Champion unless in addition to having been awarded three Challenge Certificates by three different judges, he must also have gained a prize or Certificate of Merit at a Field Trial which is recognised by the Kennel Club. This is as it should be, and in future we can but hope to see all our best show specimens of gundogs and good workers. As regards show-bred Retrievers, especially the Flatcoated, they have not suffered so much as some other sporting breeds from the show malady, as their owners have generally been sportsmen. As a matter of fact, it has for a long time been well known that most show strains of Retrievers are excellent workers and their offspring very tractable and easily broken. To breed dogs of these combined characters is thus not so difficult as one might suppose. The best of blood is fairly true to type, and although it may be safe to assert that a champion will not occur once in a hundred puppies reared, yet there is always the chance of a better average occurring with the lucky individual.

"The generality is that half of the puppies raised are good if not perfect in appearance and hold a corresponding value, whereas the other less typical animals may make workers for the less ambitious. It cannot be more strongly urged not to breed from non-typical specimens, no matter how good at their work or how well bred. If breeding is permitted with these dogs, the result will most surely be a divergence from characters and a product of nondescripts. In the production of a

Volume Three (1911-1916)

A famous Curlycoated Retriever, Trooper.

A brace of typical Curlycoated Retrievers.

thoroughly good working typical dog much credit should be reflected upon the producer. Proportionate praise is due to him who can raise stock which carry 80 points of the 100 and do well in the field. Of course, such animals are worth money, for not only are their working abilities of value, but their handsomeness must be a source of great pleasure to their owners. How to select such animals I intend to describe.

"The show judge figures in his mind his ideal and judges the dogs before him from it. Should the prize winner be far from the standard of the judge's ideal of a Flatcoated Retriever, I will endeavour to paint him for you. The general symmetry and balance of the animal as the eye catches it are of the most importance. Kindly expression in the medium sized soft, dark hazel eyes also counts for much, as it indicates temperament and disposition. The skull is flat and long with powerful jaws. The lips are firm and tight. The nostrils are fairly large. In appearance the head is long and strong, but shows no indication of flew in the lips nor squareness of muzzle; while on the other hand, it is well filled below the eyes and not sharply pointed. The teeth are large and shining white, evenly set, without a sign of being over or under-shot.

The ears are small, set low and flat to the head, and covered with short, smooth hair. The neck is gracefully proportionate in length to the short, well-set-up body, and there are no signs of throatiness. The couplings are of medium length (one might say rather short than long), and the body gives the impression of great strength. The chest is deep, the ribs only slightly sprung. The legs are straight and show abundance of bone, but not that quantity which inclines an animal to appear cloddy. The feet are of medium size, the toes close and firmly grasped. the back is short and strong, the tail of moderate length, the tip falling to the point of the hocks. The stern is carried on a level with the back. Black is the general colour. There is no trace of white, and the hair is brilliant, dense and flat. In size he appears a big dog. Such an animal as I have described is not a common article. One answering to such details would be worth quite a handsome sum, allowing, of course, that his carriage and action were perfect. The breed moves in a characteristic 'dog trot' manner, but when sent out to retrieve, a good stretching gallop is generally exercised. The standard of point values for the Flatcoated Retriever are set out as follows:

The History Of Retrievers

Skull, ears and eyes	10
Nose and jaws	5
Neck, loins and back	10
Quarters and stifles	5
Shoulders and chest	13
Legs, knees and hocks	12
Feet	10
Tail	5
Coat	10
Symmetry and temperament	20
Total	100

The weight of working dogs ranges from 50 to 60 lbs, but in show specimens size is always favoured, and 70-lb animals are not considered too big. Bitches may weigh a few pounds less.

"Before purchasing a Retriever from an unknown source, one should be thoroughly satisfied concerning the merits of the animal, as regards both work and appearance, before closing the transaction. A good price given for a satisfactory and pleasing article is never regretted, but otherwise the matter is grievous and disheartening. Probably no one has done more towards perfecting Flatcoated Retrievers both in type and work than Mr. H. Reginald Cooke. To those who have the Retriever as a gundog at heart I cannot do better than recommend them to secure a copy of Mr. Cooke's excellent little work on Choosing and Breaking a Retriever. This booklet was originally written for the use of Mr. Cooke's keepers and puppy walkers, but through the persuasion of friends interested in show and working retrievers it has been given a wider circulation. A feature well deserving support in connection with the sale of it rests in the fact that the entire proceeds are given to the Society for the prevention of Cruelty, in which Mr. Cooke is interested."

THE PERFECT RETRIEVER

I note with great interest the number of correspondents who do not use their own names to sign off their letters! Having read so much while attempting to compile this insight into Trialling history, I have discovered that the correspondent Partridge, whose letter is printed below, is in fact H. R. Cooke. The first indication of this was the fact that one of the letters from Partridge in the journal was initialled underneath HRC, which gave me my first clue. The proof is now positive. Partridge started a lengthy discussion after penning the following letter in The Field in August 1912:

"Sir, – A perfect Retriever, and up to Field

Champion Jimmy of Riverside, Champion 1912.

Volume Three (1911-1916)

Trial form." Such is the attractive summary of many an alluring advertisement of dogs for sale at Aldridges repository and elsewhere. Happy the man who possesses such a treasure, and undoubtedly, such dogs do exist. It may not be time wasted, however, to examine whether the two statements are reconcilable, and to what extent a dog 'up to Field Trial form' is necessarily a perfect Retriever.

"As spectator, competitor and judge, the writer has attended a large proportion of Retriever Trials, both public and private, since the inception of the present series some thirteen years ago. During that time very great improvement has been made. Most people that have attended the Trials will agree that:

- The handling of Retrievers has made immense strides, and men are breaking their dogs with much more regard for the requirements of modern shooting.
- The result of this careful handling is reflected in the dogs themselves in whom the virtues of steadiness, patience, obedience, restraint, quickness, and general docility, have been instilled to a remarkable degree, and it is quite the exception to see any dogs running riot at Field Trials at the present time.

"So far so good! But what about the game finding, which, after all is the raison d'être of a Retriever? Can it be said that Retrievers have attained this to the same extent as their other good qualities? The writer thinks not, though he can only guess at the cause. The statement was made at the conclusion of the Champion stake last year that only one runner was gathered during the meeting, though chances were frequent. This statement, if true, is surely a very severe indictment on what ought to be the pick of the dogs in the country. At another meeting a boy employed to carry game, picked up, with a young Retriever working behind the line, several runners which had defeated the cracks. This points to a screw being loose somewhere. Echo answers where? Many people would doubtless exclaim "the dogs are deficient in nose," and possibly this is true in many cases; but in the humble opinion of the writer the probable cause is the present insistence on dash and pace in Trial dogs, rather than for careful, quiet and patient questing. We all admire the dog showing smartness in going out, picking his game quickly, and returning right up at a gallop, but what do we often see? A bird falls, a dog is sent out, the bird has run. The dog goes out quickly and well to the fall, puts his nose down for a moment, and after a few spasmodic jumps stands still with an appealing look to his handler. The latter waves him on, and the dog then begins what is known on the training grounds as "a rousing gallop. Without actually getting out of hand he beats half the field, and finally, without having had any line, makes a cast up wind and gallops on to his bird, which he collects triumphantly. The novice spectator exclaims, "What a smart bit of work!" The old hand remarks slyly, "What a lucky fluke!"

"A well known follower of Retriever Trials summed up the position very quaintly last year by remarking "There is far to much 'Hie on' about these trials, and not enough 'Hie lost', and such would appear to be the case.

"Can therefore the failure of many dogs to find game result from actual want of nose, or from the fact that the pace demanded at Trials causes the dog to gallop over his scenting powers, and consequently over his game? The writer feels he must leave the answer to others more discriminating than himself.

"The immortal Mr. Jorrocks was wont to quote a couplet regarding foxhounds:

As well as shape, full well he knows,

To kill their fox, they must have nose.

and having the nose, or the ability to use it should surely apply to the Retriever as well as the foxhound.

PARTRIDGE."

The following reply is one of my favourites:

"Sir, – In reply to questions from a contributor in your last issue, who signs himself Partridge, on the subject of the last

Champion Field Trial stake for Retrievers, may I, as one who has handled, and also judged at Trials, venture the opinion that the fault lies not with the dog in quality of nose, or at great speed, which at times is so desirable. No, the trouble lies nearer home; it is lack of, or faulty training. I have watched the progress of Retriever and Spaniel Trials, and noticed the gradual advance made in the dog work, and in looking back feel inclined to roughly summarise, in four stages, the progress achieved from the slip Retriever of the past to the up-to-date-dog:

1. Unsteady to shot; (but) clever and fast
2. Steady to shot; (but) stupid and slow
3. Steady to shot and stupid; (but) fast
4. Steady to shot; clever and fast.

"We have not arrived at perfection in stage No.4. Our retrievers are not yet sufficiently educated, or generally speaking, clever enough to adapt themselves to circumstance, and regulate their pace accordingly.
C. C. EVERSFIELD."

Another reply states:

"Sir,– Your correspondent Partridge in your issue of August 3rd. draws a fair picture of a common performance of the present day Retriever. My own unfortunate experience is, that, so far as following by scent and retrieving a wounded bird goes, the average modern Retriever is about as useful as a camel. With his head high up in the air and his long legs carrying him at motor car speed over immense distances, any results he may get are purely accidental, and are achieved by sight, irrespective of scent.

Partridge then sent a reply to some of the letters, an excerpt from which follows:

"If Mr. Eversfield's memory will carry him back some thirty or forty years he will call to mind that the usual accessories to a Retriever at that time were a slip, or more frequently a cord for leading purposes, with a thick stick and the toe of his owners boot to control him with, the dog usually being quite unbroken, but once free he showed a nose and an aptitude to sticking to the line of a strong runner that we do not always see these days.
PARTRIDGE."

Another reply that convinced me that Partridge was definitely H. R. Cooke was this:

"Sir,– It was not my intention to encroach further on your space, but as your correspondent Breaker has put one or two questions to me, I hope you will allow me to reply.
"I am pleased that, in the main, Breaker shares my views, I can assure him that I do not, in any way, advocate the claims of the slow dog. On the contrary one of the proudest moments of my life was when a dog in my kennel, after winning an open stake, was awarded the special prize given for the dog showing most dash combined with steadiness.
PARTRIDGE."

To my mind, this statement proves that Partridge was indeed H. R. Cooke, as the Trial in question is reported earlier in this book and the dog in question was most definitely Grouse of Riverside, from Mr. Cooke's highly successful Riverside breeding kennels.

THE TRIALS IN PHOTOGRAPHS

I would like to devote the next few pages entirely to photographs. There are many Trials recorded in the journals and these are normally accompanied by several photographs. The pictorial record is just as informative and fascinating as the written one – some real characters emerge from these

Top left: Eight full champions (Flatcoated) at Riverside, 1912.
Cheshire, Shropshire and North Wales Retriever Society's Trials at Bodelwyddan, October 4th and 5th 1912. Top right: Bodelwyddan Castle. Above: L. C. and Drake with H. R. Cooke and Scout. Above right: L. C. and Colonel Cotes. Right: The judges, A. T. Williams, A Shuter, and R. E. Birch.

Above: Scenes from the Retriever Society's Trials at Oxnead, Norfolk, October 1912. Left: Mr. J. B. Warwick's Wenhaston Richard, winner of second place, retrieving to hand. Right: Captain A. Glen Kidston's black Labrador, Gwendoline, by Peter of Faskally-Juniper, the winner.

Above: Scenes from the Kennel Club Retriever Trials at Gaddesdon, Hertfordshire, October 1912. Clockwise from top left: Mr. B. J. Warwick's Wenhaston Richard; The Hon. Mrs. Edwards, Mr. C. Alington, Col. Weller, and Mrs. Turner; Mr. J. G. Mair-Rumley Hammond's Jetter, retrieving in the Junior Stakes; Mr. John Kerr, on whose shooting the Trials were held; Mr. C. Alington's Bright, retrieving in the Junior Stakes.

The Kennel Club Retriever Trials at Bygrave, Herts, October 1913. 1: The crowd following the Trials. 2: Mrs. A. E. Butter's Prudence of Faskally, by Peter of Faskally-Quest, winner of the Junior stakes. 3: Viscount Helmsley, the judge, taking a hare that has just been retrieved from the handler. 4: Mrs. Charlesworth and her Golden Retriever, Normanby Tweedledum, which she handled herself. 5: Mr. Chas Phillips' Kelton, second in the All-aged Stakes. 6: The Duchess of Hamilton's Dungavel Bacchus (third in the All-aged Stakes, retrieving over a wire fence. 7: Anxious to see the sport. 8: Dina of Northaw retrieving partridge in Junior Stakes. 9: Mr. C. Edward Cooke's Dina of Northaw, second in Junior Stakes. 10: A rest by the haystack. 11: Walking partridge through the turnips.

Colonel C. H. Weller with his Flatcoated Retriever bitch Meeru, the winner of the 1912 Retriever Championship at Oxneath, Norfolk.

pages. Likewise, the costumes of the time are a treat not to be missed.

HIGH LEGH BLARNEY

In an obituary column in The Field, in February 1913, there was a report on the death of Ch. High Legh Blarney.

"Champion High Legh Blarney, the celebrated Flatcoated Retriever, the best dog of his day on the bench, and equally celebrated as a sire is dead. Even a kennel of the size and importance of Mr. H. Reginald Cooke's is substantially the poorer by the loss of such a great dog, for the deceased Champion, after his admittance to the Riverside kennel, never knew defeat, and among his many victories were Challenge Certificates at Darlington, Crystal Palace (three times), Edinburgh, Bristol, Birmingham (twice), Crufts (thrice), Hastings, Eastbourne, Manchester etc., and, besides innumerable Firsts and Specials, he secured the 40-guinea Challenge cup for the best sporting dog or bitch at the K.C. Show. He was the sire of many winners on the bench and at Field Trials, among other notable dogs claiming descent from him being Champion Jimmy of Riverside, Blight of Riverside (winner at last K. C. show), Southwell Dolly Varden, Biddy of Riverside, Severn Darkie, Cherry Boy, Swattsfield John, Southwell Nahob, Bones, Withington Nell, Susan of Hainault, Loudwater Fly, Cumbernauld Queen, Rounton Billey, Blackmore Zulu, Drake of Riverside, Kaffir of Riverside, Ranger of Riverside, Widgeon of Riverside, Briar of Riverside, Model of Riverside, Seldom Seen of Riverside, Horton Rosette, Cherry Tart, Croghan Jet, Defaidty Don, Haylton Don, Hermit, Withington Roger, Pilgrimage, Severn Molly, Swattsfield Twinkle, Longshaw Bruce, Pioneer, Truro, Bank Beauty, Bank Betty, Roseisle, Severn Betty, Unaware, High Legh Turk, Castle Milk Perfect, etc., etc. Champion High Legh Blarney was born on 18th. February 1902; breeder, Lieut. Col. Cornwall Legh: sire, Champion Black Quilt, dam High Legh Moment, and when Col. Cornwall Legh's kennel was dispersed at Aldridges, Blarney was purchased by Mr. H. Reginald Cooke for 200 guineas."

WELL-BROKEN RETRIEVERS

In The Field on 24th May 1913 there was an amusing little report titled A Well-broken Retriever, unfortunately there was no author's name to accompany it.

"Out of a packet of letters which had been put by for some years a friend showed me the other day a note which had been sent him from a well-known dog breaker, giving the points which he expects to secure in a properly broken Retriever. They seem to me so admirably and shortly put that I quote them here as I copied them from the letter.

"The dog about which the breaker writes was a Retriever puppy of seven months, and his education was to be this – provided, that is, that he had the intelligence to learn it:

"(1) To walk strictly to heel when out with me walking and shooting.

(2) To lie down when told at my heels anywhere.

(3) To lie down at my heels when I fire a gun.

(4) To lie down in the house in one corner of the room always when with me in the house.

(5) To teach him to retrieve feather (game, not to retrieve balls and sticks).

(6) To learn him to seek and hunt feather and bring it to hand.

(7) Obedience.

And of course no broken Retriever puppy would jump up at Ladies and Co.; his manners taught him would tell him better than that."

"There is the whole duty of the retriever puppy put in a very few words. Later you may come to the consideration of the manners and the behaviour of a made dog; but these few notes as to a broken-in puppy are surely as good as they could be."

YELLOW LABRADORS

The following report is the introduction to the journals of the yellow Labrador, the date is March 1913 but there is no indication as from which publication it came. The complete report and photographs are as follows:

"THE HYDE KENNEL OF CAPT. C. EUSTACE RADCLIFFE. The first appearance of yellow Labradors in The Show Ring at Olympia a few weeks since aroused great interest among shooting men, and, as was mentioned in The Field at the time, all the men who went the round of the benches were grateful to Capt. C. E. Radclyffe for having taken so much trouble to make the group really representative of the breed.

"As regards to the origin of the variety, we

Captain Radcliffe and Dinah, a particularly good working bitch.

have it from Capt. Radclyffe himself that in April 1902, he bred from black parents, two yellow-coloured puppies, and from the dog of that litter, which he called Ben, have descended practically the whole of the yellow Labradors today."

"Ben is still alive, but he is now too old for stud purposes, and one of his sons, Neptune,

Ben, the founder of Captain Radcliffe's yellow Labradors.

Ben, Dinah, and Gypsy.

has taken his place. Every one of the Olympia exhibits was descended from either Ben or Neptune. Next to the Hyde establishment by far the best kennel of yellow Labradors is that at Lowther. A few years since Capt. Radclyffe gave Lord Lonsdale a really good dog, and he has since bought others of the same breeding, a fact proving that he has every confidence in the yellow Labrador as an aid to the shooter. A characteristic of the variety which must commend "the yaller dog" to practical men is that he possesses the typical coat of dogs which originally came from a cold country. All the Hyde dogs are descended from an unbroken line of Retrievers which were originally imported by the late Mr. C. J. Radclyffe (Capt. Radclyffe's father) nearly half a century since, direct from Newfoundland to Poole, Dorset, quite close to the Hyde.

"In those days Mr. Radclyffe, the late Lord Malmsbury, Mr. Montague Guest, and the present Lord Wimborne all bought a number of the dogs imported by Hawker, a man who owned a trading schooner which plied between Newfoundland and Poole. The yellow Labradors of today resemble Hawker's imports very closely in coat and type; but the latter were totally different from the present day Labrador Retriever of the show bench, because, coming as they did from a cold country their coat was longer and contained underneath the long hairs, a thick kind of soft, woolly undergrowth which was a natural kind of protective coat required in the cold country of which they were inhabitants. Capt. Radclyffe has visited the coast of Newfoundland and Labrador, but was unable to find any trace of species of the Retriever in Labrador itself. He declares that there is not and never has been any other type of dog in Labrador excepting what is known as a Husky or Sleigh dog, which is more like a Norwegian Elkhound or a small wolf. On the Isle of Newfoundland, however, there is still a dog resembling in type those imported in the late sixties and early seventies of the last century by Mr. Radclyffe.

"The fact that no cross of any kind has been introduced into the Hyde kennel accounts for the type and character of the original imports being maintained. Capt. Radclyffe's dogs are harder and more immune from exposure to cold and the effects of water than the present day Labrador. As a fact, many of the latter have a coat with which a dog would be absolutely unable to exist in either Labrador or Newfoundland. All the Hyde Labradors are kept for working purposes only; they are kennelled in the open, and thus retain the coarse coat which is peculiar to the strain. A particularly characteristic exhibit at Olympia was Miss P. Molyneux's Wareham Sam, absolutely perfect as regards head, ears, body, tail and coat; but his great failing is that he is too short in the legs by at least and inch and a half. He is not quite straight in front. The

Captain Radcliffe and Ben going to fish.

strain is in good hands, for there are few men connected with sport who are better known than Capt. Radclyffe. He was one of the founders of the Shikar Club, and undertook the arrangements of the first gathering at the Cafe Royal, Regent Street in 1907, Lord Lonsdale being in the chair. He has caught tarpon in the Gulf of Mexico, shot moose and caribou in Alaska, has sent falcons from the Hyde to compete with success at continental flights, and has won important pigeon shooting competitions. He served in the South African War with the

1st Royal Dragoons."

DEATH OF DUAL CH. GROUSE OF RIVERSIDE

On May 19th in 1913, Dual champion Grouse of Riverside died. His death was recorded throughout the canine press, the following being just one example.

"Mr. H. Reginald Cooke is not having the best of luck this year, for, following news of the death of his great stud dog High Legh Blarney, comes the intimation that Grouse of Riverside – relatively a greater Retriever than Blarney – was found dead in his kennel on Monday morning. A son of Mr. L. Allen Shuter's Horton Rector – Luton Melody, and bred by Miss Mabel Gray, Grouse's memory will be kept green for many years, for was he not the Flatcoated which beat Mr. Maurice Portal's Labrador Flapper and a field which also included such well-known public performers as Mr. Lewis Wigan's Sweep of Glendaruel, Lieut. Col. Cote's Pitchford Marshall; Mr. E. Wheler's Lorna, Mr. C. C. Eley's Acolyte, the Hon. Holland Hibbert's Munden Something and Mr. E. W. H. Blagg's Busy Mite at Priory Hill in October 1906. Grouse had previously been placed at Sutton Scarsdale; in fact, at six meetings between 1905 and 1909 he was three times the actual winner, twice he was third and once fourth. That was a record of which Mr. Cooke was proud; in fact no other Flatcoated Retriever has ever approached it, while his performances in the show ring were equally meritorious, for at seven shows he won fifteen first prizes, two seconds and one third. He was twice the Champion dog at Darlington and once at Manchester, and after Mr. G. Reynold Davies's special prize of £20 for the Flatcoated dog which won Field Trial honours and had also won three Challenge Certificates at any two representative shows had been on offer for five years, it was Grouse of Riverside to which the handsome special was awarded. We saw Mr. Cooke's good-looking Retriever run at each of his six meetings, and remember well how he used to work to the directions of his owner. His style was perfect; he had a wonderfully good nose, and was equally good in covert or in the open. Not once, but many times when he was down we were questioned by strangers as to the identity of Grouse. At Rushmore, Wiltshire, where he was third at the International meeting in 1907, a man declared to us that it was an education to see Grouse and his master in the field. It is no wonder that Mr. Cooke feels his loss. For eight years owner and dog had never been separated during the shooting season; Grouse was always included in invitations sent to Davenport, and up to the end he maintained his reputation. He was as good in the field last Autumn as he had ever been."

TRIALS AND THEIR MANAGEMENT

The third scrapbook then contains eight pages of letters, all covering the period from October 1913 to December 1913, and concerned with the management of Retriever Trials. The correspondence arose as a result of a letter penned by Captain Phipps Hornby, a letter which was in itself three columns long – I confess to having condensed it somewhat.

"Sir, – I am writing this letter in the hope that it might induce lovers of the Retriever and Retriever work to express their opinions as to whether the Field Trials, as now conducted, are obtaining the object for which they were originally instituted. I believe the first Trials were held in 1871 and 1872; in

The History Of Retrievers

1899 tentative Trials were held on my then estate in Sussex. In 1900 what may be termed the first Retriever Trials were conducted on the same property. I was present at those Trials, and ran two dogs. I have watched the Trials ever since, and run dogs with a certain amount of success. I now feel that, after thirteen years experience, it is time that we should ask ourselves the question – are we absolutely on the right line?

"The object of the Retriever Trials is to produce a breed of workers and not show-bench Retrievers. Are we doing this? The first essential in Retrievers is steadiness, the capacity for finding game readily and bringing it to hand without damage, not to disturb more game than possible in doing so, also endurance to enable a good days work without fatigue. From what I have seen of Retriever Trials lately, and from discussions I have heard on the subject, I am inclined to think that we are sacrificing far too much to mere pace. At present, many Retrievers at the Trials dash out at a tremendous pace, overshoot the mark, career about, scaring unwounded game, and, eventually, after a considerable time, blunder into the game they are looking for.

"I have seen Retrievers at the Trials, and winners, too, which one could not take out to a day's shooting when one is walking up game and wants to work Retrievers. When sent out, the dogs race out sixty or seventy yards or more; even then they do not begin to work or quarter till pulled up by their handlers whistle; then they race about in large circles, quarter back, towards their handler, and eventually blunder into the dead game twenty or thirty yards from their handler; in the meanwhile they have driven all other game within 150 yards away! No one would thank one for taking such a dog out shooting; Certainly, if such a dog came out to me shooting, I should politely ask the owner to take him up and not bring him out again. In my humble opinion, a Retriever, when sent out for game (which he has not seen fall), should begin to quarter outwards on leaving his handler till he gets the scent or right way of the wind. I know it is often said when a dog is a bit wild and rash in his work, "Oh, he is trying to get the wind," but is this so? Often we see this idea absolutely falsified, and only made an excuse for wild and rash work. It is a great thing to see a Retriever bring his game back at a gallop, but that is a very different thing to a dog working in mad career in search of game, over running the scent and his own nose. I know I shall be told that the best dog is one that has such a nose; he cannot go too fast for it; this is quite correct in theory, but we do not see it in practice; there exceedingly fast dogs outpace their nose. I saw one lately when sent for a running pheasant, which I had seen running, gallop over the line four times without taking the least notice; then, just as the judges called out another dog, this dog blundered into the bird, which had squatted in the roots; this dog got a prize. Very fast galloping dogs may be all very well for picking up behind the butts, grouse driving, or after a partridge drive when there is no game for them to disturb in their mad career.

"At Field Trials where I have been a spectator, I have heard other spectators make very adverse remarks to Field Trial work, when they have noticed dogs, which were far beyond the fall of the game, and not running a line, hunting any amount of unwounded game out of the field. I, too, have noticed that these tremendously galloping dogs, when working in roots, do not turn to the whistle as well as others. I think it is due to the tremendous pace they are going making such a noise in the turnips they are crashing through, that they cannot hear. Excessive pace may answer on a day with a burning breast-high scent, but how often do we get this? As Mr. Jorrocks remarks: "Believe me, my beloved 'carers', there's nothing so queer as scent, 'cept a woman."

"We do not want slow, pottering Retrievers; we want Retrievers with a certain amount of pace; but above all they should quarter outwards towards the game, which they have not seen fall. We want to make our Trials a little more like actual shooting, and our Retrievers work accordingly in an ordinary

Volume Three (1911-1916)

day's shooting when walking up game. When game is shot, Retrievers are not sent dashing out to fetch it, or hit the line of a possible runner at the risk of, in their work, flushing any amount of unwounded game. The guns and Co., usually walk on, and when near the place of the game down, may ask a dog to find it; but if it is thought there is more game in the field, which may be disturbed by dogs working, the field is shot out, and Retrievers worked to gather the game afterwards; thus, no fresh game is disturbed, and the bag not diminished by working of the dogs. At Trials now, when walking up, as soon as a bird falls or fur is shot, a Retriever is sent out at full speed to gather it. I must confess, I do not see that it shows much sagacity or nose for a Retriever to gather a bird about thirty or 35 yards away which it has just seen fall. The real test of sagacity and nose is for a dog to find and retrieve quickly game that it has not seen fall. I remember that in the first Trials Retrievers were not sent to retrieve game they had seen fall, but were taken to be tried on any other, and I really think this was far better test for a Retriever. At the recent trials at Cullompton there was one dog (I wish I was his fortunate owner), which got into the prize list, which worked in grand style; he went out at a good pace, quartered outwards, seemed always to hit the scent, and picked every bird he was sent for, and some, after a faster dog had failed. Some thought him slow, but I noticed that though he did not gallop at racing pace, he found his game and brought it nicely to hand in far less time than the dogs which raced about bounding over the roots, and he disturbed no game in his quest. I also think that too much of the work at Field Trials is done in the open. I should like to see dogs do more work in cover, when they are left to their own initiative. The time one wants a Retriever is when one cannot get the shot game oneself, such as when it falls in underwood or in bushes; this might be done by, during the day, putting into cover some of the game which has been previously killed, and then sending the dogs to find and retrieve it.

"I am a great believer in Field Trials for the purpose of improving the breed of working Retrievers; also for improving the breaking and handling of Retrievers, but in effecting this we ought to make sure that the work done by a field trial winner is such that we should like to see the dog do when out for a days shooting. The following remark has often been made to me: "Oh, yes, the Field Trial dog is all very well, but he is not always what one would take out for a days shooting." There is no more charming dog or companion than a good Retriever, and those who have his welfare at heart will, I hope, give their views and opinions, so that by making these opinions public, we may make sure we are on the right line, or if not, that these opinions may enable those who have the management of the Trials to frame rules and standards for Trials, which will make the winner as near perfection as a shooting Retriever as is possible.
G. PHIPPS HORNBY, CAPT."

Captain Hornby certainly got his wish when he asked for views and opinions – they were numerous. I hope the ones that I have selected are of interest.

"Sir, - The thanks of all interested in real Retriever work are certainly due to Capt. Phipps Hornby, and evidently very many will agree that the answer to the question "Are we absolutely on the right lines?" is in the negative.

It is unfortunate that one generally receives the same sort of account from a person who has been to a Retriever meeting for the first time (they probably do not go again), "No I do not think much of the trials, and I could show you far better work at home." The plan of holding a conference at the end of his season to discuss the whole question is a good one but would it not be as well if, through the medium of your columns, some practical suggestions and remedies were made now, in order that the ground might be prepared for such a conference? My own views in the matter of making the Trials a genuine test of real Retriever work are as follows:

- There should be a small amount of walking up and driving to test for steadiness, marking etc. and to collect some dead game;
- Dead birds and fur should be placed for the dogs to gather (unseen by them) in (a) roots, to test for quartering of ground, obedience to whistle and hand and for nose; and (b) in thickish covert, to test for courage for facing rough places.
- There should be runners for every dog in every stake; and for this I can only echo the old suggestion that there ought to be a hamper of pinioned birds.
- In addition to the above, I should like to see all dogs tried in water, and if at all possible, the handlers killing the game.

ANDREW PEARSON, October 25th 1913."

"Sir, – Whatever we try to do to improve the conditions of Trials, I am perfectly convinced in my own mind that we can never carry them through on lines nearer approaching an ordinary shooting day than they are at present. I do not mean to say that they are similar, as they are very far from being so. At a shoot, the dog is sacrificed for the bag, at a Field Trial, the bag is sacrificed for the dog, and all our sympathy must surely go to the keeper of the beat. A bird is dropped thirty yards or more in front of the line in the middle of a root field teeming with birds, on an ordinary shooting day who would be the plucky (or rather foolhardy!) guest who dare send his dog that has not even marked the fall? In a Field Trial, the line is stopped, and if the dog has marked it no harm results, but should he not have done so, he must necessarily hunt the ground, and if he fails to find another is sent and so on. In the meantime birds are getting up all over the field, especially if this particular one happens to be a runner! How many hosts on an ordinary shooting day would stand this?

"But things like this are bound to be in every famous history"

"How often have I turned and looked at the face of the keeper, who has worked like a Trojan to get the stubble driven in, and now sees his birds pouring out in streams. He well deserves our sympathy. I quite agree with all your correspondents who condemn the dog that dashes out in the tearaway fashion and seems to have no idea of working his ground, but I cannot agree with Mr. C. S. Wentworth Reeve that judges encourage this. My experience is that such dogs are very rightly penalised and always get their deserts. No doubt there are a lot of such dogs, but I honestly think that it is only from excitement and keenness to work, and that many of these dogs on their owners shooting never get out of hand at all. But when a dog is used to picking up what is shot, or at any rate a proportion of it, and then on a Field Trial day goes for hours merely watching other dogs retrieve and work on each side of him, it is not unnatural for a highly strung one to lose control of himself and gallop wild. The judge can see it all, and naturally penalises him, but knows in his own mind that he is a downright good dog; but he is there to judge him on what he sees, and I have no hesitation in saying the dog gets what he deserves. I lately ran a dog at a meeting, was down from 10:30 am to 3:30 pm (with interval for lunch), and never had a bird given me. What I expected happened, and the judge very rightly knocked him out, but he is the best dog I ever had. Field Trials will prosper so long as we have as judges men who break and handle their own dogs, who can at once see the faults and good points at a glance, and, who will penalise for any mistakes your correspondents take exception to. Many of them are not wilful, but, as a well-known handler said to me once, it is only "anxiety to please". We hear a lot about a dog being too fast for his nose. In my opinion this dog lacks sense, as it is only on a cold scent that he is too fast when he should slacken his pace. He comes off on a good scent, but has not the reasoning powers to slow down when scent is poor. A dog cannot be too fast if he is always under control, works and quarters his ground as he goes out in a proper manner, and regulates his pace according to the scent. Some do this but very few.

"Another Handler is quite right in condemning the system of exchanging dogs before every one of them has been down for a preliminary test, and this is an instruction every society should give its judges. I also think dogs are very often given too much time over a runner when apparently making nothing of it; but there is no reason why several should not be tried on the same bird, as judges can thereby frequently note how each dog frames in his work, and mark accordingly, even though the bird is never found. I should like to see the use of blank cartridges dispensed with, it is quite an unnecessary evil, and judges are quite competent enough to notice all that goes on between handlers and their dogs without the necessity of that nuisance. By all means have the meeting, but do not instruct judges as to the methods by which they must judge. The one and only remedy is to select the men in whom every confidence is put by the competitors.
ERNEST TURNER, November 1st 1913."

"Sir, – As one of the sporting public, who hailed with deep satisfaction the Kennel Club rule that no show-bench gundog could win the title of Champion without a Field Trial certificate, I now venture to voice the opinion of my brother breeders against the present mode of judging at Trials. From observations and information throughout the seasons of 1912 and 1913 I can but come to the conclusion that the Trials as run at present, are anything but fair and satisfactory. I make no insinuations that the judging is not all that it ought to be as far as honour goes. A judges position is an unenviable one. He is a mere man, and as such liable to prejudice. A Labrador lover is naturally prejudiced in favour of a Labrador, and the same applies to a Flatcoat judge, and the same might, and would apply, only they are in such a small minority, to our newest breed, the golden-coloured Retriever.

"At a certain Trial this year a dog was awarded a Certificate of Merit. The only mistake that he made as far as the public saw was that on one occasion he brought back two birds and he had only been sent to retrieve one! Presumably he was given a Certificate for doing all he was asked to do (and a bit more!). Another winner of a Certificate was a dog that had run in. Again at Trials, I have seen a dog put on a bird and fail to get a line, and after anything from a quarter of an hour to half an hour, a new dog called up. The first dog that had everything in its favour remains in, and the owner of the second is informed that his will not be wanted again.
EBELGEE, November 1st 1913."

"Sir, – Having read all the letters in The Field re the recent discussion on Field Trials, their management, judging etc. I have come to the conclusion it is nothing more or less than a clap-trap controversy of certain men who wish to have Trials to suit their own special stay-at-home favourite dogs. I should say the judges know which style of working dog is required, and the common-sense competitor brings forward which they think most fit. Some shooting men enter their dogs simply to get used to the public hum of excitement and nuisances, put it which way you like. This dog may be a promising one, but not ready. This same dog might run through with flying colours, or might disgrace himself and handler. Still, if he does, what have the onlookers to do with that? If everyone were like them, do all the talking but not the performing, Retriever Trials and all other Trials would be a long way further behind than they are at the present moment. Now men who have these very good dogs at home, do for goodness sake bring them out next year, and I hope they will get a fair trial, and here's luck to him who wins; but allow me to express my candid opinion, they will go home with a lot of excuses for their dogs faults, or their own handling.

The History Of Retrievers

ALWAYS LOOKING FOR A BETTER, November 8th 1913."

"Sir, – In view of the number of unsuccessful applications for nominations at the various Retriever Trials, I would suggest that a rule might be made at those meetings where two stakes are on the programme prohibiting an owner from running the same dog in both stakes so long as any unsuccessful applicant for a nomination is on the list.

"If an owner is lucky enough to get a nomination in both stakes, and has only one dog to run, let him choose whether he will have a go with his young dog at the Senior stakes, or, if not good enough, let him elect to run his dog in the Junior. This would give a few more owners a chance. The question of the same owner running the same dog at several local meetings might also be considered. A man can play for only one county at cricket, however many residences he may own in various counties, and, personally, I think if an owner has drawn a nomination at one local meeting, he should not be allowed to run the same, or any other dog, at any other local meeting till all applicants for nominations at such meeting who have not been so lucky have been satisfied, though I am afraid that the opposition to this suggestion will be too strong for it ever to become law.

GUNNING CAMPBELL, January 10th 1914."

And so it goes on... In all honesty, we who compete in Trials today could ask ourselves if things have really changed all that much.

WYTHAM RETRIEVER TRIALS, 1914

"The fourth Championship Retriever Trials were held at Wytham Abbey, Nr. Oxford on 6th/7th January 1914. The judges were, Capt. C. C. Eley, Mr. Maurice Portal and Mr. H. Reginald Cooke. There were nineteen entries and the card was made up with: six Labrador bitches, ten Labrador dogs, two Flatcoat bitches and one Labrador x Flatcoat dog.

"The results were as follows:-
1. Mr. Archibald Butter's Labrador dog Butter's Patron of Faskally.
2. Col. Weller's Flatcoat bitch, Meeru.
3. Mr. C. Arlington's Labrador dog, Bright.
4. Capt. Burrell's Labrador bitch, Broome Park Sikh.
Reserve: Mr. W. M. McCall's Labrador dog, St. Mary's James."

Mr. Charles Butter, on whose grounds, Wytham Abbey in Oxfordshire, the Championship Retriever Trials of 1914 were held.

Patron of Faskally (belonging to Mr. Archibald Butter), the winner of the 1914 Retriever Trials.

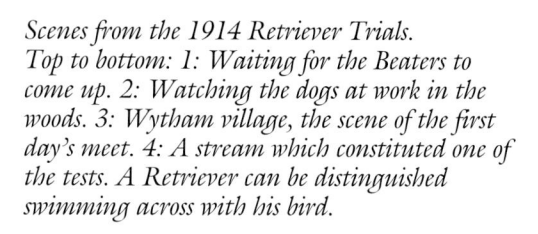

Scenes from the 1914 Retriever Trials. Top to bottom: 1: Waiting for the Beaters to come up. 2: Watching the dogs at work in the woods. 3: Wytham village, the scene of the first day's meet. 4: A stream which constituted one of the tests. A Retriever can be distinguished swimming across with his bird.

KENNEL CLUB RULES

On June 6th 1914, there was a great deal of debate concerning the role of the Kennel Club in the making and enforcing of rules governing Retriever Trials.

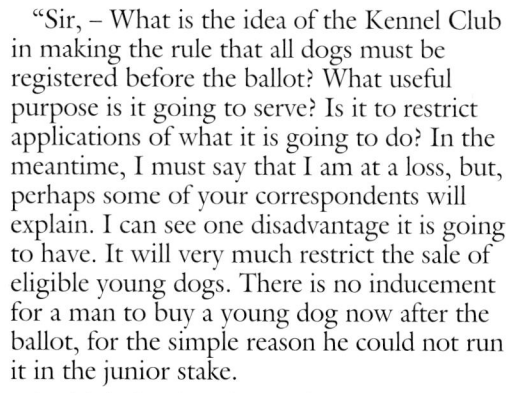

"Sir, – What is the idea of the Kennel Club in making the rule that all dogs must be registered before the ballot? What useful purpose is it going to serve? Is it to restrict applications of what it is going to do? In the meantime, I must say that I am at a loss, but, perhaps some of your correspondents will explain. I can see one disadvantage it is going to have. It will very much restrict the sale of eligible young dogs. There is no inducement for a man to buy a young dog now after the ballot, for the simple reason he could not run it in the junior stake.

"I think the abolishing of blank ammunition is a good idea, but I do not like forbidding a handler to carry a gun. I think you rob a dog of a certain amount of interest when it sees its master without a gun, it is reversing the order of things; we will have to give the keepers the guns now, and the masters will walk in line picking up the game. But the rule may be a means towards an end. We shall never get ideal Trials till the handlers are allowed to kill the game. An idea that I heard some time ago occurred to me as a good one. Let the different associations combine and rent a shooting for the purpose of holding the Open meetings (and some of the private ones for that matter), and then they could say how the meetings were to be conducted. Then the handlers would shoot the game, and the dogs would be tested in a legitimate way. The thing might be run as a syndicate and made to pay.
A. AITCHISON JUN."

The History Of Retrievers

The Championship Retriever Trials at Wytham Abbey in January 1914. 1 and 2: Mr. C. Alington's Bright, who took third prize, retrieving pheasant. 3: Spectators and guns moving to a fresh beat. 4: Giving bugle call for beaters to start operations. 5: Colonel G. H. Weller's Meeru, second in Championship. 6: Mr. A. E. Butter's Patron of Faskally, winner of the Championship Stake and Cup. 7: Mr. W. M. McCall's St. Mary James, winner of the Reserve prize. Opposite page: Scenes from the Championship.

Mr. Charles C. Eversfield

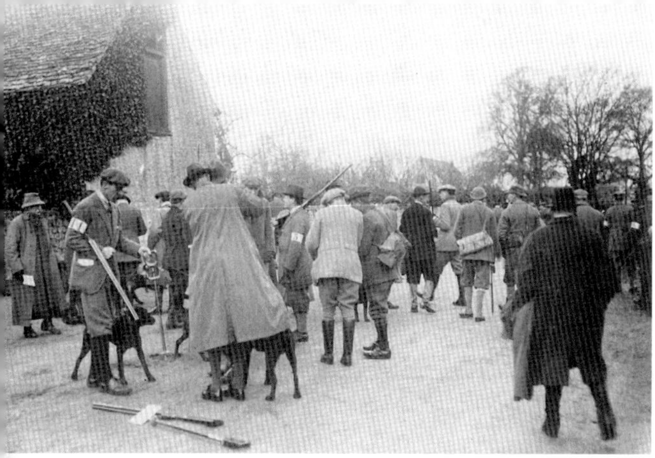

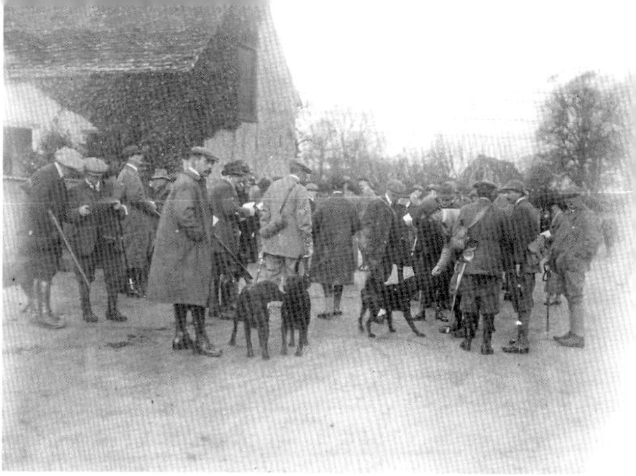

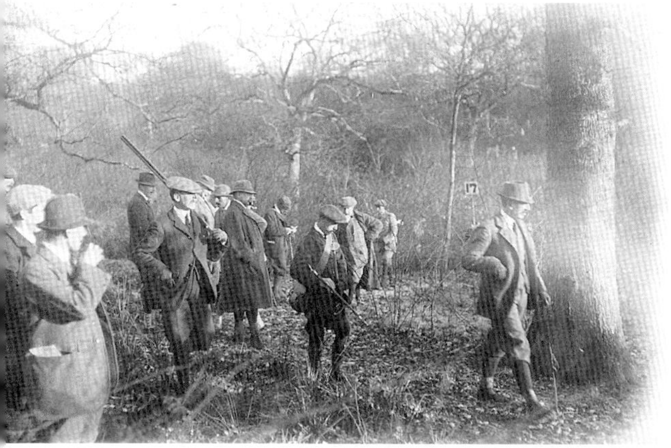

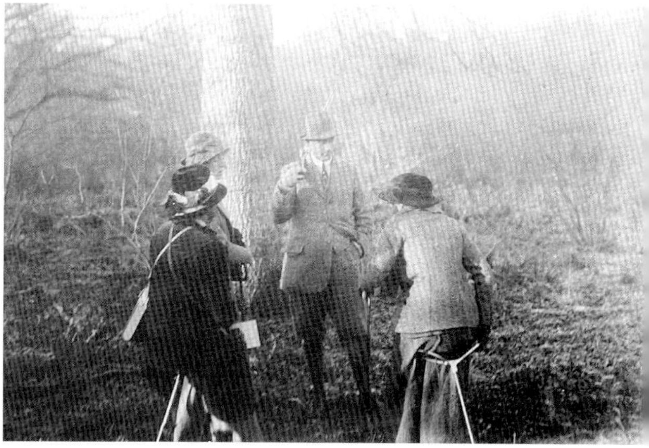

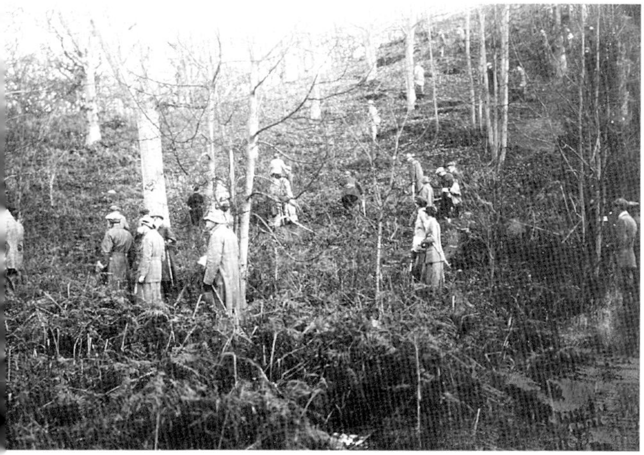

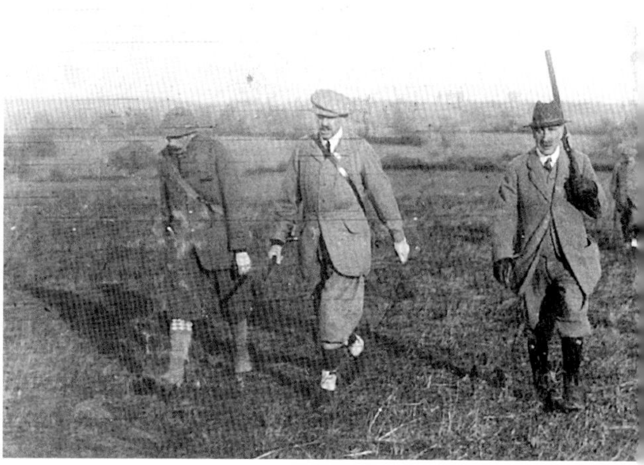

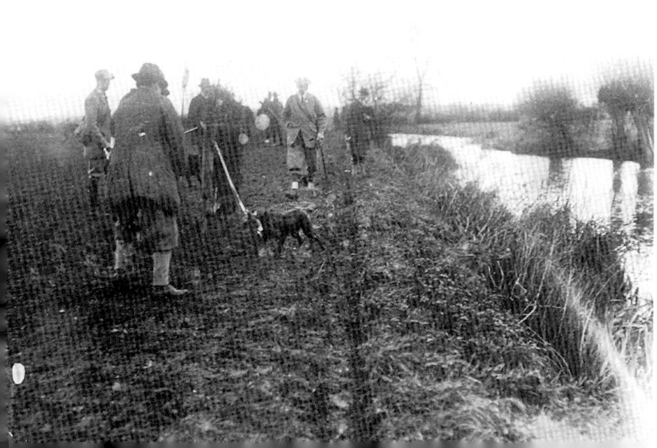

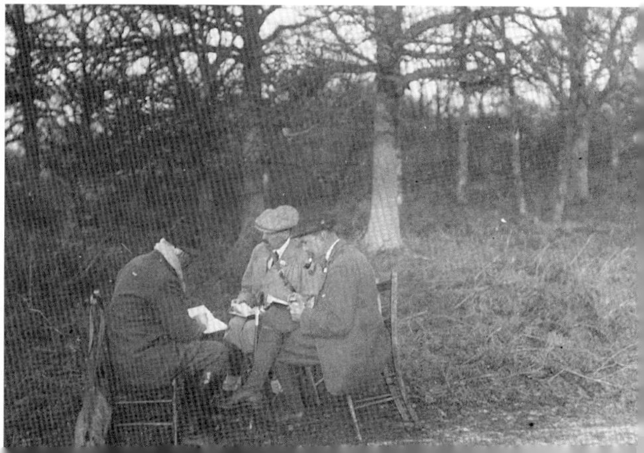

Mr. H. Reginald Cooke's 'Riverside' Flatcoated Retrievers. a: Ch. Wrangler, Ch. Roddy of Riverside, and Kaffir of Riverside. b: Susan of Riverside. c: Broom of Riverside. d: Drake of Riverside. e: Blight of Riverside. f: Southwell Peter.

Volume Three (1911-1916)

OBITUARIES

Throughout 1914 and 1915, several well-known figures in the Retriever world died. Some deaths were due, at least in part, to the war, while others were unrelated. One of the first obituaries recorded during this period covers the death of Mr. Charles C. Eversfield (pictured page 98) on December 28th 1914, a fact recorded by the Morning Post.

"The prominent Field Trials judge, breeder and exhibitor Mr. C. C. Eversfield died suddenly last week at Denne Park at the early age of 43. His decease was hastened by his recent hard work at the front, and by anxiety for his relatives and others in the fighting area."

The canine press also reported in length about Mr. Eversfield's contribution to Field Trials and the breeding of Retrievers.

"Mr. Charles Eversfield, whose death was announced in yesterday's Morning Post, was the owner of the strongest kennel of sporting Spaniels in the United Kingdom, and at the Championship meeting held at Wytham under the management of the Kennel Club, in January last, the Denne Spaniels won each of the three stakes.

"Mr. Eversfield was an expert motorist and immediately the war broke out he placed two cars at the service of the War Office, volunteering to drive one himself. It was during a short holiday leave granted for Christmas that he died. Mr. Eversfield was in his forty third year, and was a bachelor."

In April 1915, Mr. Gladstone, a regular sight at a Field Trial, died. His death was recorded thus:

"The Field Trial movement has lost a good friend by the death of Mr. W. G. C. Gladstone, who has been killed in action, and members of the Cheshire and North Wales Retriever and Spaniel society are not likely to forget that it was entirely due to his kindness that they were able to institute Retriever Trials in the autumn of 1909. He not only placed his beautiful shooting at Hawarden at the service of the committee, but instructed his head gamekeeper, Nichol – who is so well known in connection with Labradors – to spare no effort to make the meeting a success."

While the deaths of some of the Trials' key members, as well as the war itself, made an impact on the Retriever community, there seems to have been a concerted attempt to minimise the effects of the war, as this extract from the July 1915 edition of The Field, shows:

"The dropping of the chief Open meetings during war time has not quelled the spirit of competition among the owners of Retrievers, and while watching the judging of the excellent groups of Retrievers at Richmond this week, we were invited to two matches which are to be contested early in the shooting season. One is for £25 a side between teams of Labradors, each owner being allowed to name three dogs, while the other has been made by two of the most prominent Flatcoated Retriever men in the country.

"Their match, which is fixed definitely for Wednesday 1st September, on ground not far out of London on which there is a first-rate crop of partridges, is for a purely nominal amount, and a judge has already been nominated. Not unlikely each party to this match will run a half-bred. Each match is certain to arouse interest among Retriever men; their decision may lead to other contests, though, with Major W. G. Eley on Military Service it is not likely that the long delayed match between a dog from his kennel at Escrick and a Flatcoat representing Mr. H. Reginald Cooke will be held even this year. It has been frequently postponed for a perfectly good reason; when it does come off it will arouse interest, for owners will be 'up'. There are few better amateurs. Finally, we hear of an old lover of the Flatcoated Retriever who is on the lookout for a really good Curlycoated dog with which to have what he calls a fair go at the Labradors. He has set himself a task beyond a doubt, but it is not absolutely hopeless."

A GROUSE DRIVE IN WAR TIME

Of all the articles, cuttings and excerpts contained within the journals, the following has to be my absolute favourite. The Major referred to in the article reminds me very much of a friend within the gundog world, who is himself affectionately known as 'The Major', and sometimes 'The Big Green Gun'. The grouse drive took place at Newtonmore, Inverness, in August 1915. Events are not so far removed from the present day, apart from the delivery of the morning paper and the mail at lunchtime.

"It was the first drive of the season in the district of Badenoch. our host, on short leave from Kitchener's Army, had travelled up the previous Sunday to whip up guns from his neighbours – no easy matter when guns are scarce. On the appointed morning we motored to the lodge, and had scarcely a mile to walk before we reached the first butts. On our way thither sundry old cocks crowed defiantly close to the side of the path. One in particular stood on a hillock and cried "go back" repeatedly within twenty yards of the party. This was too much for Major C. T. Dugdale of the New Army, who with his brown cocker, was casting longing eyes at the old warrior. Our host gave permission for the execution, and our friend clipped in a couple of cartridges and walked a few yards nearer the old cock. The latter raised his head higher and rose cackling, dipped below the hillock, and vanished before a shot could be fired. Applause and laughter followed, and the Spaniel, giving tongue lustily, went off in pursuit. Our host beckoned us on, and looking round, we saw the cocker receiving his first hiding of the day, accompanied by language somewhat unparliamentary. The Major never heard the last of that old cock all day.

"We halted close to the butts and drew. No. 3 fell to my lot, and from previous experience I knew that I would be in the thick of it all day. The Major was on my left, H. R. Cooke on my right, accompanied by a famous bitch who had distinguished herself on the bench and in the field alike. It was a glorious morning with wisps of mist rising from the hills and a slight breeze blowing from the east – just the wind we would have chosen for the drive.

"The programme for the day was as follows. Above us rose a steep hill, covered with heather now in bloom. To the east lay a succession of slopes and flats, all of which were to be driven in succession towards the hill. Beyond the hill is a deep, narrow corrie, which is also driven towards the same beat, and thus the whole of our birds would be collected for a great evening drive on the way home. On a favourable day, the scheme works to perfection. In the distance the Cairgorms towered upwards, and here and there a snow field on the nearer Grampians bore witness to the severity of the early spring. From the flats below us a flock of Golden Plover rose whistling in shrill chorus, circled round, and came like greased lightning down the wind over the Major's butt. They were closely bunched and after his two shots the air seemed to rain plover for a moment. As a matter of fact, he had killed eight with the two barrels. The Spaniel was now whining low and plaintively, but an occasional smack from the leader kept him in the butt. Then a sharp whistle from the head keeper, flanking on the left, brought us to attention, and the first pack of the day swung round the hillock in front of my butt and slanted towards my friend on the right. I secured a brace and he killed three with his four barrels; the remainder swung down the line to our host, who, with his usual accuracy, accounted for four. This was a good beginning for the day, but an old cock, neatly flanked in from above, rocketed down the line a few minutes afterwards and escaped unscathed.

Volume Three (1911-1916)

"Then came a few odd birds, leaving toll at every butt as they passed. An old blackcock followed, and this I secured as it passed high and slanting on the left, falling close behind the Major's butt. This was too much for the Spaniel and he dashed in boldly, followed by his indignant owner. Meanwhile grouse were passing every minute, and my own young dog was getting jumpy. The Cocker was now mad with excitement, and now being tethered, whined and shrieked loudly as the grouse fell around him. The major and I agreed to pick up in common as our birds were mixed, and we got our number in short time, thanks to the exertions of our respective dogs. The Cocker was invaluable at the pick up, and did his best to secure the largest share of the spoils.

"We lunched after the third drive in a cosy little bothy close to a burn, and the exploits of our various dogs formed the subject of much good humoured chaff during the meal. The morning paper and our hosts letters arrived as we concluded our repast, and, our hearts warmed by news of victories, we started for the great corrie drive, which was expected to yield good results. The Major was on the warpath again, leading the way, Cocker at heel - shooting at birds breaking back, here being permissible. On our right towered a great hill, on the lower slopes of which the grouse were already streaming up in front of the beaters. The Spaniel had proved himself a wonderful worker and saved two runners from being left behind. He was earning his keep today with a vengeance, and his little black eyes were fairly dancing with mischief and devilment. On the way to the butts a young hare proved too tempting for him, and off he went in full cry, but, fortunately lost her in a peat hole before he had done any harm. More thumps greeted his return, but we were soon settled in our places, all wild dogs tethered and ready for the sport to begin. We had not long to wait, and a succession of rocketing coveys breaking off the tops as the beaters circled round gave us some pretty shooting, though the proportion of kills to misses need not be chronicled.

"Then came the last drive of the day, a drive which will live long in my memory. The sun was now blazing in full summer heat, and scarcely a breath of wind stirred the heather. The butts were on the north side of the hill and the Major and I were almost on the top. We had a longish wait here as most of the beaters were old men and boys, the able bodied being engaged in sterner work. They had to make a long detour to reach the south side of the hill, and meanwhile we basked in the sun and smoked. Suddenly, we were roused by the keepers whistle once more, and, jumping to my feet, I saw a long line of dark forms in the distance at the far end of the hill. The drive had begun. The pack came straight along the top on their way home to the corrie, passing on both sides of me, and giving several butts a good chance. I killed one far out in front with the first barrel, missed badly with the second, and only secured one behind. It is of the first importance in grouse-driving that a pack should be fired at well out in front, so as to give other guns a chance. And now pack followed pack till our guns were hot and the birds streamed homewards to their respective beats. It was a glorious half-hour such as one remembers in happier times, before the war-cloud burst upon the world. We could enjoy it with a clear conscience, for few are shooting this year except the aged, the infirm, and those on leave. Yet it is not the same to any of us, though for a brief space we may forget.

"However, in the great drive, there was little time for thought, and as many of our birds had fallen in a deep gully behind the butts, the pick up was no easy matter.

The total bag for seven guns was 217 brace of grouse, a blackcock, and a dozen hares, and, as all had a fair share of the shooting, we wended our way homewards feeling that we had done our part in reducing the numbers of the grouse.

H. B. MACPHERSON."

CROSS-BRED RETRIEVERS

The third journal ends with a report on a

meeting called by Mr. T. W. Twyford at Crufts Show. February 10th. 1916, the reason for the meeting being the registration of cross-bred Retrievers. The report on the meeting is lengthy, I have selected one or two extracts followed by a sample of some of the correspondence in The Field that appeared in the following weeks.

"The Chairman (The Hon. A. Holland-Hibbert), explained that Mr. Twyford was more or less responsible for calling the meeting together, and asked him to make a statement. Mr. Twyford said he had sent out some 43 circular letters, to which he had received some 35 replies, the balance being made up of people who were abroad on duty. As it was impossible to read all the letters, he would briefly indicate the opinions of the writers. Mr. Burdett Coutts wrote in favour of something being done to remedy their complaint against cross-breds being allowed to be shown in pure-bred classes. Mr. R. R. Ballingal was also strongly in favour of altering the present rule, and the Earl of Chesterfield expressed much the same opinion. Some of his correspondents were in favour of a Labrador club being formed, but all, whether or not in favour of a club, agreed that the Kennel Club should be petitioned to alter or rescind the rule complained of. The gamekeepers were the strongest supporters of the idea of having a club, they numbered in their ranks some of the strongest supporters of Labradors.

"Mr. W. H. Leslie, supported them and favoured the rescinding of the rule against which they were protesting, but he thought that if, by crossing, a better working dog could be obtained, there was not so much harm in it. The resolution to be submitted to the Kennel Club would appeal not only to those interested in Labradors, but also to the Flat- and Golden-coloured Retriever people, who, together with them, recognised the importance of the rule being rescinded or amended.

"If they united in a joint petition to the Kennel Club, their movement would have all the greater power behind it, and would be all the stronger lever towards securing the removal of conditions they consider to be unjust. They were going to send the whole of the correspondence to the Kennel Club, so that those in authority might judge the views expressed – forcibly expressed in some instances – as to the damage that accrued from the present state of affairs.

"The whole crux of the meeting, concluded the chairman, was whether it was a good rule that cross-breds should be shown as pure-breds. If a cross-bred was a pure-bred, then the Kennel Club was right; but if a cross-bred was not a pure-bred then they were right in their protest."

Other letters about cross-bred Retrievers are included towards the back of the third scrapbook.

"Sir, – Many owners of Retrievers besides myself will doubtless have read with interest and satisfaction your remarks on this subject in last week's The Field, and thanks are due to you for giving publicity to this question. Most people are aware, but it may not be generally understood, that before a Retriever can compete, either at a Field Trial or on the bench, he must be registered at the Kennel Club. His owner must fill up and sign a form, giving full particulars of the dog, must pay a fee of two shillings and sixpence, and if all is found in order, he receives from the Kennel Club a certificate of the registration of the dog. Hitherto this system has worked well.

"Recently a new situation has been created. By way of improving the working qualities of their dogs, breeders have been crossing the two varieties (Labrador and Flatcoat), the idea being to preserve the good qualities in both breeds, delete the defects, and it may eventually be proved that the cross-bred dog will be the best Retriever for work. The question is asked, why are the produce of the cross invariably registered as Labradors? The answer is quite simple. Everyone who has tried the experiment, knows that the puppies of the first cross invariably resemble the Labrador in shape and characteristics to a much greater extent than the Flatcoat, and quite naturally the breeder of the puppies registers them in the breed which they most resemble."

The result of such registration gives rise to a ridiculous position, as I will endeavour to show, quoting one quoting another:

"At the recently held exhibition of the National Gundog Society, the winner of some prizes and the challenge prize in the Labrador classes was a half-bred Labrador and Flatcoat. He is a particularly nice retriever, but has no claim whatever to be classed as a Labrador pure and simple. On his sires side he comes of a strain of pure-bred Flatcoated retrievers, going back very many years. I myself bred and owned his Grandsire (Jimmy of Riverside), his grandson takes honours in the show ring, and wins at Field Trials as a Labrador! Could absurdity go further? I am aware that the Kennel Club has an existing rule that a cross-bred can be registered thus:

- Bang (Flatcoat) Bob
- Kate (Labrador)

But, as it has on several occasions fallen to my lot to check the Retriever records and pedigrees before publication in The Stud Book. I can testify to the fact that the rule is more honoured in the breach than in the observance and as no penalty is inflicted on the delinquents the rule is worth than useless.

"The remedy seems to me to be quite simple. Let the Kennel Club be requested to open a register for interbred Retrievers. The term interbred is perhaps more euphonious than cross-bred, and owners could then register their cross-bred dogs under this heading without attaching any stigma to them. The register for pure-bred Labradors and Flatcoats could still remain, and, as a result, breeders would see exactly 'where they are' and emerge from the existing chaos. Unless something of this sort is done, The Kennel Club Stud Book will be rendered useless for all practical purposes, and I most strongly urge those in authority to take immediate steps to rectify the evil.
H. REGINALD COOKE."

The following letters were written in response:

Sir, - In your last issue Mr. H. Reginald Cooke makes the statement that the Kennel Club's certificate of registration of a dog 'is a guarantee that the dog is registered as a pure specimen of his variety.' But is this so? On page 234 of History of the Kennel Club by Mr. E. W. Jaquet, will be found as follows: "A resolution, its object being to correct a widespread misapprehension that the registration is a guarantee of the pure blood." It was carried in the following terms: Registration is only intended to furnish evidence of the identity of a dog and a record of its pedigree. This rule was adopted in 1899 and has been in effect ever since I believe.
J. SCOTT McCOMB."

"Sir, – I have been laid up for some time and fit for nothing, but reading an account of the National Gundog Show Society's exhibition in one of the Sporting papers has so infuriated me that I feel I must let off steam. I hold that at Retriever Trials everyone wants to see the best dog for shooting purposes on the day win, and that the judges job, is, if they can, to spot the dog quite apart from his looks or breeding. But can folly go further than the following?

"Labrador Retrievers - Limit dogs, 1st Mr. Alan Shuter's Horton Max, also 1st. in Open dogs, 1st in Field Trial class, also Challenge Certificate for best dog. Judges comments: A much improved type (of what?), full of quality, beautiful head and fair body.

"What could the judges have been looking for? Horton Max is a half-bred, and his performances in the field are confined to, I think, fifth position, in what must have been a poorly represented field in the only Trials held last year. What will Archie Butter, Maurice Portal, Charles Arlington, Major Eley, and so on think when they return from the front and find their favourites are out of type?

"When the war is over are Field Trials to be bothered with judges who look for type in a half-bred, and give a Field Trial prize to a dog who has won nothing?

Of course things will right themselves again after the war, and the best dogs for work will win again when we get going. I well remember the first trial I went to with Meeru. A very superior person came up to me and asked "What is that brute?", I very humbly told him, and she won the trial. So no doubt it will be again, but I hope the war ends soon.

G. H. WELLER."

4 EXTRACTS FROM VOLUME FOUR (1916-1923)

This journal begins with several obituaries, casualties from the War, all of whom were sportsmen and prominent figures within the gundog world. One of these reports, dated September 1916, is reproduced here.

THE LATE LORD FEVERSHAM

"Retriever men, and especially those who have followed Field Trials, will regret to hear it is announced that the Earl of Feversham was killed in action while leading his battalion of the King's Royal Rifles in last Friday's (September 15th) fighting. At the time of writing there is no official confirmation, but there is reason to believe that the sad news is all too true. It was by the wish of his Lordship that he was attached to the King's Royal Rifles after he had done so much towards strengthening the regiment of his county, the Yorkshire Hussars, and he was given the command quite early in the War, and saw a great deal of what he called 'hot work' around Ypres. No more fearless leader ever went into action, and he was adored by his men, among whom were his own gamekeepers; they wanted no persuasion when the question of enrolment was put to them, and hundreds of men of the North Riding ranged themselves on the side of their young county leader. It was in January of last year that he succeeded to the Duncombe estates, which are among the fairest in the county, on the death of his Grandfather. As Lord Helmsley he had gained a fair reputation as a polo player, though his weight was against him, and he had difficulty in getting ponies equal to carrying him through strenuous games on the chief London grounds. No doubt he felt more at home in the shooting field in the company of the red or biscuit-coloured Labradors of which he was so fond. Gordon, who had the charge of the dogs at Nawton Tower and Duncombe, declared that Lord Feversham spoiled his Retrievers by kindness. There was certainly no harshness in his methods of either handling or breaking, and the writer always considered him one of the best six amateurs yet seen at Field Trials. He was a proud man when the Yorkshire meeting held on his grandfathers estate at Helmsley in the Autumn of 1913 his Nawton Pruna (a really smart bitch) divided first and second money with Lord Lucas's Wigglesworth, and that first rate form was confirmed three weeks later when she won the Nomination stake of the Retriever Society on the Polars shooting of Mr. Frank Mew near Newport, Isle of Wight. Major the Hon. Ulric O. Thynne's Muntham Peter was second, and Mr. Charles Eversfield's Denne Nora third. Mr. Alan Shuter's consistent performer Horton Rosette shared fourth honours with Capt. W. M. Burrell's Broome Park Sikh. It is sad to think that three of those five owners have sacrificed their lives for their country. That win qualified Pruna for the Championship stake at Wytham Abbey, and she well earned a Certificate of Merit. Nawton Boxer was another useful Retriever sent from the Helmsley kennel. Lord Feversham was on the committee of the Retriever Society, and had been mentioned as a possible successor to Mr. Maurice Portal as the President. He was made Master of the Sinnington hounds in 1904. Four years later he was joined in the mastership by the late Mr. Percy C. Sherbrooke, the partnership continuing until the death of Mr. Sherbrooke in 1915, when Viscount Helmsley (as he was then) became sole master. In January of last year he succeeded his grandfather as Lord Feversham, and though serving his country at the front continued the Mastership of the Sinnington. Lord Feversham, besides being a hunting man, took great interest in pony breeding, and had served the office of President of the National Pony Society.

"On succeeding to the family estates, some 40,000 acres in extent, the late Earl inherited what remained of the noted herd of Shorthorns. Situated as it is close to the ancestral home of the Shorthorn, it was natural that Duncombe Park should have had long and intimate association with the great cosmopolitan breed. The Duncombe herd was established early in the nineteenth century, the foundation stock including purchases at Mr. Robert Colling's sale in 1818. It was always strong in Bates blood, and as late as 1880 the Third Duchess of Underley was bought for 2000 guineas; indeed, the first importation of Cruickshank blood was made in 1892 when the young bull New Year's gift, bred by Lord Lovat and bought when a calf by Queen Victoria, was purchased at the Windsor sale for 1000 guineas. The herd was finally dispersed in March 1915. In 1904 Lord Feversham married Lady Marjorie Blanche Eva Greville, daughter of the fifth Earl of Warwick, and leaves two sons and a daughter. His successor to the title is not quite ten years old."

RETRIEVER RUMOURS

Entries regarding the sale of prominent Retrievers still appear from time to time in Mr. Cooke's scrapbooks, as this one from The Field, May 1917, demonstrates.

"In order to replace to some extent the deceased Ch. Withington Dorando in their kennel, Capt. and Mrs. Quintin Dick have purchased from Mr. A. Nichol his son, Brayton Sandow, who is descended from four champions – Ch's. Withington Dorando, Peter of Faskally, Manor House Belle and Brayton Swift.

"Sandow is perhaps more distinguished as a Field Trialler than a show dog, although he has won a few prizes, but his breeding should show, and is already showing, itself in the young dog as a sire, for he is the sire of that crack young Labrador, Brayton Siddy, who by a slip we said was sired by Ch. Withington Dorando. The purchaser of Brayton Siddy, we notice, is Mr. H. Reginald Cooke, who owns the finest kennel of Flatcoated Retrievers in the world, and who, it would seem, is now determined to have a kennel of Labradors of equal merit.

"Mr. A. Nichol has replaced Siddy in his kennel by a beautiful bitch in Selo, which he has purchased from Major Why Corrie."

A FISHING RETRIEVER

The following article, which was pasted in the scrapbook, was taken from The Sporting and Dramatic News, June 1917, entitled 'A Fishing Retriever'.

"The dog here shown is a Flatcoated Retriever named Kim of Riverside, bred and owned by Mr. H. Reginald Cooke, of Davenport, Bridgnorth. Kim is a son of Kaffir of Riverside, his dam being Dinah, a daughter of the well-known Field Trial winner Grouse of Riverside. As a puppy Kim showed a fondness and aptitude for retrieving fish, and in time became quite clever at it. The dog is his owner's constant companion on fishing days, and has been the means of landing many fish which would not otherwise have been creeled. He is equally good with the gun. The pictures are of the Worf, a Shropshire trout

Kim, the Fishing Flatcoat.

and grayling stream."

SPORTING DOG SALES

An article headed 'A Boom in Dogs' from The Field, December 2nd, 1918, shows how popular the Retriever breeds had become by this time.

"Everything points to a very big boom in sporting dogs, and, while the demand for Terriers is already vastly exceeding the supply, we know that it is next to impossible to get a really good gundog even at a price which would be considered exorbitant in pre-war days. Spaniels are especially difficult to get, and a friend in the West Midlands who naturally regrets that he cannot supply his patrons with what they are constantly asking for. "Selling hot cakes", he writes, "is a mild occupation compared with what I am being called on to do in the way of selling broken dogs". And now there is quite a good prospect of the revival of Field Trials on broader and more popular lines, it is certain that men who have held on to good strains will receive the thanks of others who have been absent from English sport for a considerable time. It is a good sign when colonials write us or call for information as to where representative kennels of certain varieties can be seen, and, at the recent meeting of the Pointer and Setter Society it was gratifying to meet such a man as Lieut. Col. E. S. Clifford, of the Canadian Forces, and to hear that the object of his visit to Aldridge's Repository was to seek membership of one or other branches of the International Gundog League. Retrievers are his favourites, and he is now a member of the Retriever Society, and hopes to be able to meet the members at the general gathering to be held in London next month. He is especially anxious to introduce Field Trials on English lines to the notice of Canadian enthusiasts, and told us of a meeting which was being promoted as mobilisation was begun, and, at which there was an entry of sixty. Dogs of the Riverside strain are very popular in Canada, and we were pleased to hear a very high character given to several Flatcoats which were direct imports from the Cheshire establishment of Mr. H. Reginald Cooke. Colonel Clifford is an owner of the right sort, and as long as he is kept in England he will try to be in touch with canine affairs."

POST-WAR TRIALS

On the 11th and 12th of November in 1919, the Kennel Club held the first Retriever Trials since the war, at Lowther Castle, Penrith. Unfortunately, as the article shows, the Trials were abandoned after the first day due to heavy snow falls.

"The week at Lowther to which Retriever men and women had looked forward so much fizzled out practically on the Wednesday morning, for though Lord Lonsdale did not issue the order for dispersal till twenty-four hours later, it was his anxiety to cause visitors as little inconvenience as possible which caused even that delay. On assembling in Lowther early for the second day of the Kennel Club meeting, the prospects of being able to go on seemed very small, though quite a good proportion of the handlers having further interest in the stake were in favour of resumption, and that view was placed before our host, who, while expressing no surprise that some of the hardy souls were prepared to brave the elements, pointed out the certainty of some dogs being favoured at the expense of the others. The line taken by so sound a judge as Lord Lonsdale silenced all argument, and the fifty or sixty enthusiasts who had reached the Trial ground by various routes from Penrith, even with thick snow falling, retired to the tents so thoughtfully provided, and waited for the arrival of the very excellent luncheon sent out from headquarters, and to which all were invited by Lord Lonsdale. One of the subjects discussed with freedom and thoroughly ventilated by some of the best authorities in the country is mentioned by Mr. H. W. Carlton in a letter appearing in this week's The Field, the views of other men may be given later. We and others who preferred listening to taking part in the discussion were greatly interested. The wait of six hours was in no way dull, but everybody welcomed the appearance of Mr. Reginald Heaton late in the afternoon with the news that after careful consideration, it had been decided to postpone resumption of the stake until Thursday morning. Conditions then showed no improvement, and at eight o'clock a telephone message from Lowther to headquarters brought about a scramble for breakfast, and in less than an hour some of the southerners were already on their way home. The message was to the effect that the two meetings were abandoned; a wise decision, for there seemed to be no sign of the weather breaking, and the convenience of men assembled in Westmorland was certainly worth considering. With the Kennel Club stake in an unfinished condition, Mr. Jaquet and the members of the Field Trial Committee were in difficulty, and it certainly was a pity that the proposed water tests on the second day could not be carried out; had that been possible the judges would have been able to make their awards and give the Certificates of Merit which were undoubtedly earned. Apart from complimenting Lord Lonsdale and his head gamekeeper, Mr. Robinson, on the way in which all their very perfect arrangements panned out, nothing more need be said of "a week" which promised to give Retriever men and women something to talk about for many days to come, but which, worse luck, ended in disappointment. The Retriever campaign, therefore is finished and done with, for no more meetings are announced."

OUTCROSSING DEBATE

Between November 1919 and March 1920, outcrossing was the topic for lengthy discussion and an enormous amount of correspondence. In the journal, there are eight pages of letters, to and fro, under the heading 'Retrievers and their Making'. The Kennel Club at this stage had not announced their intentions but on 14th June 1920 the following letter from Mr. Chesterfield, the Chairman of the Kennel Club Field Trial Committee, was published in The Field.

"Sir, – Some weeks since numerous letters appeared in your columns with reference to the merits of the present-day Retriever. Many of your correspondents seem to have come to

The Kennel Club Retriever Trials at Lowther Castle, Penrith, November 1919. The Trials were stopped after the first day because of a heavy snow storm. 1: Snow plough clearing a way through the park at Lowther castle. 2: Lord Lonsdale, one of the judges, leading the field to fresh ground. 3: Following the Trials (The highlighted figure is H. R. Cooke). 4: Mrs. Quntin Dick chatting to Sir Arthur Hazlerigg. 5: Lord Lonsdale blowing his small horn to get the field to follow.

111

the conclusion that, regards nose and other qualities, the Retriever of today has deteriorated, and suggested an outcross with a view to their improvement. Without wishing to enter onto the merits of the question, and at the same time being anxious to do something to meet the views referred to above, which seem to me to demand more than passing notice, as chairman of the Field Trials Committee of the Kennel Club I ventured to bring the matter to the notice of the General Committee with the result that the following resolution was unanimously passed: "That as there is a demand for an outcross or outcrosses in the breed of Retriever, that such outcross or outcrosses be allowed, and that some distinctive name and classification be made on the registers, and that the selection of such name shall be referred to the Field Trials Committee." There was a discussion at a later date with reference to the name, and no better name having suggested itself for these dogs, the Field Trial Committee of the Kennel Club adopted the name of 'Retriever outcross'. When registering these dogs at the Kennel Club and in entering them at Field Trials it will be necessary to state the name and breed of dog used to obtain the outcross, whether sire or dam. Lastly, at a meeting held on 10th June the Field Trials Committee of the Kennel Club passed the following resolution: "In future the stakes at the Kennel Club Retriever Trials will be open to Retrievers pure-bred, inter-bred, and outcross. An outcross Retriever is one whose sire or dam is a pure-bred retriever."

"I should like to make it quite clear that the decision to allow Retriever outcrosses to compete refers only to the Kennel Club's own Field Trials, and is not obligatory on other meetings held under Kennel Club rules by other societies. Each individual society can make its own regulations as to whether or not Retriever outcrosses can run at its meetings.

"Trusting that our action and the lead so given may commend itself to the many owners and breeders of Retrievers and that it may result in the desired end.
MR. CHESTERFIELD."

Mrs. Quntin Dick with Blanchary Bolo, by Scandal of Glynn.

STUD BOOKS
The International Gundog League held a meeting on November 2nd, regarding the establishment of a stud book:

"The most momentous meeting in the history of the International Gundog League was held at 12 Grosvenor Crescent, S.W., by invitation of Mrs. Quintin Dick on Tuesday afternoon, and we were pleased to notice that the whip issued to members through The Field had been effective. Mr. B. J. Warwick, the official chairman of the three societies, must have been well satisfied with the result of his efforts to secure a really representative attendance. He met with marked success and everything he had hoped to be able to do was done.

Volume Four (1916-1923)

"The subject occupying the most time was that of the establishment of a stud book, and though the details supplied by the secretary were not quite so convincing as had been hoped would be the case, the fact that the societies affiliated to the league promised support up to £60 turned the scale, and it was decided to go on with the scheme. We are now at liberty to give the result of the secretary's inquiry of members whether or not they would support the issue of the publication to the extent of subscribing a guinea for the first volume. The number of inquiries posted was 150; ninety answers were received, and, of those, exactly eighty were in favour of the stud book being established.

Mr. J. Russell and Mrs. Colman of Crown Point.

MRS. QUINTIN DICK

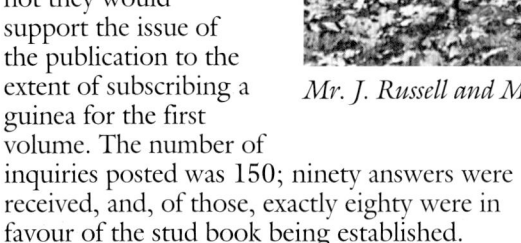

Mrs Quintin Dick is a lady who appears regularly in print and in photograph throughout the scrapbooks. She was greatly involved in the Retriever world, and she achieved quite a lot of success with her dogs, such as winning the Retriever Championship stake at Crown Point with her Labrador dog Branchory Bolo, in December 1920. Crown Point, owned by Mr. J. and Mrs. Colman, was known as one of the best-known East Anglian shooting grounds, as this article demonstrates.

Right: The judges of the 1920 Retriever Champion Stake at Crown Point, Norwich: Mr. Portal, H. Reginald Cooke, and Mr. B. J. Warwick.

The History Of Retrievers

"The whole of Mr. Russell Colman's well-known mixed ground had been secured by the Retriever Society's president Major Astley, and the excellence of the arrangements of the head gamekeeper made the meeting one of the best and most easily worked of the season. What is known as the Sewage Farm beat – the last taken on Wednesday afternoon has its drawbacks but there was no denying its value as a drive, and only approaching darkness prevented the judges from actually finishing the stake there. Several birds which might have provided convincing tests had to be left. The weather was delightful, and the crowd, while not large, was very enthusiastic."

FIELD TRIAL AWARDS

A letter from Lord Lonsdale in The Field, published in December 1920, continues the debate about which qualities should be considered desirable in a Trial dog.

"My Dear Sir, – My ideas as to how awards should be given for the best Retrievers shown and run at the Field Trials are as follows: There is a very close link between brilliance and lunacy. To my mind a Brilliant Lunatic that is thrashed to the mind of a trainer is a dangerous stock breeder. A sensible dog without extreme dash and sense is of far greater value to the shooting public than is the most racing dog 'wonderfully broken' yet naturally wild, for it is the capability of breaking a lunatic rather than the production of a valuable Retriever. The idea of racing over game for a Retriever is, to my humble mind, wrong. A really good nature with common sense and natural instincts, easily broken although not Derby Speed is a far more valuable dog than what I can only describe as a Brilliant Lunatic, who, if lucky, brings off a big thing, if unlucky, is useless, and probably the very last dog you would select yourself to take shooting, especially in your friends' presence. The most valuable animal is a general ability dog – brains, natural speed, nose and sagacity; and therefore I put your questions in the following order:

1. The most valuable dog is the dog that can be taken out by anyone shooting with a view of finding game when dead or wounded;

2. When guns are posted, the handler should not be allowed to make signs, or speak to his dog, and, if he does so, he should lose marks, for it is obvious that the best dog is the one that requires no special care when behind the guns;

3. Speed out and returning is of the greatest value, for a dog wanting in speed will, by the time he is three years old, become a 'potterer', but the speed should not be a mere handler's training, and it is somewhat dangerous to imagine that the speed is everything. The best dog out that steps on his line quickly, picks up his game, or loses, and returns fast is an advantage, but a dog which is merely trained for speed and runs over game becomes difficult to control when out, and is, from my point of view, a dangerous dog and tiresome for an ordinary individual to handle, and, therefore, not in the best interests of a gundog.

4. A dog that runs a hare and does not stop when whistled to or told, should, in my opinion, not be allowed to run again.

5. A hard mouth should obviously be wiped out and not allowed to run again.

6. A handler should not be allowed, under any pretext whatever, to go in advance of the guns that he is with.

7. Any dog that gets out of control must not be allowed to compete again, for it must be clearly remembered that, from my humble point of view, the best dog for shooting purposes is the one that is steadfast, and the worst dog is the one that is a 'trip' – a trained dog, wild and impossible for the ordinary individual to handle. Therefore, he becomes a useless dog for the purpose required.

8. Obviously, nose and hearing, and obeying when they do hear, is the essential starting point for all dogs. I hold the view that has a naturally good nose and sagacity is a more valuable animal for gun purposes than a dog trained for 'trick' shooting.

The 1920 Champion Retriever Trials at Bixley. Above left: Mrs Quintin Dick. Above right: Mrs. Dick working her dog; Left: Tag (Stake Winner). Below left: At the water test. Below right: Blanchory Bolo retrieving.

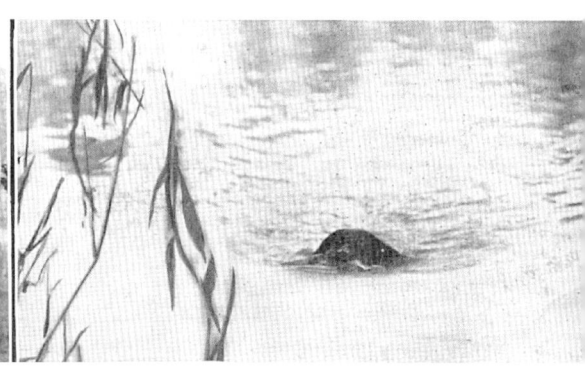

9. Remember this: you go shooting for pleasure; your dog should be unnoticeable until wanted. To have to keep one's eye on your dog and another on the object of your shoot spoils your pleasure, believe me.

Yours truly,
LONSDALE."

THE TRIALS OF OCTOBER 1921

The following was published in The Field, October 1921, under the heading, 'Retriever Trials (An Interesting Programme)'.

The History Of Retrievers

"The Trial campaign begins today (Saturday 1st October), and, thanks to the determination on the part of each secretary not to be 'left', it has been found possible to present a complete list of the fixtures in good time for issue on the opening day. It is a list which Retriever men – and women – may well be proud, for, while being in advance of any issued even before the war, it shows that, even in these times, there are owners who generously and in the best interests of sport are ready to sacrifice their own shooting in order that the continuity of the Trials may be preserved. In this connection it may be mentioned that the members of the Retriever Society have been most fortunate, for though it was not till within a few days of the date on which entries had to be closed that ground was really secured, it was an old supporter of the society and a life member who came to the rescue. Mr. G. Fydell Rowley entertained the society as long since as 1906 – a meeting memorable for the victory of Mr. H. Reginald Cooke's Flatcoated Retriever Grouse of Riverside over the great Labrador Flapper. That a return visit was possible fifteen years later proves that the owner of Priory Hill was not unmindful of friendship started in the early days of the trial movement. Is Pocklington still at Priory Hill was a thought which recurred to us on hearing that a return visit had been arranged, and was the gorse in which Grouse of Riverside did such good work still available? We have little doubt that the ground is very much as it was fifteen years since, and that the meeting of 1921 will be quite as successful in every way as was that of 1906. The full list of meetings arranged is as follows:

DATE	SOCIETY	ESTATE	TOWN
October 1st	Herts, Beds and Bucks.	Shardeloes	Amersham
	Northumberland	Harehope	Alnwick
October 4th	Yorkshire	Duncombe	Helmsley
October 5th	Eastern Counties	Lexham	Kings Lynn
October 6/7th	Midland Counties	Chetwynd	Newport, Salop
October 11/12th	Scottish	Dupplin	Perth
October 14/15th	Gamekeepers	Castlemilk	Lockerbie
October 15th	Down House	Shetterton	Bere Regis
October 18/19th	International	Priory Hill	St. Neots
October 20/21st	Cheshire	Bryn Tanat	Lluasaintffriad
October 21/22nd	Western Counties	Dumbleton	Evesham
October 25th	Horsham	Cowdray Park	Midhurst
October 27/28th	Labrador Club	Luton Hoo	Luton
November 1/2nd	Kennel Club	Crown Point	Norwich
November 9th	Golden Coloured	Godersham Park	Canterbury

Retriever Club: the Championship will be run as usual under the management of the Retriever Society, probably in December."

The Cheshire, Shropshire and North Wales Retriever Society's Trials at Brogyntyn in October 1921. Top left: Tolz of Riverside (winner of divided first and second prizes). Top right: Baron of Bryntanat (winner of divided first and second prizes). Above left: The line. Above right: In the roots. Below left: The guns. Below right: By the river Tanat.

The History Of Retrievers

At Brogyntyn 1921.
Above: The ladies: Lady Harlech, Mrs. Ormrod, and Mrs. Reginald Cooke.
Left: The judges: Lord Harlech, Mr. R. E. Birch, and J. H. Hulme.

Volume Four (1916-1923)

The 1922 Cheshire, Shropshire and North Wales Retriever and Spaniel Society.
Above: H. Reginald Cooke is proposing a vote of thanks to Captain and Mrs. Quintin Dick.
Right: Tommie Cooke, H. Lister-Reade, Mrs. Cooke, H. Reginald Cooke, and Eileen Flower.

The History Of Retrievers

THE FIELD

Throughout the journals, there are cuttings taken from The Field magazine. It is unsurprising then that H. Reginald Cooke included the following obituary among his cuttings.

"To our very great regret, Mr. Walter Baxendale, Kennel Editor of The Field since March 1908, passed away at his residence, Flackwell Heath, on Wednesday December 21st, 1921, just after our issue for December 24th had gone to press. He had been at home ill for some time but with characteristic loyalty he supervised the department, which for nearly thirteen years he had so admirably conducted, almost to the day of his death, some of his notes appearing in last Saturday's paper. Alas for the hopes thus raised! Our old colleague has gone and will be sadly missed, for by his geniality, his good fellowship, his willingness to assist in many ways he had endeared himself to us all. By others too his loss will be greatly felt, for he had occupied a prominent position in the dog world, having been secretary of the International Gundog League and also of the Retriever Society, while to followers of Field Trials and supporters of dog shows, few men were better known, or, we may add, held in greater esteem. It was to Mr. Rawdon B. Lee, author of Modern Dogs, and for many years Kennel Editor of this paper, that Baxendale practically owed his introduction to The Field. Lee fully recognised Baxendale's ability and gave him much encouragement. This measure of kindness was amply repaid by our late comrade, for during Lee's long illness Baxendale took charge, practically con amore of the Kennel Department. It was then that his capacity for work and general knowlegeableness came to be fully realised, and on Lee's death the post thus rendered vacant was at once offered to him. Mr. Baxendale was born in Halifax on May 3rd 1863, and consequently was in his 59th year. The funeral took place on Saturday December 24th at Little Marlow, a part of the country well loved by our old friend."

THE FIELD TRIAL COUNCIL

In 1923, the very first Field Trial Council of Representatives was formed. The following rules were a result of that first meeting.

"The Field Trial Committee of Representatives shall consist of delegates representing Field Trial Societies, or societies providing stakes at field trial meetings. The object of the council shall be to submit recommendations to the Field Trial committee of the Kennel Club, upon any matter dealing with, or arising out of, Field Trials. An intimation of the recommendations of the Council shall be sent to the Secretaries of the clubs who have nominated delegates. Invitations to elect delegates shall be sent out by the Secretary of the Kennel Club. The secretary of each club shall intimate to the secretary of the Kennel Club in each year, the name of the delegate or delegates appointed to the council, and this notice shall be countersigned by the President or Chairman of the society. Societies consisting of up to 100 members may elect one delegate, and societies with over 100 members may elect two delegates. The council shall meet each year in February, and the Chairman may call a meeting at any other time, or the Secretary of the Kennel Club shall call a meeting on written request from six delegates. Seven days notice of meetings shall be sent to the delegates."

5 EXTRACTS FROM VOLUME FIVE (1923-1925)

The fifth scrapbook opens with a cutting taken from the October 1923 edition of The Field. Like so many before it, this article is concerned with the constitution and running of Field Trial competitions.

"In most respects the Field Trial season, which opens this week, shows marked improvements over previous years and indicates in no uncertain manner the widespread development of the movement. An examination of The Field fixture list for the current month leaves no room for doubt as to the strong and increasing hold Retriever competitions have on the gundog community, and nothing could more forcibly illustrate the progress made than the rapid growth of provincial meetings, forming as they do, such a valuable nursery ground for the open events culminating in the Championship fixture of the International Gundog League.

"Despite the vapourings of interested critics, the net result of the development of Field Trials has been a much higher aggregate standard of work, though a survey of recent criticisms shows there still remain a few who desire to have these working tests remoulded on lines more in accord with their individual ideas – and needs. It is not surprising in a period like the present, when Field Trials have assumed such intensive proportions, that a set of obstacles has been created to promoters by the unavoidable clashing of dates. In endeavouring to adjust dates during October to the mutual satisfaction of all concerned, the efficacy of the present system is being sorely tested. This question of the conflict of dates is a pressing one, and it cannot be doubted that it would be for the good of the movement were the whole matter of date adjustments taken in hand and controlled by an independent governing body, such as was proposed by prominent Field Triallers in the columns of The Field some months ago.

"There are many other questions in connection with Field Trials which impatiently await solution. Above all, there is one of pre-eminent insistence which may very properly be termed the problem of the Retriever Field Trial world. Needless to say, reference is made to the difficulty experienced by the leading societies and clubs of making adequate provision, in a competitive sense for the large number of applications for nominations, which have become the rule rather than the exception, as the result of the popularity of Field Trials for gundogs. To the specialist club devoted to fostering the welfare of the Labrador Retriever, an association owing its undoubted prominence to the enthusiasm of its president, Mr. Holland Hibbert, unquestionably belongs the credit of presenting to the Field Trial community the most comprehensive programme yet devised in this regard. The Labrador Club, by arranging for two Trial meetings in the one season, has established a precedent in advance of anything yet tried and characterised by a fitting recognition of the needs of its supporters. The tendency on the part of the specialist clubs to promote working competitions exclusively in the interests of the breed or variety espoused is very noticeable and is coincident with, and the natural corollary of, the general development of the Field Trial movement. The Labrador Club occupies an enviable place in this category and very marked success has attended the annual Trials of the Golden Retriever Club. Appropriately enough, it is for the ultimate good of the breed that the recently constituted Flatcoated Retriever Club indicate that Working Trials will form an integral part of its programme, an announcement that will be doubly welcome to the adherents of this handsome and useful gundog. With the assured active support of that staunch enthusiast Mr. H. Reginald Cooke, the coming year should prove the dawn of a new era for, and a decided revival of popular interest in the Flatcoated variety."

The Flatcoated Retriever Field Trial Association was formed later that year.

KENNEL CLUB FURORE

Here is a copy of a circular letter issued by certain members of the International Gundog League in October 1923. The letter was written as a response to the Kennel Club's action of appointing a Flatcoated Retriever Field Trial Council of Representatives without consulting the other Field Trial societies, and, by these means, attempting to gain control of Field Trials.

"Sir, – It is probably well known to you that, during this summer, the Kennel Club has formed a Field Trial Council of Representatives, and rules and regulations governing it have been issued, whereby the Kennel Club has taken steps towards securing the control of Field Trials generally, which action has been taken without the expressed approval of the Societies concerned. A letter stating the facts regarding this action, none of which have been refuted, appeared in The Field of the 28th June from Mr. E. G. Wheler-Galton, and several others commenting thereon have since been communicated to that publication. The controlling power of the Kennel Club rests solely upon their power to refuse registration to dogs not conforming with any of the rules that they may make, and hence to exclude them from all Field Trials and shows held under those rules. We, who have been actively connected with Field Trials for many years, as owners, handlers, judges and officials are convinced that the well-being and progress of gundogs would be endangered by all Field Trials being placed under the sole control of the Kennel Club. Their guardianship of dog shows makes it undesirable, since the interests of exhibitions and Field Trials are by no means always identical. Moreover, it is admittedly impossible for the Kennel Club General Committee to do more than delegate the management of Field Trials to their Field Trial Committee. Such delegated poers can at any time be curtailed, altered, or withdrawn without notice or appeal. It has been frequently stated that there exists a widespread demand for a central body of some kind for the purpose of securing, so far as may be considered advisable, uniformity of action as regards the management of Field Trials by the various Field Trial societies. It seems therefore very desirable to ascertain the strength of any such opinion and it is also of the greatest importance to consider the best form that any such body might take.

"With these ends in view, we venture to bring those matters to your notice, and to suggest that you should express your opinion by replying to the enquiries that will be found in the enclosed post card. This circular letter is being sent to all members of Field Trial societies whose names and addresses we have been able to procure in order to ascertain to what extent they may desire to join hands in the formation of a representative Association to facilitate arrangements regarding Field Trials, and for the protection of mutual interests. In our opinion, a controlling body of the nature of the 'Jockey Club' possessing executive powers would, under present conditions, by no means receive unanimous support, and we suggest that the body should be of a purely advisory character and that it should be formed of representatives elected by Committees of Field Trial Societies. We do not think that a central body operating in London can successfully control and manage Field Trials, as they cannot be acquainted with local requirements. In the event of it being denied to form any such Association the following procedure would seem to be advisable:

(a) That an Advisory Association be formed to be called the 'Field Trial Association';

(b) That a register and Stud Book be instituted for working gundogs only, and be controlled by the association;

(c) That the management of Trials be left entirely in the hands of each promoting society;

(d) That offenders be dealt with by the society where the offence is committed.

"Should sufficient support be forthcoming, it is proposed to summon a conference shortly of those who are willing to accept the above proposals. It is with the greatest reluctance that the responsibility of issuing this circular has been undertaken, but it is felt that the recent actions of the Kennel Club have made it necessary. Our sole object is to preserve the working qualities of Gundogs. We would like to make it clear that we have no desire to work counter to the Kennel Club or any other body, and we will co-operate with them when possible, provided that all societies are left free to manage their own affairs.

"As a guide to our future action, we shall be grateful if you will answer and return as soon as possible the enclosed list of enquiries with your views, to Captain Cowan D.S.O.R.N.

Claverdon, Warwick, who has kindly consented to act as our Hon. Secretary. Should no reply be received from you it will be presumed that you are not interested in the matter.

Yours faithfully,

W. ARKWRIGHT, H. REGINALD COOKE, CHARLES. C. ELEY, A. G. HAZLERIGG, F. C. LOWE, E. G. WHELER-GALTON."

K.C RETRIEVER TRIALS 1923

Despite the commotion caused by the Kennel Club's actions, their Trials, held between October 9th and 11th at Ruckley Grange in Shifnall (Shropshire), were well attended.

CORRESPONDENCE

Following the circulation of the above letter to all gundog enthusiasts and the Kennel Club, there followed several pages of letters which were published as a result of the circular. Also included were statements from The Field, The Shooting Times, The Sporting Chronicle, and Country Life. All these were very lengthy and even word-for-word discussions were printed at length. There follows just a few examples.

From Country Life, November 1923.

"The battle which has recently begun following years of simmering revolt is whether or not the Kennel Club shall exercise control and be the final arbiter in all disputes. Obviously, it is the proper authority so to act, but there are strong symptoms that it has gone the wrong way to establish its authority, in what, after all, is a department of work outside its natural sphere. In these democratic days there can never be government without the consent of the governed. That the governed have been left too much out of the reckoning is equally a fact. Where the Kennel Club seems to have erred is in having failed to include in its cabinet the best talent of the party whose affairs it seeks to administer: at

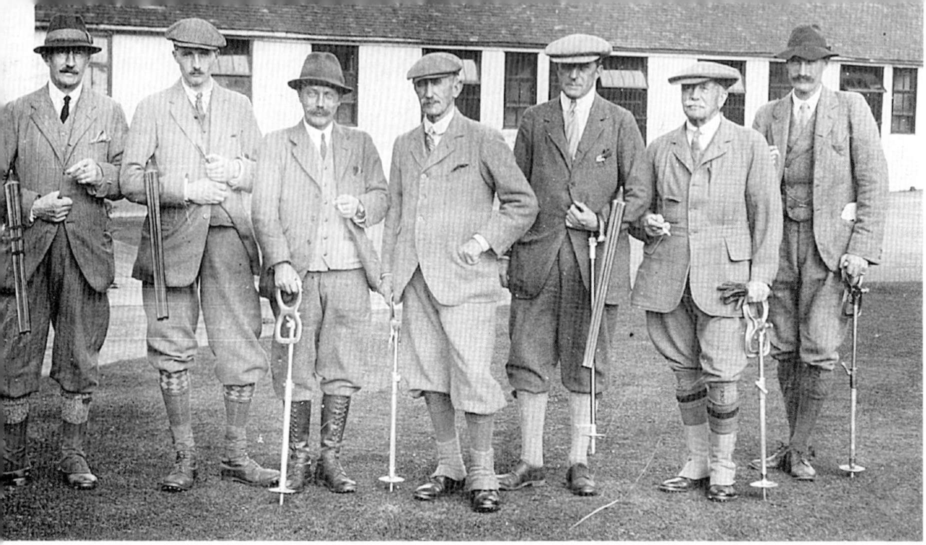

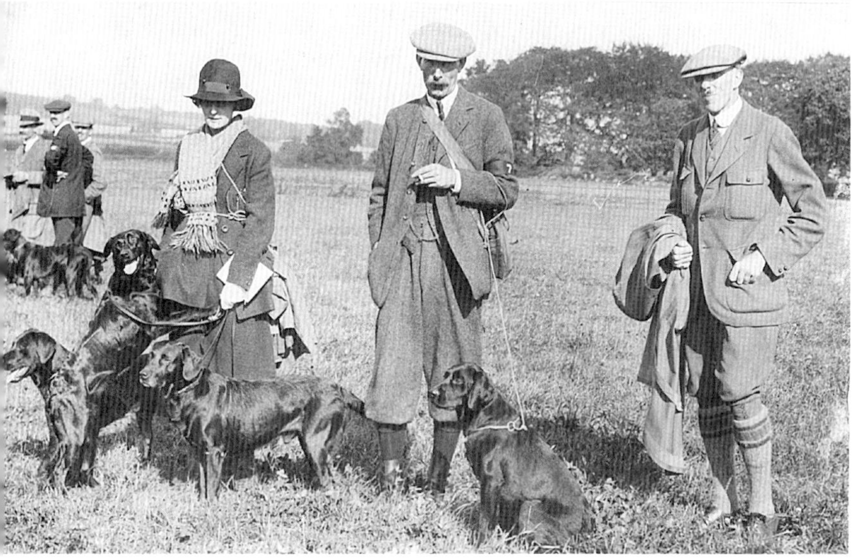

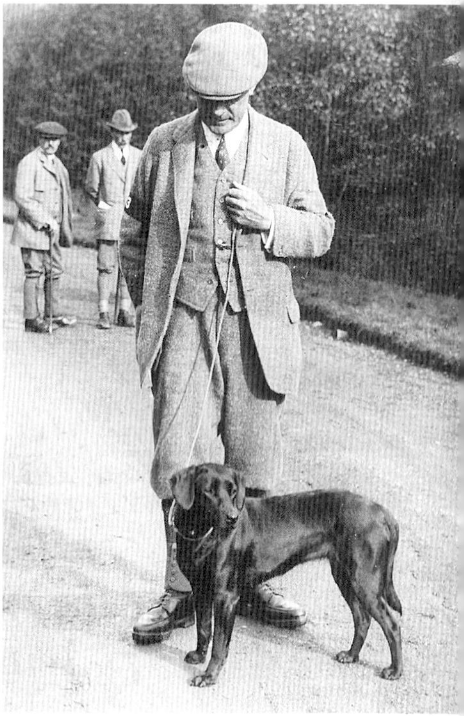

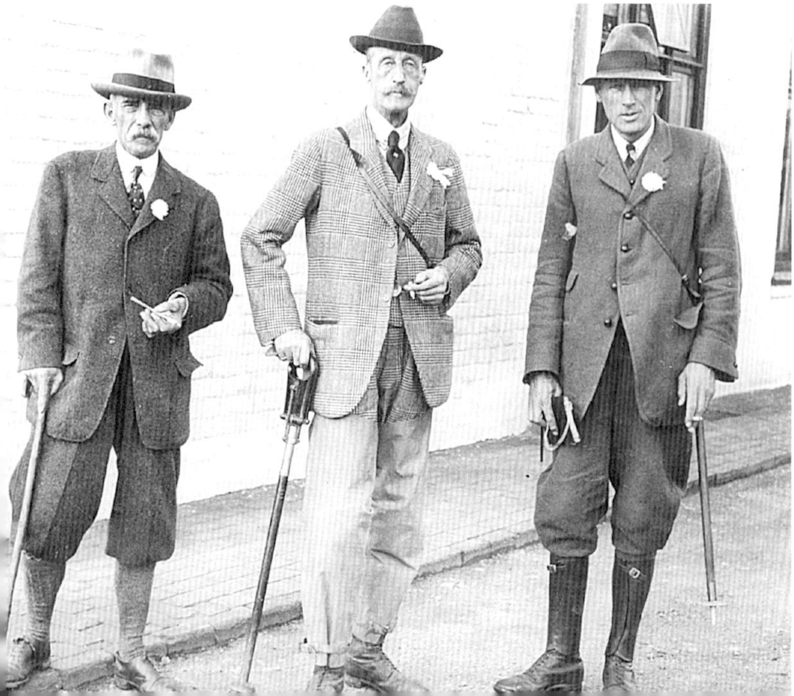

The Kennel club Retriever Trials at Ruckley Grange, Shifnal, Shropshire in October 1923. Opposite page, top left: The guns: General Hoare, Hon. Scott, Lord Bradford, Col. Sandeman, W. Clarke, J. Reid-Walker, Hon. Bridgman. Opposite page: Mrs. Quintin Dick and dogs, with Mr. C. Alington and the Secretary of the Kennel Club. Reginald Corket and Vici of Adderley. Opposite page, bottom: The judges of the Shifnal Trials: Colonel Phillips, Lord Chesterfield, and W. S. Medlicott. Above: Spectators at the KC Trials.

any rate, it has failed to secure their allegiance. True, it has drastic powers of compulsion, which, in its present temper, it might be tempted to use, but in that direction lies chaos and other evils. To speak very bluntly, the Kennel Club is accused, so far as Dog Trials are concerned, of being run by a Clique. Certainly there is a clean-cut distinction as to whether a person is within or without the Magic Circle."

From The Field, November 1923.

"The procedure required by the Kennel Club's Field Trial Council, should any Field Trial society desire to bring forward a recommendation or amendment is Cumbrous, irksome and Dilatory. The recommendation must first be adopted at a meeting of the society; it must then be submitted "in an orthodox manner" – whatever that my mean – to the Kennel Club's Field Trial Council of Representatives, who, in turn, will submit it to the Kennel Club's Field Trial Committee; assuming it has not been referred back, of course, through the recognised channel, the recommendation may the possibly be turned down by the Kennel Club's General Committee, by whom the right of hearing an appeal (under rule 9) is specifically reserved. The waste of time and trouble thus entailed would place Field Trial Societies at a serious disadvantage."

FIELD TRIAL DEVELOPMENT

That so many Field Trial enthusiasts felt so strongly about the Kennel Club's actions, may in part be due to the manner in which the Field Trial movement developed.

The first Field Trial was held near Bedford in 1865, by Mr. W. Brailsford of the Knowlton Kennels, the most noted gamekeeper of his day in the Midland Counties. After 1866, the Shrewsbury (or National) Society held a Field Trial meeting regularly and this society was the arbiter upon all matters concerned with working dogs. The first Retriever Trial was held in 1870 at Vaynol and another at Rhiwlas shortly afterwards. Both of these Trials had not been seriously undertaken and were failures.

The Kennel Club was founded in 1873 and in the same year imitated Shrewsbury in inaugurating it's own Trials. In 1895 Mr. F. C. Lowe and William Arkwright founded the International Shooting Dog Club. This new club regularly held Autumn Trials on grouse and encouraged brace stakes. It changed its name a few years later upon becoming a branch of the International Gundog League, in company with the Sporting Spaniel Society and the Retriever Society. Soon after the establishment of the International Gundog League there followed a rabies scare and the regulations consequent from that virtually robbed it of its International status.

It was not until the year 1900 that the Kennel Club first allowed the title of Champion to be gained at Trials but it was still excluding any mention of Field Trial classes in the Stud Book.

Given the above, it is unsurprising that the various Field Trial societies were so fiercely protective of their societies' autonomy. Having fought so hard to achieve recognition and status, and achieving both without the assistance of the Kennel club, the Field Triallers were not about to hand over control without a struggle. In February 1924, this culminated in the formation of a breakaway Field Trial Association, as this cutting reports.

"At Aldridges on the 12th February 1924, probably the most influential and representative meeting of persons interested in gundogs which has ever been held. Its purpose was to inaugurate the new Field Trial Association and, considering that so drastic a step is of necessity a repudiation of Kennel Club domination, the quality of the gathering proved how deeply feeling has been stirred. Severance of working gundogs from the show-bench control is regarded as the only possible haven of safety. Mr. E. Wheler-Galton, who was voted to the chair,

Mrs. Ernest Turner, Honorary Secretary of the Flatcoated Retriever Society.

emphasised at the start that neither he nor his associates desired other than friendly relations with the Kennel Club. Their aim was to exclusively to insure that freedom of action which, judging by all too eloquent symptoms was being threatened at the moment. Debate was concentrated on fifteen numbered items which covered the proposed constitutional basis of the proposed Association.

"In essence the Association was to consist of one representative from each of the Field Trial Societies. Consideration was mainly directed upon the policy of keeping a register and stud book. Negotiations had been opened with Field Press Limited, who were prepared to keep the register and stud book for a very low fee and to publish monthly the registration effected. A resolution was passed unanimously authorising arrangements for its inception. All other items on the list were similarly approved and the principal resolution was then proposed viz. that the Field Trial Association should be formed on the basis laid down. This was put to the vote and carried unanimously."

KENNEL CLUB RESPONSE

Following the issue of the Kennel Club of its report of proceedings devised to bring rival factions into harmony, the fifth journal now presents us with a verbatim transcript of the Chairman's opening speech. There is none of the olive branch about this oration, in fact, it is a purely fighting speech, carrying, besides an undertone of extreme irritation, not to say irritability. Those of us who stand aside from any extreme partisan feeling in this dispute cannot help regretting that Lord Chesterfield did not draft beforehand a much more closely reasoned statement free of personality and addressing itself exclusively to the points of objection which have been raised.

For example, the case where Field Trial Societies are invited, or required, to forward a list of their prize winners to the Kennel Club. Apparently this is solely a measure of assistance to the society, whereby the registration and general credentials of the competing animals are verified in the register. The secretary in due course issuing his report that everything is in order: but instead of the reply being sent in that innocuous form it goes out as permission to hand over the prizes: This remarkable discord between process and language was brushed aside as immaterial, yet behind the word 'permission' stands an assumption of power which invites question.

In the same way, it may seem to the ruling spirits in the Kennel Club the most natural thing in the world that their body should assume the control of gundog Field Trials. There are others who have still to be convinced that such a development would be beneficial. Approximately, what they say is that the Kennel Club is so essentially tied to the principle embodied by the show-ring that it is incapable of the wider outlook which alone can safeguard sporting utility. Reduced to its simplest aspect, the issue is one of confidence. You cannot force anybody to like you but there are methods by which mutual appreciation can be built up. Whether the speech that has been issued in pamphlet form exemplifies such methods is open to question, however.

The judges of the Golden Retriever Club Trials at Syncombe, Henley-on-Thames, September 30th to October 1st 1924. Mr. C. C. Eley, Mr. H. Reginald Cooke, and Colonel E. Godman.

KENNEL WORLD

Moving on to September 1924 and there are several more pages of correspondence regarding this issue. I insert an observation from The Kennel World, given the column title of 'A Controversial Matter: The Kennel Club v The Field Trial Association.'

"Some months ago it will be remembered the controversy that had arisen between the Kennel Club and the newly formed Field Trial Association as to the control of Field Trials. Since that time there has been so much correspondence written and published on either side that unless one is devoting oneself to the subject specially, it has become almost too intricate to follow. Just in the nick of time, as the whole crux of the matter is reaching a point near that of breaking, a letter has come to hand from the secretary of the Field Trial Association which gives clearly and concisely, a resume of the whole situation.

"Rather than break away from the Kennel Club, the Field Trial Association has suggested and asked for a conference between a certain number of their members and the same number of members of the Kennel Club Committee to discuss this whole matter with a view to a peaceful settlement, but, this has been refused by the Kennel Club through their secretary, unless it is taken for granted that: (1) The Kennel Club retains control over the registration of dogs; and (2) Retains the penal powers governing disqualifications and suspension for which the Kennel Club shall be the final court of appeal.

"SOCIETY'S HISTORY. Now look back. Until the establishment of the Kennel Club Council of Representatives every Field Trial Society had full freedom of action to carry on its Trials just where and when it desired and to deal with cases of unfair conduct should they arise, entirely independent of the Kennel Club. Then this club instituted its council, and

Volume Five (1923-1925)

Above: The judges of the Cheshire, Shropshire and North Wales Retriever Society's Trials of 1924, held at Capesthorne, Shropshire. Colonel F. J. Raitt, Mrs. Quintin Dick, and Colonel E. Godman.
Top right: Tommie Cooke, H. Reginald Cooke and Toby. *Right* Tommie Cooke, Mrs. Rushby, Lady Harlech, H. Reginald Cooke and Toby.

immediately attempted to secure full control over all Field Trials by reserving to itself overwhelming representation in proportion to other societies, appointing the chairman and secretary, excluding the press from all meetings, and issuing all notices calling or appertaining to such meetings itself. This was obviously too autocratic an action for any group of men to stand, and the Field Trial Association came into being as a purely advisory body to assist those societies who desired freedom of action, without the least intention or wish to control or judge others."

The single Spaniel Championship Stakes winner with his handler, the Duke of Hamilton's FTCh. Reece of Avendale.

RETRIEVER TRIALS OF 1924

The world of Retrievers was not totally preoccupied with the Field Trial Association fight with the Kennel Club, however. Time was still found to organise Trials and to enjoy oneself. The Golden Retriever Trials were held on September 30th, while the Cheshire, Shropshire and North Wales Trials were held over October 7th and 8th.

FLATCOATED RETRIEVER TRIALS

The first Flatcoated Retriever Field Trial was held at Auchencairn on October 17th 1924, and was reported thus:

"It has been depressing to see how the old and once popular Flatcoat has fallen from public grace as far as Field Trials are concerned but the success which attended the first Trial should do much to and lead to it once again taking its full share in modern gundog progress. The meeting which was pronounced a resounding success, afforded the keenest enjoyment to all present. There was a full card consisting of seven dogs and seven bitches. Full awards were given at the end of the day including five Certificates of Merit. At the close, Mr. Ernest Turner fittingly conveyed the indebtedness of all to Sir M. Hollins and Mr. Ainsworth for so generously placing such excellent ground at the disposal of the Association, adding a special tribute to Mr. P. Fitzsimmons for the ability with which he had directed the beating arrangements. The judges were thanked on the call of Mrs. Fletcher, while Captain Beaumont Neilson proposed a hearty vote of thanks to Mrs. Turner for the able manner in which the meeting had been conducted."

THE LATE MR. SIDNEY GRAY

An obituary regarding Mr. Sidney Gray was included towards the end of this journal because of the gentleman's connection to Mr. Cooke's Riverside kennels. The obituary reads as follows.

"A brief announcement a few weeks back of

The Late Mr. Sidney Gray.

the death of Mr. Sidney Gray came as a shock to many of his old friends in the doggy world. Mr. Gray was responsible for the breeding of many noted Flatcoated Retrievers, his Luton Melody being the dam of the famous Dual Champion Grouse of Riverside who was sold for a great price to the Riverside Kennel and earned undying fame with the brilliant record he put up at Field Trials and on the bench.

"Another dog of note bred by Mr. Gray and sold to H. R. Cooke was Hermit, at a very big figure. At one time Mr. Gray had some good Clumber Spaniels, and latterly, Labradors. He was a shot of the old school, always taking careful aim, a good judge of distance, and killed his game clean and well with his favourite Langley hammerless which he had used constantly since 1900. He always had his cartridges loaded with 41 grains of Schultze powder and 1 ounce of No.6 shot, and his good work with this charge led many coverts to its use. He was sound judge of gundogs in general and Flatcoats in particular."

TAIL DOCKING

In September of 1925, there began some correspondence regarding the docking of Retrievers tails.

"Sir, – It is probable that everyone owning a Retriever and those interested in their various breeds will welcome the announcement appearing in the present months issue of The Kennel Gazette on the subject of docking the sterns of such dogs. This announcement, of course, does not apply to those people who keep Retrievers for work and sport only. In such cases, it does not in the least matter what sort of stern a dog possesses, but where Retrievers are intended for exhibition the case is altogether different. One of the points looked for by judges in a perfect Retriever is a short, straight stern, and many dogs possess perfectly natural sterns of this description, but more often it is the case that dogs have an unsightly 'kink' or twist in their sterns and such sterns are often operated on by unscrupulous owners with a view to winning prizes, and it is to be feared that this dishonest practice has increased in recent years. It is most satisfactory therefore, to find that the Kennel Club has taken up this matter, for the practice is manifestly unfair to those exhibitors who show their dogs in their natural state, and it is greatly to be hoped that the pronouncement now made by the Kennel Club Committee, who will doubtless deal with any cases brought before them, will have its due effect.

H. REGINALD COOKE."

At the Cheshire, Shropshire and North Wales Retriever Trials, at Western Park, Shropshire, in October 1926. Lord Bradford and Colonel H. Wilson.

KENNEL CLUB DEFEAT

At the very end of the fifth journal, the Kennel Club versus the Field Trial Association argument once more rears its head. This time, however, in November 1925, the debate appears to be settled, as the title of the following article indicates – 'Exit the Kennel Club's Field Trial Council.'

"It would appear that, without a discordant voice raised in protest, even by its sponsor, present at its obsequies, the Kennel Club's unpopular Field Trial Council of Representatives is now a thing of the past. This significant decision was adopted unanimously at the Kennel Club meeting although the Council was inaugurated on the initiative of the Kennel Club itself as a means of solving all problems and of bringing the whole Field Trial community into unison. Its genesis was inspired by uncontrollable ambition, and it was inaugurated on the very definite promise that it was to be an 'independent body' with power and authority to deal with Field Trial matters, and to be entirely outside Kennel Club control – a thoroughly representative council having the trust and confidence of all members of Field Trial Societies. The formation of the Council was at first accepted with a certain measure of satisfaction by the many prominent Field Triallers unattached to the Kennel Club. Most promises made by the council were not ratified and it was early apparent that the covert objects for which the council was instituted were more ambitious than practical, more imaginary than actual.

"This Field Trial council of representatives in its constitution as a dependent nursling of the Kennel Club was not long in manifesting its purely subsidiary character. So far as being independent and having freedom of action, it

Volume Five (1923-1925)

Mrs. H. Reginald Cooke and Mr. H. Reginald Cooke at the Cheshire, Shropshire and North Wales Retriever Trials.

was officially acknowledged to be merely an advisory board whose sole pretension to independence lay in the questionable privilege of being permitted to offer recommendations, which might be summarily turned down and dismissed while those responsible for its existence sought to exercise the power of ultimate decision and to retain the entire authority and the dominating control.

"The institution of the Field Trial Council was the practical protest against control, and the futility of the Kennel Club's Field Trial Council of Representatives became more and more patent. Henceforth the fraternity of gundog people will have a voice in the conduct of their own affairs. Aiming at complete harmony they can work for the welfare of gundogs and the Field Trial movement unhampered and unrestrained."

6 EXTRACTS FROM VOLUME SIX (1927-1932)

The sixth scrapbook opens with a picture of Mrs. Cottingham, a society lady, with some of her dogs.

HYSTERIA IN DOGS
This heading, published in 1927, immediately caught my attention, and, as I read on, I discovered that there were several more types of hysteria in dogs! These were stomach hysteria, ear hysteria, nerve hysteria and others! Much was written on the causes and cures, and various remedies were printed to aid the dog owner to control or cure the various forms. Mr. Cecil French (Doctor of Veterinary Science, McGill University, Montreal) wrote columns of informative theories and observations including the following excerpts.

"It has been assumed by most of the writers in Our Dogs that this so called 'hysteria' is specific in nature – implying that it is caused by one definite factor, ranging all the way from ejaculation of some mysterious effluvia by toads to reflex irritation of the brain through infestation of the aural passages by ear-mites and in general infection by some undisclosed ultra-microscopic organism. But can this trouble rightfully be regarded as of a specific nature?"

"On one occasion in the early days of my practice I was called to attend a case of 'nerve-seizure' in a nursing bitch. I wanted to use morphine hypodermically but did not happen to have a supply of that drug with me. On the other hand I did have some apomorphine, and, knowing that I should get a certain amount of narcosis from its employment fell back on it and gave a dose hypodermically. The resultant quick ejection of the contents of the stomach brought almost immediate cessation of all the nervous phenomena long before any narcotic effect of the drug could have been exerted."

After several reports about canine hysteria, several readers wrote in with their home made cures for the condition.

"It may interest you to know that I entirely cured some Fox Terrier Puppies who had these screaming fits for no apparent reason (they did not have worms) by pouring down their ears the recipe as below as soon as I could catch them after they started the attacks.
Napthol, 1 dram
Ether, 3 drams
Olive oil, 10 drams.
That is very satisfactory and should be noted by other readers."

"During my 35 years experience with dogs I have had this distressing state of things occur at various times to dogs in my possession. In every case I have traced the cause to the stomach. In one case I traced it to the dog

Volume Six (1927-1932)

Mrs. Cottingham and some of her Golden Retrievers.

coming from town life and eating large amounts of grass. Quite recently I was run out of stale brown bread and the last three dogs to be fed were given hound meal for their supper. (I always feed stale brown bread which I am generally fortunate enough to get a good supply of). Now these three dogs were given hound meal covered with meat gravy – a thing they had not had before – and about midnight I was fetched out of bed by their continuous howling, and on going to investigate the cause I found these three dogs in an awful state of hysteria."

"TREATMENT FOR HYSTERIA. First of all give the dog a dose of Castor Oil – and then seven grains of Hydrated Chloral in half a wine glass of water every morning for a week and afterwards an occasional dose as a preventative. Get the Chloral made up in liquid form and keep the bottle well corked.

"If the dog froths at the mouth the dose should be increased to ten grains of Hydrated Chloral. During the treatment keep the dog very quiet in his kennel, only allowing him out for short intervals. If the dog has been fed on biscuits previous to the fits – change the food and feed on rice and any meat that can be obtained."

"We were out yesterday (August 12th) and one after the other all the six Pointers and Setters collapsed, symptoms sometimes barking fits and foaming at the mouth, or else

a few whines and then into water if they could find it. Collapse with complete powerlessness. The dogs appeared to recover very quickly and be none the worse, and then on came another fit. The symptoms are identical with those we have seen so much of in the past, and we would advise all who have this trouble to contend with to treat the dogs ears with:
Borasic Powder, 2 ounces
Iodoform, 4 drams.
Even in cases where no hysteria has so far been seen it would be advisable to treat all dogs with this prescription."

FAKENHAM TRIALS, 1927
At the Eastern Counties Trials, held at Sennowe, Fakenham in Norfolk, Mrs. Quintin Dick, who featured earlier in the journals, made her first appearance as Lady Howe. Among the other distinguished guests were Lady Naylor-Neyland, Captain H. W. Lance and Mrs. Coleman, Lady Anne Bridgeman and the Earl of Bradford. The Trials were held on the 4th and 5th November, 1927.

RISE OF THE LABRADOR
In February 1928, the following article appeared in The Daily Mail, describing the lapse in popularity of the Flatcoat, alongside the meteoric rise of the Labrador.

Lady Howe (formerly Mrs. Quintin Dick) with her champion Balminto Jock at the International Gundog Trials at Idsworth.

"Flatcoated Retrievers, which, in the early years of this century seemed to be invulnerable, have been side-tracked latterly, Labradors having eclipsed them completely alike on the show bench and at Field Trials. Even the Golden Retrievers surpassed them in numbers at Crufts. Yet the Flatcoats are undeniably pleasing, both in disposition and appearance. Their heads indicate high breeding and kindly natures. Their shoulders, fronts and quarters are so formed as to suggest ability to stay and gallop.

"Retrievers have become so indispensable a part of the shooting mans entourage that it is somewhat difficult to realise they are a product of the nineteenth century. Older sportsmen were content with training Pointers or Setters to pick up as well as point. That classic work on Dog Breeding first written by General Hutchinson in 1847, though revealing that the Retriever proper was then known, makes it clear that many men still used the other dogs for the purpose. The author remarks that from education there are good retrievers of many breeds, but it is usually allowed that, as a general rule, the best land retrievers are bred from a cross between the

Volume Six (1927-1932)

Left: Lady Anne Bridgeman, with her father, the Earl of Bradford, and a keeper. Pictured at the Weston Salop Labrador Trials.

Below left: Lady Naylor-Leyland, at the North Wales, Cheshire and Shropshire Retriever and Spaniel Trials at Capesthorne. Lady Naylor-Leyland entered her Retriever May, seen in this picture.

Below: Captain H. W. Lanes and Mrs. Colmon, at the Eastern Counties Trials of 1927.

The Eastern Counties Society Trials at Sennowe. The Eastern Counties Retriever Society held its Working Trials the other day at Sennowe, near Fakenham in Norfolk. The judges were Mr. H. R. Cooke, Sir Arthur Hazelrigg Bt., and Mr. Walter Marchant. The trials were held in Sennowe Park by permission of Mr. Thomas Cook, who is a member of the Royal Thames Yacht Club, and who acted as one of the stewards at these Retriever Trials.

Volume Six (1927-1932)

Setter and the Newfoundland, or the strong Spaniel and the Newfoundland."

A QUAIL IN SHROPSHIRE

In September of 1928, H. Reginald Cooke wrote to a magazine with the following news. He pasted the subsequently published letter into his journals.

"While shooting on September 1st, one of my Retrievers flushed a quail when hunting for a wounded partridge on a rough grass field. Later the same day I heard from a farmer that, when cutting a field of barley on an adjoining farm, about twenty of these birds rose out of the standing crop, and he thought that some of them were young birds. The quail is an unusual visitor to this part of Shropshire. On September 18th 1915, one was shot which rose on a stubble field, but since that date I have not heard of one being seen in this neighbourhood.
H. REGINALD COOKE."

DISTEMPER CURE

In 1923, The Field set up a fund for the prevention of distemper in dogs. Mr. F. W. Dunkin and Dr. Laidlaw worked for five years under the auspices of The Field Distemper Fund, and in 1928 a report was published on the result of their findings, with the title of ' Dog Distemper Immunisation Found Possible.'

Mrs. Allen Shuter with Labrador, Flatcoated and Golden Retrievers.

"The method consists of a double inoculation. The first is made with an inoculation is made with a vaccine which is, in fact, the inactivated virus of distemper. The second is made, after an interval of about ten days, with an attenuated strain of living virus.

Mr. F. W. Dunkin (left) and Dr. Laidlaw. A vaccine has been found which, it is claimed, will prevent distemper in dogs. The discovery is the result of five years' research work at the laboratories of the Medical Research Council at Mill Hill, London. These events occurred in 1923.

The Champion Retriever Trials at Idsworth, Horndean, Hants, December 1928. Above left:: Hon. Mrs. Grigg. Above right: Spectators.

The dose of living virus is a hundred-fold that would infect a dog not previously treated with the vaccine, but as a rule it is followed by nothing more than a trivial and transient disturbance of health. Dogs which have undergone this double inoculation have proved to be completely resistant to the disease thereafter."

CHAMPION RETRIEVER TRIALS, 1928
These were held at Idsworth, Horndean in Hampshire, on December 4th and 5th.

JUDGING COMPLAINTS
In 1929, the subject of what constituted a fair Field Trial again reared its head. Under the caption 'Judges and Judging at Retriever Trials', the following correspondence was published in The Field.

"Sir, – In asking you to give space to this letter in your columns I feel I am treading upon very dangerous ground, because any criticism of judges or judging at Field Trials savours of discontent or disappointment, if nothing worse. Nothing, however, of this description exists in the mind of the writer, whose experience of Field Trials covers many years, and whose sole desire is to recall some results of that experience and to offer a few suggestions to those who may not be able to look back so far, but who willingly and unselfishly undertake the responsibilities of a judge – a somewhat thankless task at all times.

"Judges may be divided into two classes: Firstly, the 'old hands', who have little or nothing to learn, men who have shot since their boyhood, who have constantly broken and handled their own dogs, who take a delight in watching all kinds of dog work and have made a life study of all the faults and virtues of their dogs. All honour to them!

Above: A scene from the Champion Retriever Trials at Idsworth, Horndean, Hants, December 1928.
Right: Sir Malcolm Murray.

The History Of Retrievers

Above and right: Scenes from the Champion Retriever Trials at Idsworth, Horndean, Hants, December 1928.

Volume Six (1927-1932)

Mr. H. R. Cooke, Lady Howe, W. S. Medlicott, John, and Mrs. E. E. Turner, at the Champion Retriever Trials of 1928.

Secondly, men who are equally fond of dog work, but who through force of circumstances or lack of opportunity for handling their own dogs, have not had the experience of the men previously mentioned. Such men are sometimes called upon to judge at Field Trials, and appear somewhat apprehensive of their own judging abilities, though most anxious and willing to do their best.

"To these latter perhaps I may be permitted to offer a few suggestions based on experience gained at many Field Trial meetings, but I fervently hope that these suggestions may not be construed as instructions, which I am not sufficiently presumptuous to give. My suggestions are as follows:

"Go to a Field Trial with an absolutely unbiased mind, with the fixed determination of sorting out the best dogs irrespective of breed or ownership. Decide in your own mind to endeavour to get the best out of each dog and his handler, and not resort to laying 'traps' such as hiding up birds which have been handled.

"Let every handler work his dog in his own way. If you have reason to think that he is spoiling his dog's chance you can make your own deductions.

"Climatic and scenting conditions vary very often during a day. On the first day of the Trials, therefore, it is desirable to try each dog in the stake as soon as possible without undue haste. To enable this to be done a judge should put aside as soon as he possibly can any dog that has done well in a few early tests. Such a dog can be more freely tried later on, and his temporary retirement will enable the judges to get more quickly through the card in the first round.

"When two dogs are working under a judges he should try them alternately, although not necessarily at the birds nearest each dog.

"Each judge, without interference, should endeavour to see as much as possible of the work of the dogs under the other judges. This is very helpful when the final summing-up takes place.

"If a dog is asked to hunt for a bird which he has not seen fall, and he makes an honest and hardworking attempt to find it after a long hunt, give him due credit, even if he does not recover the bird. This is one of the few chances a judge has at Field Trials of testing stamina and determination.

"Insist on a water test wherever possible. A dog who does not willingly enter water is unworthy of a prize or certificate. Have the water test in the morning or midday, so that the dogs may go home dry. If a natural and fair water test can be provided (they do not always go together) so much the better, but, failing this, a few birds thrown into the nearest pond or river will suffice to satisfy the judge. This is a natural test, but it provides the means, at any rate, of giving all the dogs an equal chance.

"If a judge suspects a hard mouth in a dog he should confer with his CO-judges, who should take into consideration the nature of the ground from which the bird has been retrieved. There may be some good excuse for the dog, but if the judges are satisfied that the bird has been 'pinched' the dog should at once be discarded. A hard mouth is a retrievers worst fault.

"Dogs should be tested both in walking up game and at a drive if the Trial ground can provide both. Give credit to the dog who marks and goes to the fall of a running bird, taking the line straight away, with his nose down, and eventually getting the bird. This shows brain and nose, and is the dog everyone wants. Discriminate between such a dog and the dog that misses the fall of the bird and then goes on a wild gallop with head up. He may by chance gallop on to the bird in another part of the field but this is blundering and not true retriever work.

"In the final summing up a judge should bear in mind that Field Trials were originally instituted in order to discover the best dog to take out shooting. He should therefore select a good mannered, level-headed dog, quiet, watchful and steady under all circumstances, but quick and alert to do his work when required. Such a dog is a treasure. PARTRIDGE."

MRS. COTTINGHAM

Halfway through the sixth scrapbook, Mrs. Cottingham again makes an appearance, this time pictured with some Golden Retrievers. The accompanying text reads:

"At Woolley Hall, Maidenhead, Berkshire, Mrs. Cottingham with some of her Golden Retrievers. She gives much time and care to the interests of the Golden Retriever, and in addition to showing and judging, Mrs. Cottingham superintends the training of her dogs for the Field Trials. The puppies shown are the progeny of Ch. Cubbington Diver of Woolley and Ch. Reine of Woolley."

COUNTESS HOWE

The former Mrs. Quintin Dick, now known as Lorna, Countess of Howe, now becomes a regular feature in the journals, as this, one example, amply demonstrates.

Mrs. Cottingham with some of her Golden Retrievers.

TOBY OF RIVERSIDE

On June 12th 1930, it was reported that Dual Champion Toby of Riverside had died.

"Mr. H. Reginald Cooke has recently sustained a severe loss by the death of Dual Champion Toby of Riverside, one of the best Flatcoated dogs ever produced from the Riverside Kennels. Toby was 12 years old when he died, and was sired by his owner's Punch of Riverside from a bitch named Dart, formerly owned by Commodore Ellison. R. N.

"As a combination of good looks and working ability, Toby was probably never surpassed in the breed. Only exhibited at five shows, he was never beaten, and won Challenge prizes at Birmingham, Manchester and Kensington. He then retired from the show bench. His career at Field Trials, though brief, was equally successful and after winning several stakes and being frequently placed, his

The History Of Retrievers

Lorna Countess Howe, arriving at the Kensington Society Show in 1930.

owner adopted him as his own special shooting companion and Toby was his aide-de-camp at all shoots both at home and elsewhere. Fortunately, the dog has left some good stock in the Riverside Kennels which are much prized."

SIZEWELL TRIALS, 1930
These were held on October 16th and 17th, at Sizewell in Suffolk.

"The Flatcoated Retriever Associations 7th Field Trial Meeting was held at Sizewell, Suffolk by permission of Mr. C. R. Aldrick, Mr. C. J. Scott, Sir Gerald Talbot and Mr. E. Turner and it was very successful. The judges were Lord Henniker, Captain E. H. Buxton and Major I. B. Winch.

"In the nomination stakes there were 17 entries, with three absentees. The weather was perfect from a spectators' point of view. It was quite hot on the first day, and scenting conditions were very poor in consequence. The venue was excellent. There is every kind of cover, both for walking and driving. The missing link was a water test, which was conspicuous by its absence on this portion of the ground. Water could only be had for the dogs by going to the farmstead, and this was not always convenient for the handlers. The work on the whole was fairly good, a big improvement on last year being noted. Game was plentiful, but the judges' task would have been easier had a few more birds been

Scenes from the Flatcoated Retrievers Trials at Sizewell, Thorpeness, Suffolk, in October 1930.

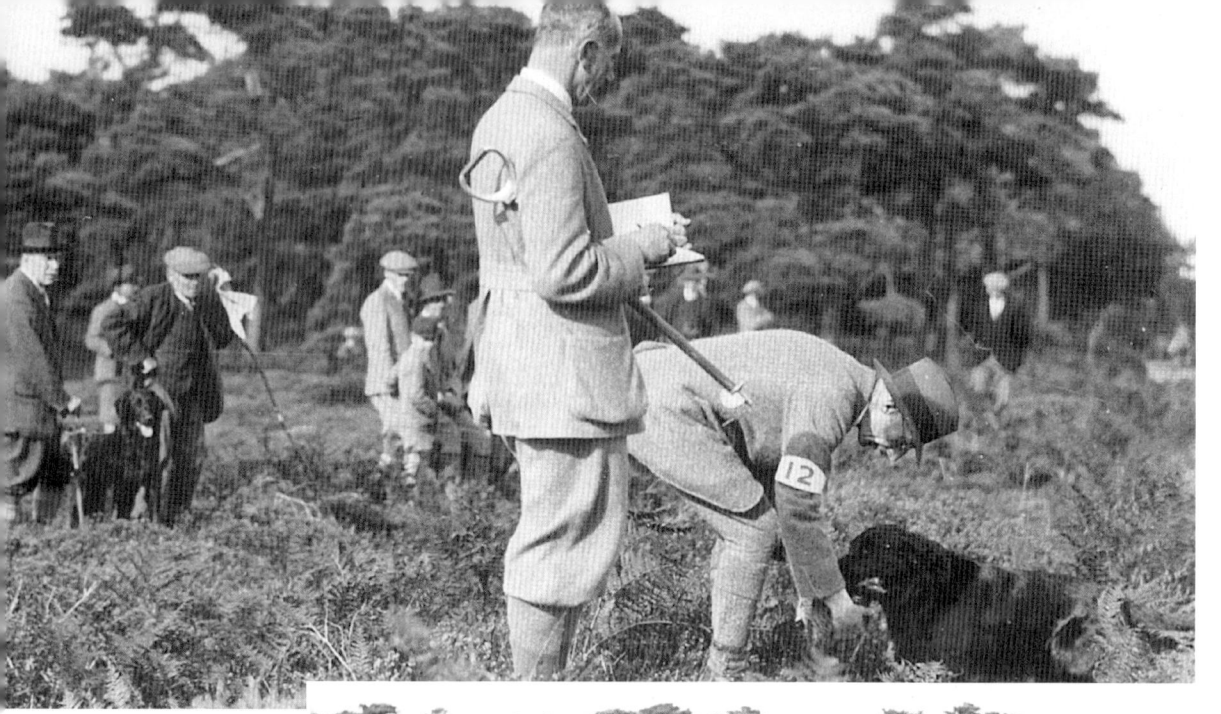

Scenes from the Flatcoated Retrievers Trials at Sizewell, Thorpeness, Suffolk, in October 1930.

brought down on the first day. A decided improvement was noted on the concluding day, and the judges were able to give their awards when lunch was taken.

"After the luncheon, to which a large and representative company sat down at Cliff House, Sizewell, with Mr. G. Stuart-Ogilvie in the chair, Mr. R. E. Birch expressed the thanks of the Association to the shooting tenants for the time and trouble they had taken in arranging the Trials, which had been a great success. Mr. Ogilvie said he greatly appreciated the kind words of Mr. Birch, and he wanted to say on behalf of Mr. Aldrick and himself how pleased and honoured he was that they should have had as their guests such illustrious representatives of the finest sports in the world. He could assure them that if at any time they honoured them again by coming and trying that admirable shooting, they would be only too pleased to receive them. The health of the judges was proposed by Major H. F. Fletcher, and in his reply Lord Henniker said he could assure the company on behalf of the three of them that the trials had afforded them a great deal of pleasure. The judges would like to thank particularly their stewards and those who had helped them in what was not always an easy task.

"Replying to the thanks proposed to him by Major Fletcher, Captain G. H. Gibson, the secretary, said that the arranging of that meeting had proved no trouble to him. On the other hand, it had afforded him the liveliest pleasure."

POETRY
The sixth scrapbook ends with two poems. The first was published in Punch in July 1931. The second has no named provenance, but is marked as making its first appearance in February 1932.

From Punch

"In days devoid of hurry
And leisurely of life,
When Squires were Squires in Surrey
And Lairds were Lairds in Fyfe,
Or ever cars ran hooting,
Or maids desired to vote,
No gentleman went shooting
Without a Wavycoat.

"Up in the morning early,
Their titled ways men took,
In whiskers combed and curly,
In Billy Coke (or Cook),
To manors (with a rental
That gave the squire his due);
And, bold and black and gentle,
The Wavycoats went too.

"There, grandsires hale and Tory
Rammed powder home and shot;
There youth in all it's glory
Breathed 'Breechloaders – why not?'
But, ramrod in the barrel,
Or cartridge in the breech,
In wavywise apparel,
Would be the dog of each.

"For, when the gun was frequent,
From Frant to John O' Groats,
No nose as sure ('Hie-seek') went
As his old Wavycoats.
In mustard and in Mangels,
He stuck to lines like wax
To lines and tortuous angles
That Euclid's self might tax.

"Men say his day is over;
They add that pace and style
In covert, corn and clover
Can beat him by a mile,
And that his case is Cave
The Labrador, and that
His coat that once was Wavy
Has fallen very Flat.

"Yet, when I go, at hearty
Invites (per dreamland posts),
To join a shooting party
Of dear bewhiskered ghosts,
On Manors with a rental
To pay a squire his due,
Then, wise and black and gentle
A Wavycoat comes too."

The History Of Retrievers

From February 1932

"A RETRIEVER'S 'IF' (WITH APOLOGIES TO RUDYARD KIPLING)

"IF you can keep your seat when all around you,
The pheasants or the grouse are falling 'plop',
And IF you're sent for birds they haven't found, you
Don't rush and gallop all about the shop.

"IF you can mark the kill and judge the distance
And can remember where the dead bird lies,
And do not need too much of man's assistance
When shifting winds the elusive blood scent dries.

"IF, when you get your nose down on a runner
That hides away among the turnip roots,
You do not lift your head when some fool gunner
At other birds puts up his gun and shoots.

"IF, when your handler sends you for a pheasant
Which your nose tells you has not fallen there,
Although your instinct says it would be pleasant,
You do not try to catch that tempting hare.

"IF, maybe sent to fetch a wounded bunny,
You do not drop it, just because it squeals,
This may appear to the spectators funny
But please remember how your master feels.

"IF, where the lovely water lilies quiver,
Concealing from your sight some fallen duck,
You hunt right out and get it and you never
Complain if someone says ''twas only luck'.

"IF persevering for your master's pleasure
You find some long-lost bird beneath a log,
When you're returning with your hard won treasure
You'll hear your master say, 'A damned good dog'.
'MUIR GLEN'"

7 EXTRACTS FROM VOLUME SEVEN (1932-1935)

This volume begins with several pages of pictures and text regarding the Flatcoated Retriever Trials of 1932. These were held at Great Bromley Hall, Colchester (Essex), on October 25th and 26th.

WATER TESTS IN FIELD TRIALS

During the early 1930s, there appears to have been some debate about including water tests in Field Trials. Where is was felt that a water test was necessary, some hosts, whose grounds may not have had a suitable naturally occurring feature, resorted to alternative means for the water test. This seems to have caused some controversy, as this article in the January 1934 edition of The Field shows.

"A suggested remedy for Artificial Methods.

"For the benefit of those who are not able to see many Field Trials, I will briefly state what happens at the various meetings all over the country as regards water tests.

"These tests in certain cases are absolutely natural; that is; nothing is done other than that which might be done in any ordinary day's shooting. The dogs in the stake are tested throughout the day's shooting in retrieving game shot across water or on to water while they are in the line, either after a drive or during walking up, and are not called into the line for the sole purpose of being put into water. This kind of test took place at the 1932 Championship Retriever Trials at Sir Ernest Will's shoot at Littlecote, and never was there a better, the dogs being in and out of water at all times during both days. There is another excellent water trial at Lilford, but, unfortunately, it is very rare indeed that such a water test can be provided, and elsewhere it may happen that artificial tests have to be 'made up'.

"Such tests generally involve resort to a pond, lake or river, sometimes large, sometimes small. The owner, or keeper of the shoot knows it will be impossible to bring game to the guns so that they can shoot it into or over the water. So the keeper takes a bag full of dead birds to the waters edge, and possibly 50 to 200 spectators crowd round, sometimes very near the edge, sometimes held back; press and other cameras get ready; and judges call on handlers to have their dogs – perhaps numbering from 12 to 20 ready in number order close at hand. When ordered the dog is taken off the lead and told to sit. A bird is then thrown into the water and the dog is sent.

"Sometimes, even, birds are scattered about in the water before the dogs arrive on the scene. No shot is fired, unless asked for by the handler in order to encourage his dog, when one of the guns looses off into the sky or on to the water near the bird; sometimes stones, etc. are illegally thrown in by handlers. Alternatively, there may be a combination of the natural test and the artificial test. At times an attempt is made to have a purely natural

Left: Miss Janet Crossman, and Mr. R. E. Birch (foreground), two of the judges at the 1932 Flatcoated Retriever Trials of 1932.

Below: Another three judges of the 1932 Trials, Mrs. Venalles Kynke, Major Stafford Brown, and Sir T. W. Stanton.

Spectators, dogs, handlers and guns at the Flatcoated Retriever Trials of 1932.

test; this fails, and perhaps only two or three birds fall right for a water test, so others have to be thrown into the water by hand. In all three cases the water has to be deep enough for dogs to swim in.

"Now as regards the purely artificial test, or the combined artificial and natural test. Those in favour of these might say that a dog shows that he will go into water when ordered to do so no matter whether he is at a shoot or not. This proves obedience, and shows whether he is a good swimmer or a bad one; from this it can be seen if he will retrieve in or across water correctly; and often a judge will learn from such a test whether a dog can be directed by signal to any given point in water or on the land beyond it, and he can gain some knowledge of the quality of the dogs intelligence and nose in the water. Finally it will show how much he will persevere, and how long he can last, especially if swimming among thick sedge and reeds. But now to take the arguments against the purely artificial test. The whole thing is a 'fake' and the wise dog knows it. So that all the good points mentioned about it above, should count nothing, because none of it can possibly occur in the real shooting field. The real performance in the shooting field is for a dog which has either seen or has reason to believe that a bird or game has been shot over or across water, to go in and fetch it out. And I contend that you can't blame a dog if he will not carry out the latter part of the performance without the shooting part. Some will say: 'But your dog must pick up if required after a shoot'. I can only reply here, for want of space that if you use a good shooting dog for picking up after a shoot he will not long remain a really first-class Retriever, or very rarely so.

"It is surprising to me that many more dogs don't refuse water in this test. They are suddenly taken off from the excitement of the shooting field to a dull cold performance, told to fetch a bird they have seen thrown in, which is probably cold and manhandled, and as often or not there is a good crowd of people all round the edge of the water. All this combined does occasionally cause a really good Retriever, and one known in the district to be an excellent water dog on a shooting day, to refuse water, so he has had to be put out of the awards, however well he may have done out shooting. I do not mean to convey the idea that many Retrievers refuse water, for astonishingly few do; but I have personally known several good water dogs refuse this test. I can't say definitely why., but I believe it is because they know they are being fooled and that it is not the real game. The crowd round and the special anxiety of a handler performing before a crowd also probably have something to do with it. Generally speaking, this test is of little use to a judge, because it is not real shooting and is, therefore likely to cause false awards to be made. Under this test judges often openly admit that they only require to see whether a dog will swim to order; if they do even the worst of swimmers are allowed to pass the test and so get into the awards. In some cases they are obviously very poor water dogs and could never last long in water. I have therefore, come to the conclusion that if the purely natural test can not be provided it would be much better to eliminate altogether any water tests where acts never performed in the shooting field have to be employed. It would be much more satisfactory for owners of shoot, who so generously provide ground, for judges, for those responsible for Trial arrangements, and probably for most competitors, but above all for the welfare of Retrievers. As a remedy – all Retrievers should if possible be proved to be good shooting dogs in water – could not water test trials, for water testing only, under absolute natural conditions, be held at suitable places in different parts of the country? At such meetings dogs destined to run in ordinary Field Trials could have the chance of obtaining a life water certificate to be produced when awards at Field Trials were made. And these permanent water certificates might also be gained at any Trials if conditions were available.

W. S. MEDLICOTT."

Volume Seven (1932-1935)

THE RETURN OF THE FLATCOAT
The changing fortunes of the Flatcoated Retriever seem, once more, to have reached a high point in January 1934, as described here in this cutting from The Field. How times have changed!

"That Flatcoated Retrievers are capable of putting up a good entry at a show when their owners are so disposed was apparent from the excellent support given to Crufts. The Flatcoated Retriever Association, however, is more interested in Trials, as may be seen from the annual report that has recently been issued. This contains a record of the trials since 1924. Mr. H. Reginald Cooke is president; the secretary is Capt. G. H. Gibson, Bradwell House, Witham, Essex."

PERSONAL TOUCH
One of the many delightful features about these scrapbooks is the personal items they contain. As an example, there follows four letters to H. Reginald Cooke, congratulating him on a recent Field Trial Win.

The History Of Retrievers

[Handwritten letter on Daisy Bank, Lower Withington, Chelford letterhead, dated 23 Jan 1935, addressed to H.B. Cooke Esq.]

Daisy Bank,
Lower Withington,
Chelford.

23 Jan 1935

H. B. Cooke Esq

Please accept my very sincere congratulations on Quick's win yesterday. Although I was not competing, I was very glad you won, and I was also very pleased to hear you are getting so much better & I hope you will soon be well again. It seems a long time since I first came to Riverside as a very green youngster, with my first flat coated bitch "Jet of Daisy Bank". The most faithful friend I have ever had. You were visiting the kennels at the time I came & you said I could use any dog I liked. I picked "Black Quilt" & got a very good result — won if the nine pr fee — broke my school boy savings. It made me two of the soundest friends I have ever had, yourself & your kennel manager. I ran "Old Adam" because W. Birch asked me to, he had not been at any work since last yrs trials. On Monday, my Dr would not allow me to go so I quit [loaned] him & packed him off to Massey & told him to take him & have a go. I understand the dog did very well but when he got his birds he was looking for me & did not know who to give up to, he is the meanest shooting dog any one could have and when I first had him. He was about the wildest fool I ever saw and

It has all been done with being kind & to him. I often think I may be quite wrong, that a many good dogs are spoiled by too frequent use of harsh treatment.

Massey tells me he never ran a day at trials were the judges were more fair to every dog & the meeting was a great success. This was very pleasing to me, for I never mind how low I am in the awards when it is by merit but I don't like the other way. Hoping you will soon be restored to good health, and that Mrs Cooke who has always been so very nice to me is in good health.

Yours truly
J. H. Hulme

156

Volume Seven (1932-1935)

Ask your host before you bring a dog

A cartoon from 1935 illustrating the debate.

A PERSONAL HISTORY OF THE FLATCOAT

In 1935, H. Reginald Cooke wrote the following article for Dog World. It was published under the title of 'The Genesis and Progress of the Flatcoated Retriever – A beautiful, useful and clever dog that has faced many difficulties and overcame them.'

"As in the case of most breeds of Retrievers the origin of the Flatcoated Retriever is somewhat obscure but is generally supposed that he was the result of across between the Newfoundland and the Irish or English Setter, the idea doubtless to combine the retrieving characteristics of the Newfoundland and scenting qualities of the Setter. Some considerable time must have elapsed before settling down to a type but eventually the late Mr. S. E. Shirley of Ettington took up the breed and by spending much time and money on his kennel produced a large number of dogs of a settled type.

"The early Flatcoats were large, coarse dogs, lacking in quality and activity, and comparatively useless for sporting purposes,

Volume Seven (1932-1935)

but Mr. Shirley, by careful selection in breeding, produced dogs of a much better make-up and more adaptable for sporting purposes. In fact, it may be said that Mr. Shirley was the 'Father' of the breed, and it is due to him that the Flatcoats became popular and were in constant use by sportsmen of that day. Unfortunately, after Mr. Shirley's death the kennel was not kept together. All the dogs were sold and passed into other hands, but in many cases the new owners carried on the breed and, in addition to using their dogs for sporting purposes, began exhibiting them at the shows.

"It is probable that about this time a slight strain of Labrador blood crept into the breed, for one dog belonging to Mr. Shirley, named Paris, was undoubtedly a half-bred Labrador, and so, also, was Mr. S. T. Bartram's Zelstone, a dog famous in those days. Mr. Shirley evidently experienced the difficulty of obtaining an outcross of blood, and, with that object in view, bought a dog with the curious name of Ploughchain, which was afterwards changed to Rightaway, but much to Mr. Shirley's disappointment he mentioned in a letter to me that he found that this dog was closely in-bred to inmates of his own kennel. General Hutchinson, in his book on dog training published in 1847, gives us pictures of various crosses. Shortly after that date Dr. Bond Moore owned and worked a number of Retrievers, but they were very large, coarse dogs and other noted dogs of that day were Mr. Megrick's Wyndham, also Mr. Brailsford's dog of the same name (Wyndham) and another was Major Allison's Victor.

"Perhaps the strongest pillar of this breed of all time was Ch. High Legh-Blarney, bred by Colonel Cornwall Legh, of High Legh, Cheshire, and owned after the death of the breeder by me. Blarney lived at a time when a great deal of coarseness permeated the breed. He was a prolific sire and all his stock showed great quality and were invariably good workers. My two dogs, Dual Ch. Grouse of Riverside and Dual Ch. Toby of Riverside were two Retrievers which distinguished themselves both in the field and on the bench.

Other good dogs were Champions Horton Rector and Shotover, Ch. Pettings-Mallard, Black Drake and Ch. Jimmy of Riverside, all of which transmitted their good qualities to their descendants and helped to maintain the type, which had been showing gradual improvement.

"The Flatcoated Retriever was first introduced as a defined breed at a dog show held in the Cremorne Gardens, Chelsea in 1873, but in the first volume of The Kennel Club Stud Book in 1874, the varieties were all classed together. This particular breed was originally termed Wavycoats but now the 'wave' is discouraged and 'Flatcoat' is their accepted designation. In colour they are usually black, but in the early days of the breed a good many liver-coloured specimens appeared, this colour apparently being a throwback to the Irish Setter. These liver-coloured dogs were often very handsome, the colour being favoured by many sportsmen, as dogs of this colour were less conspicuous on a moor when out shooting.

"The Flatcoats suffered greatly on the outbreak of the Great War. At that time, many of the breed were in the hands of Gamekeepers who, when they left for the front, put down their dogs or sometimes sold them to people who took no interest in breeding. Consequently, the breed lost a full six years fostering as well as training and has been at a disadvantage compared with other breeds which were in the hands of wealthy owners of large kennels and consequently a better start was made at the conclusion of the war. Nevertheless, renewed interest is being taken in Flatcoats, thanks to the efforts of the Flatcoated Retriever Association, which was started in 1923 and supports the breed by offering special prizes at the shows and holding Field Trials annually.

"The first Field Trials for all breeds of Retrievers were held on the property of Mr. Ashton-Smith at Vaynoe Park, North Wales in 1871 and 1872 and they then seem to have been dropped till the International Gundog League was formed. This league was formed by the late Mr. W. Arkwright of Sutton Scarsdale, Derbyshire, in the year 1900. In the first year of its constitution the president of the Retriever Branch was Mr. B. J. Warwick. In the constitution rules the object of the Retriever branch of the I.G.L. was described as follows:-

• To promote the breeding of pure Retrievers and to develop and bring to perfection their natural qualities.

• In order to carry out these purposes a working Trial, if practicable, shall be annually held.

This was the commencement of the Field Trials for Retrievers.

"As regards the show-bench Flatcoated Retrievers of the present time, it is probable that the type has never been better. At one time these dogs were bred with too narrow heads but breeders soon saw the error of their ways and heads are now better proportioned and well balanced. In the size of these dogs too there has been an improvement. Many of the dogs were formerly too large, but breeders have realised that size can be reduced, the dog at the same time being possessed of the requisite bone and strength. A medium-sized dog of correct proportions will 'kill' his gigantic brother at work.

"In conclusion, I think it would be difficult to find a dog more loyal or of a sweeter disposition than a Flatcoat. Clever, very sagacious and anxious to please, he is at all times a friend and charming companion.

H. REGINALD COOKE."

WINNING FLATCOATS

H. Reginald Cooke achieved great success with his Riverside Flatcoats, and, as if to prove his points about Flatcoats, the Dog World article is followed by a photograph of Field Trial Ch. Quick of Riverside, along with the following annotation.

"Winner of the Flatcoated Retriever Association Nomination Stake, The Challenge Cup for the Best Working Retriever, the IGL Silver Medal at Birdsall, Malton (Yorkshire), in October 1935."

Champion Q0uick of Riverside, Field Trial Champion at the 1935 Flatcoated Retriever Trials at Birdsall, Malton, Yorkshire. The dog was the winner of the Flatcoated Retriever Association Nomination Stake, winner of the Challenge cup for the Best Working Retriever and holder of the IGL silver medal.

The 1935 Flatcoated Retriever Trials at Birdsall. Top: The guns. C. Hudson, Captain Davy, Colonel Brewis, Captain Slingsby, Colonel Unett, and Captain Bunburg. Below right: The judges. Lord Middleton, Captain Medlicott, and J. Bell. 121. Right: Lord Middleton, the donor of the ground. Far right: Mrs. E. G. Oliver, The Hon. Secretary.

8 EXTRACTS FROM VOLUME EIGHT (1936-1941)

The eighth and penultimate scrapbook of the series contains several accounts of some of the more famous dogs mentioned throughout the journals.

GUNDOGS OF CHARACTER

This scrapbook begins with an account of the famous Labrador Flapper. The following was published in The Field in 1936, under the heading 'Flapper: A Labrador Retriever, always ready to do his best and go on working.'

"I was fortunate enough to get Flapper in 1903 and he was then aged between eight and nine months. This was my first breakaway from the Alnwick Castle breed of Flatcoated Retrievers which left little to be desired in working qualities. I soon found that I had nothing to regret and found Flapper to be one of those adaptable dogs with plenty of brains and an exceptionally nice temperament, always ready to do his best and go on working, a nice sensible dog.

"His advent into the I.G.L. Field Trials, held at St. Neots in October 1906 was pure chance. In those days Labrador people were not popular and greatly in the minority, we were placed second. I ran him the same year at the Kennel Club Trials at Horstead Hall, Norwich where once again he was second. In 1907 the Kennel Club Trials were once again held at Horstead Hall and I ran Flapper there, his only outing that year. He was placed first, and won numerous specials. I ran Flapper in 1908 at the I.G.L. Trials, Six Mile Bottom on October 15th & 16th where he once again took first prize. Here he had what I thought to be the hardest bit of work to do – a partridge tipped in one wing by the right-hand gun in a field of potatoes, of which the haulms were rough and somewhat mildewed. I had not seen the actual fall, but was certain that the bird was an active runner. However the judge told me it was a dead bird, and roughly where it fell, and I begged to differ as to it being dead, so when Flapper found the fall and began to work away out, slowly at first, I was told it looked like a rabbit – there were several about. Flapper kept crossing over drills, then up a bit and going faster, then slower, finally, the pace increased and about 200 yards out I saw the bird jump up in front. That ended an anxious five minutes. The other judges were watching, and I thought the dog would be high up.

"Flapper was the sire of a great many puppies, very many of which I met out shooting, and I think the outstanding factor was that they were not on their toes but very sensible Retrievers, with good noses and showed an evident desire to please. Sometimes a whole litter by Flapper did well, and the

Volume Eight (1936-1941)

Flapper, Major Maurice Portal's best Labrador.

outstanding litter was one of five which the Duchess of Hamilton bred in 1907 by him, out of her Dungavel Juno (a good consistent winner at trials 1907-1910): three of the litter – Dungavel Dido, Phoebe, Jet – all won at Trials. The fourth was owned by that gallant Admiral Craddock who lost his life in H. M. S. Good Hope in the battle of Coronel – a very good shooting dog and never separated from his owner until war broke out. I once made a tentative offer to buy: but, as I expected, the reply was 'No price would buy her'

MAURICE PORTAL."

THE FIRST DUAL CHAMPION

The next personal account to be featured was written by H. Reginald Cooke, and was about his Champion Grouse of Riverside; the first dog to be made a dual Champion.

"As years go by one is apt to cast one's memory back into the past and make a survey of one's canine favourites, and having been associated with the breed of Flatcoated Retrievers for 53 years. I have yielded to the invitation of the editor of The Field to describe some of the exploits of one of my best dogs.

"Such a dog was my Flatcoat Dual Champion Grouse of Riverside. I bought this dog from his breeder, Miss Gray, of Luton, Bedfordshire, whose Father was one of the best judges of a gundog that I ever met. This dog was about ten months old at the time, and I bought him one Saturday afternoon in the summer, taking him that evening to London, where I had been staying. The dog stayed in my room that night, and next day I took him into Hyde Park and being Ascot Sunday, the park was very crowded but Grouse was not at all upset. A few days later I took him to my home in the country and in September he came out shooting. He had previously been quietly handled and I found he knew something about the game. His mouth was very tender, His pick-up and delivery perfect, and he showed a good nose and was quick and methodical in his quest, but a hare going away from him was too much for him and he had several chases which would have done credit to a Waterloo Cup Winner!!! However, I took

Below: Dual Champion Grouse of Riverside.

him out with a check-cord and, after a few admonitions, he absolutely reformed, and became a very steady dog, so much so that at some of my shoots at home I left him at a stop between two guns heading the covert whilst I walked up with the beaters, and I found he had never moved, although sundry hares and pheasants had run past him.

"Grouse's first appearance at Field Trials was in 1905 when he competed in the I.G.L. Retriever Society's Trials at Sutton Scarsdale, Derbyshire. On the first day of these trials I was handling Grouse, and the dog worked nicely throughout the day, but on returning to a friend's house where I was staying I found a somewhat urgent telegram calling me home. This was awkward, for I either had to withdraw the dog from the stake or make some other arrangement. Fortunately amongst the spectators at the meeting was a gamekeeper I knew who asked me to let him handle the dog on the following day, and together they captured the fourth prize – not bad work considering that neither the man nor the dog had previously seen one another.

"Grouse's next appearance was in 1906, when he ran at the I.G.L. Retriever Society's Trials. In this stake he was placed First and also took the £20 special prize given for the dog which had won certain prizes on the Show Bench. He also took the special prize for the best looking dog running at the meeting. A spectator at the meeting who contributed an article in the Estate Magazine that year described Grouse as follows: Grouse of Riverside as a perfect Gentleman's dog – in excellent coat and condition and training – and in looks bad to beat as his championships prove.

"Grouse next ran in 1907 at the I.G.L. Retriever Trials at Rushmore, Wiltshire. Here the dog won third prize and the prize for the best looking dog at the meeting. In 1908, Grouse again ran at the I.G.L. Retriever Society's stake, where he again won third prize. In 1909 he competed in the Open stake of the Cheshire, Shropshire and North Wales Retriever Society. In this stake he was placed first and also won the prize for the best looking dog at the meeting. The following week he won the I.G.L. Retriever Society's Open Stake where he also won the challenge cup and the special prize given for the Retriever showing most dash combined with steadiness. Grouse did not run again at Trials.

"On the show bench, Grouse only competed at four Championship shows when in my possession, and he won Challenge prizes at the Ladies Kennel Show in London, Darlington and Taunton and thus became a Full Champion. I believe I am correct in saying that he was the first gundog to become a Dual Champion.

H. REGINALD COOKE."

CONDOVER RETRIEVER TRIALS, 1937
These were held at Condover (Shropshire) on October 1st and 2nd.

COUNTESS HOWE
The photograph shown here was published in 1939, accompanied by text reading:

"On Wednesday next, Lady Howe will be judging the Labrador Retrievers at Crufts and on Thursday she will be one of the three judges who will make the award for Best in Show."

In the same year, Countess Howe featured in the May 15th edition of The Times.

"Lorna Lady Howe is now making arrangements for the first specialist championship show of Labradors that is to take place on June 29th in the grounds of the Brine Baths Hotel. under the auspices of the Labrador Retriever Club. It is an attraction for Retriever enthusiasts, being close to the kennels of Mr. H. Reginald Cooke, doyen of Flatcoat breeders. We have just heard of a new sphere of usefulness for Labradors. One of the dogs of this breed from the Police Training

Above: The Condover Retriever Trials, Shropshire, October 1937.

Right: Lorna Countess Howe on Jock. On the following Wednesday next, Lady Howe would be judging the Labrador Retrievers at Cruft's Show and on Thursday she would be one of the three judges who make the award for Best in Show.

School at Newbury having been the means of discovering shortages in the underground cable at the new Broadcasting station of the Post Office at Cooling, near Rochester. By locating 14 shortings, the dog saved digging up about two miles of cable."

THE SHOOTING MAN'S SERVANT

The eighth journal ends with a report written by the kennel correspondent attached to The Field. It was published in June 1939.

"John Meyrick wrote a little book on dogs as long ago as 1861 that is still worth reading. He was first brought under my notice by a parson friend whose devotion to dogs and sport sometimes incurred the mild censure of his parishioners, though he was exemplary in his duties. Ever since dog showing and Field Trials became common we have had clergymen as members of an honourable fraternity.

"There is the well-known story of Parson Jack Russell, after whom strains of Fox Terriers are still called. Early one hunting morning he received a call from his Bishop. 'Tell his Lordship,' he instructed the servant 'That I am suffering from scarlet fever and it might be safer if he did not see me'. He was at the time in his hunting coat.

"In 1861 Retrievers had not been long enough in the making to have acquired a pronounced individuality, although Meyrick explained that the term applied exclusively to the cross between the Newfoundland and the Setter or Water Spaniel. The Newfoundland used was the smaller variety now known as the Labrador. Apparently, shooting men at that time had not altogether made up their minds that the results of these crosses were the only dogs that could be suitable for retrieving, for Meyrick wrote: 'I have heard of a cross between the Terrier and Beagle being used for this purpose. Almost any dog with the requisite qualifications of strength to carry a hare, a good nose and sufficient intelligence can be taught to retrieve. I am myself possessed of a first-rate Retriever of that maligned race, the bulldog '

"Ten years later at the show at Crystal Palace, we find well-filled classes for Retrievers, divided into Curlycoated, Smooth or Wavy. These in their turn were divided into blacks and other than blacks. One of the exhibitors was Mr. S. E. Shirley, M.P., a founder of the Kennel Club who devoted himself to the improvement of the Wavycoated, now called Flatcoated. Before long, his strain earned a reputation that was well deserved, and a little later Major Harding-Cox's Flatcoats were prominent. Before the end of the century was reached the Flatcoats were very much the rage, high prices being paid for them, and several were credited with earning vast sums at the stud.

"All these old breeders have disappeared, the only survivor being Major Harding-Cox, who no longer keeps dogs, but the continuity is maintained by Mr. H. Reginald Cooke, whose Riverside kennels were established some 40 years ago from Mr. Shirley's strain. Since he began innumerable dogs of the highest class have passed through his hands, and he has resisted the charms of the Labradors that rather more than 25 years ago began to supplant the Flatcoats. Mr. Cooke has recently expressed the opinion to me that the Flatcoats are now as good as, if not actually better than, they ever were in most respects. Down to 1914, although not so conspicuous at shows, they were largely kept by gamekeepers, numbers of whom gave up their dogs on joining the Forces. Latterly there has been a distinct improvement."

H. REGINALD COOKE

This article, about H. Reginald Cooke, was printed in Our Dogs in December 1937.

"Mr. H. Reginald Cooke was born in 1859 at Arden House, Ashley, Cheshire, and was educated at Eton and Trinity College, Cambridge. He whipped in at the Trinity College Beagles, and also represented

Volume Eight (1936-1941)

Cambridge in the High Jump against Oxford in 1879 and the two following years. In 1881 he won the High Jump for Cambridge against Oxford and in the same year took his B.A. Degree.

"He established his kennel of Flatcoated Retrievers in the year 1881, shortly before the death of the late Mr. S. E. Shirley, of Ettington, who was the founder of the breed. Since that date he has exhibited and judged at all the leading shows, and has also run dogs and won at Field Trials, at which he has also judged many times.

"Up to date the Riverside Kennel has won 336 Challenge Certificates, which is probably a record for a Kennel in which only one breed is kept. On one occasion, Mr. Cooke bought four puppies from one litter sired by his dog, Ch. Dancer of Riverside, and up to date has won 39 Challenge Certificates with the four!

"Mr. Cooke was president of the Flatcoated Retriever Association since it was originally established by Lady Howe, but resigned in the year 1936. He was a member of the committee formed in 1900 by Mr. W. Arkwright, of Sutton Scarsdale, Derbyshire, which originated the International Gundog League, and caters for Field Trials of all gundog breeds. Now he is vice president of the Cheshire, Shropshire and North Wales Working Retriever and Spaniel Society, of which he was president for many years.

"Mr. Cooke's favourite recreations are hunting, shooting and fishing. He resides at Dalicote, Bridgnorth, Shropshire, but his kennels are at Riverside, Nantwich, Cheshire, under the able management of J. Salter."

END OF AN ERA

In January 1941, Mr. H. Reginald Cooke decided that he would not be exhibiting any of his dogs in the future. The Riverside Kennels had then been in existence for 60 years. However, Mr. Cooke continued to breed working dogs and retained most of his Stud Dogs.

Mr. Cooke was not allowed to retire quietly. His announcement, that he was to cease exhibiting, seems to have prompted much of the canine press into publishing articles about his contribution to the world of Retrievers, as well as other articles about developments in the respective Retriever breeds in general.

One example can be seen in this article, published by The Kennel Gazette in February 1941.

"When Mr. Cooke started, he sat at the feet, as it were, of Mr. S. E. Shirley, the Warwickshire gentleman who founded the Kennel Club in 1873. Mr. Shirley was a supporter of Bulldogs as well as Flatcoats, but it was in connection with the latter variety that he will best be remembered. He took them up at a time when they were really in the making. Few serious attempts were made to produce a specialised Retriever until about 1881 when the Labrador was used as the principal foundation, he being crossed with a Setter to give us the Flatcoats or a Spaniel to give us the Curlies. Forty years ago, several Flatcoated Breeders were helpful members of the Kennel Club Committee. Lt. Col. H. Cornwall Legh who was a Trustee of the club had a leading kennel in Cheshire, and after his death when his dogs were put up for auction, Mr. Cooke bought Ch. High Legh Blarney, a dog that exerted a great influence upon his and other stock.

YELLOW RETRIEVERS

Another article from that time described the development of the yellow and golden-coloured breeds of Retrievers.

"There has been so much controversy in The Field on the subject of these breeds of dogs that I have been asked to contribute an article on the subject. First let me say that the letter from Lord Ilchester in THE FIELD of June 14th was correct, and undoubtedly my description of his Father's breed of yellow Retrievers was misleading. I did not really mean that the coats of these dogs were short

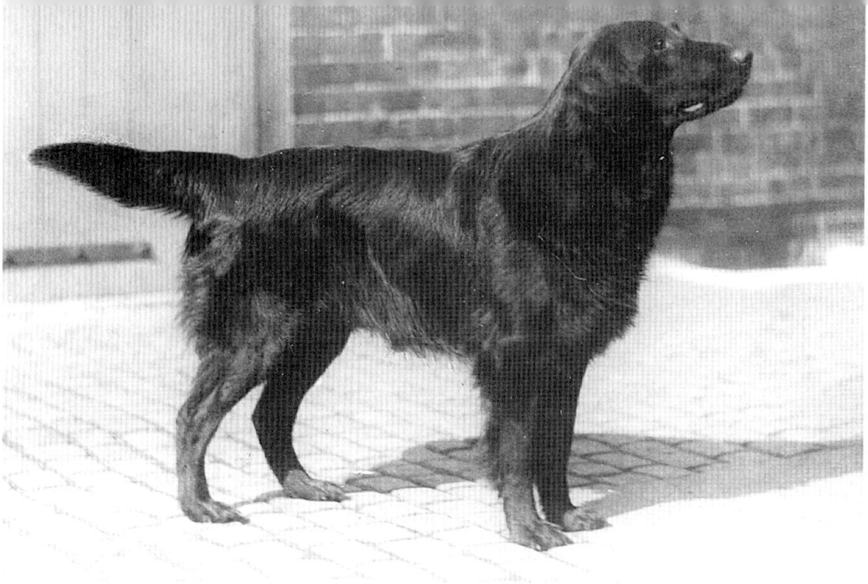

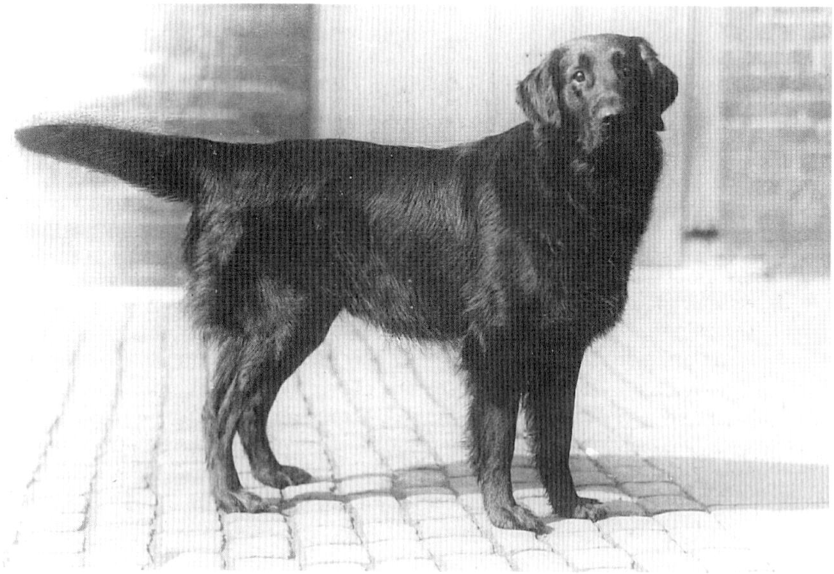

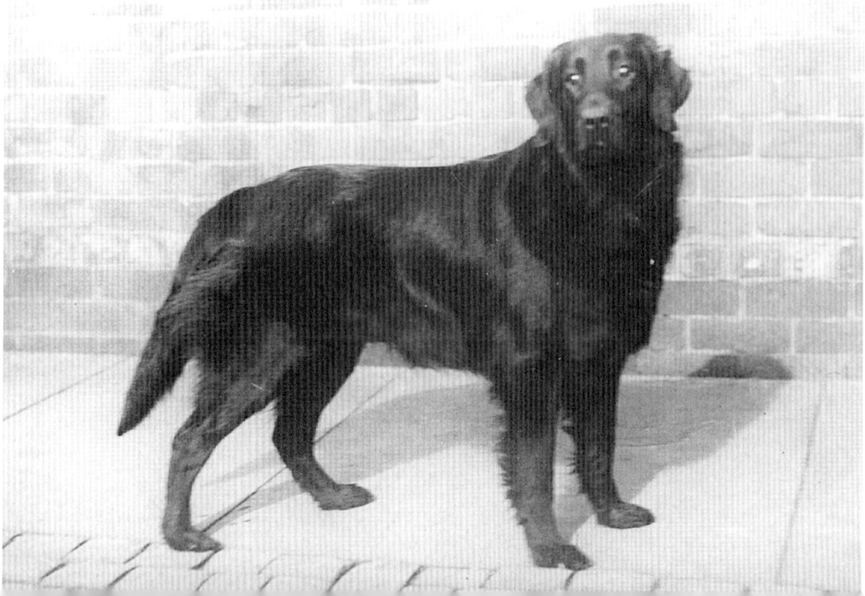

The Riverside Champions. Opposite page, top: Kiss of Riverside, winner of 19 Championship prizes and never beaten. Opposite page, centre: Mate of Riverside, winner of 5 prizes. Opposite page, bottom: Dipper of Riverside, winner of 10 prizes. Above left: Wimpole Peter, winner of 12 prizes. Above right: High Legh Blarney, winner of 14 prizes. Right: Nancy of Riverside, winner of 3 prizes. Bottom: Black Quilt, winner of 7 prizes.

The History Of Retrievers

Eight Riverside Retrievers, all of which are Champions.

like a Foxhound, but rather that the hairs were fine and straight, in fact, as far as I can remember after some 50 years, the coats of several I saw were more like fine and long-coated Labradors than anything else. (In my letter to The Field of March 29th, I actually stated that both Lord Ilchester's and Lord Tweedmouth's dogs were a type of the Flatcoated Retriever). In the last century when I first remember Retrievers, most of those seen in the field were either the long Wavycoated black Retrievers which we used to call the Wavycoated Newfoundland Retrievers, or the black Curlycoated Retrievers. The latter were good dogs when well broken, but were hard to break and had a tendency to be wild and often hard mouthed. This breed I seldom see in the field today. At that time a few well known sportsmen owned a number of black dogs imported from Newfoundland which were known as the short coated Newfoundland Retrievers. Of these owners, the best known were the Duke of Buccleuch, Lord Malmesbury, Lord Wimborne and a few others including my Father. When and why these dogs began to be called Labradors I could never find out. But on visiting the coasts of Labrador and Newfoundland many years ago I was surprised to be laughed at when asking to be shown a Labrador Retriever, which was unknown in that country. The original shortcoated Newfoundland dog was black, and often had a small white patch on its chest. I also saw some with one or more white feet. Their coats had long straight hairs, under which was a thick, woolly coat like that of an otter, and no amount of water seemed to penetrate this undercoat. Thus these dogs could withstand any amount of cold and wet. I am glad that my dogs still retain this undercoat, although it seems to be disappearing in the modern show-bench dog, which today we call a Labrador.

"It is often very hard to trace the origin of any particular type, or breed of dog. Originally there was presumably only one type of wild dog. It puzzles me how dogs like Pugs, and Bulldogs can be descended from ancestors which had to hunt and catch their own food. When we come to types which have started within the living memory of men, such as yellow Labradors, we can, however produce facts to produce the origin of these freaks. And I think it can be safely said that I started the first kennel of these dogs at the end of the last century, with two yellow pups born in a litter of Black Labradors. And since then I have bred other freak dogs, such as pure-white Labradors, and also white Wavycoated Retrievers. My friend, the late Mr. Austin Mackenzie, of Carridale, actually started a breed of pure-white Labradors which were very handsome dogs. My great trouble at first was to keep the yellow Labradors pure and true to type. This did not apply to my own kennels, but only to cases where dogs passed into the hands of strangers who, I regret to say occasionally crossed the true Labradors with other breeds. Hence, we sometimes see today a so-called yellow Labrador with a thin coat more like that of a pointer, which is quite wrong.

"Once I remember sending by request to a leading show a type of what I thought was a perfect specimen of a Yellow Labrador. This dog was not awarded a prize, and on being asked why this was so, the judge said 'Oh, that type of dog is different to what we now give prizes to, it is an old fashioned type of Labrador.' I must admit that the old type of short coated Newfoundland dog was different to Labradors of today. If anyone has the back volumes of The Sportsman's Magazine, I think about 1860, they can find there illustrations of the shortcoated Labradors which show these dogs as I remember them. At the time of writing this I have not my library at hand, so cannot refer to the magazine for dates, etc.: and I may be far off the mark of quoting 1860 as the date of these illustrations.

"As regards the origin of Lord Tweedmouth's yellow dogs, I have heard all kinds of tales. In my records of dogs, which also I have not at hand, I have and interesting letter from Lord Lonsdale, in which he describes how Lord Tweedmouth took a party of friends to a great circus in London. There they saw three yellow dogs performing on the stage. Lord Tweedmouth was so delighted with them that he insisted on buying all three dogs, and these were the ancestors of his breed. As this happened before I was born I cannot personally vouch for the events described, but it is clear from Lord Ilchester's letter in The Field that at some periods these dogs were crossed with Bloodhounds and Labradors. It is, therefore, certain that there must have been variations in the type of these dogs coats, if in no other respects. The well-known

Lord Lonsdale with Rads, a yellow Labrador Retriever who was presented to Lord Lonsdale in 1905 by Major Radcliffe.

photographer of animals and sport Mr. W. A. Rouch, has just written me a letter and enclosed some photos of my dogs which he took in 1907 and 1908. I am sending these to The Field in case any of them are suitable to show what the original type of Yellow Labradors and old Wavycoated Retrievers were like.

"I well remember showing that great sportsman the Hon. A. Holland-Hibbert, a young yellow Labrador bitch called Dinah from the first litter of all yellow ones I bred. He said 'That is the most beautiful creature I have ever seen, and if she belonged to me I would build her a silver kennel.' Again, I can recall a scene in 1905 when I arrived at Lowther Castle to take part in one of those splendid old shooting parties, the like of which I fear we shall never see again. I took with me one of my yellow dogs, and presented it to my host, saying: 'It is only right that the yellow Earl should own a yellow dog, so please accept the first one I ever gave away.' Lord Lonsdale was so pleased with it that afterwards he never moved without that dog going with him, and he could be seen on the moors or in the London Parks with 'Rads', as he named the dog, which he said was an abbreviation of the donor's name.

"And lastly, to give you some idea of what people thought of those early yellow Labradors, I may quote the following incident. A certain very wealthy Oriental Prince, who figured in a celebrated lawsuit in England, and who was over here, asked to see my yellow dogs. I did not want to sell any at the time but he would not take 'no' for an answer. Finally, he had a solid silver model made of one dog, and went away with three of the yellow dogs, leaving me with a cheque for over £500 in exchange.

MAJOR C. E. RADCLIFFE."

The Earl of Ilchester, another well-known breeder of yellow Labradors, also decided to write his own account of the breed. Again, this was published in The Field, appearing in November 1941.

"A good deal of hearsay of much later date has recently been introduced into the discussion in your columns on the origin of yellow Retrievers. May I, therefore, intervene, as I am probably now the only person who was closely connected with both the Tweedmouth and Ilchester breeds, within eight or ten years of their commencement. Here is the story as I used to hear it.

"Sir Dudley Marjoribanks, later created Lord Tweedmouth, in the late sixties owned a black bitch, which on one occasion, possibly not the first, produced yellow puppies in a black litter. There were two: Crocus, the dog, was given to his son Edward Marjoribanks; Ada, the bitch, to his nephew, my Father. This was probably about 1868.

"Ada, when probably about six or seven years old was included in a portrait of my Father, painted by the Hon. H. Graves. I can quite well remember her: a broadish head, with a long, soft, smooth coat, reddish, but certainly far lighter in colour than the 'Golden' Retriever of the present day. She died about 1880 or 1881, as an oldish dog. About that time my Father owned a brown dog. He was never used for the stud, not having been broken and, being of very uncertain temper, afforded a contrast to the sweet disposition of the yellow strain. Even in those early days, the yellow colour was curiously self-assertive. A yellow bitch put to a black dog invariably produced yellow puppies, the black bitch to a yellow dog, usually, but with much less certainty. I remember that a black dog, Sweep, belonging to Mr. Montague Guest, I think a Smoothcoat, sired one or two of my Father's best litters. He occasionally used Black dogs for a change of blood, and sometimes Labradors, in the later days, but never the Bloodhound strain.

"Sir Dudley's purchase of one dog, or more, in Brighton, probably took place about 1871 or 1872; one preferably, as had there been several, more, doubtless would be known about them. The Czar's entry of a Russian Retriever at the Crystal Palace show about that time, may have led to the belief that the

Brighton dog was Russian. But, anyhow, I well remember being told, as a boy, that there was a similar yellow brees in the Caucasus – sheepdogs. Colonel le Poer Trench set out to find a specimen of this race, and bought some home many years later. I was in close correspondence with him at that period, and may even have suggested to him the possibility of fresh blood from that source. Unfortunately, he chose the season of the year when the dogs were far away from civilisation in the high mountains. He arranged to buy one, unseen, but heard nothing more of the dog nor of his money!

"The Colonel's dogs were certainly nearer in shape, colour and texture of coat to the original breed than the vast majority of the present yellow Retrievers. The Ilchester dogs, however, never had woolly coats. The pale colour, with certain exceptions was certainly a characteristic of the early days of our breed, but they were never cream coloured or albino. A very pale dog was given to my Father at the end of his life (the dog died about 1912), but it was a complete outcross. About the same time, he had another present, a dark-red bitch, quite different in shape, with some curl in the coat and with more resemblance to the present Golden Retriever. I believe this came from Alma, Lady Breadalbane; but of this I am uncertain. We had three generations of that strain, all bitches, but they produced few puppies and the line died out.

"All this time, the Tweedmouth breed was thriving equally with our own; and interchange of blood took place from time to time. Guisachan also developed a deer-tracking strain, and introduced some Bloodhound blood to assist it. There was a large kennel still in being when I was last there shooting Woodcock in November 1904, a year or more before the sale of the property by Edward Marjoribanks, second Lord Tweedmouth. Big dogs of the original breed were there, trackers and some smaller ones of the 'Golden' type. The source whence this latter strain emanated, I do not recollect, or perhaps, never knew. I understood, when the Guisachan kennel was dispersed, that the personal favourites went to Hutton, Lord Tweedmouth's Castle in Berwickshire; that the late Lord Harcourt had his pick of the remainder; and that what was left, including the trackers were sold to the purchaser of the property, Lord Portsmouth, or were thrown into the deal. Lord Harcourt was a breeder of small black Spaniels, and may for that reason have preferred the smaller type. I discussed the earlier problems with the late Lord Tweedmouth on several occasions; but he was, unfortunately, unable to throw any fresh light upon them.

THE EARL OF ILCHESTER."

9 THE FINAL YEARS (1945-1951)

Sadly, as we reach the end of these journals and I turn the opening page of book nine, the final book, I am presented with several pages of obituaries of friends and colleagues of H. R. Cooke. I realise that this lifetime's record of Retrievers, Trialling, showing, breeding, and much more besides, is almost over.

In 1946, H. Reginald Cooke suffered a fall while out shooting and was confined to his bed. This rendered him inactive for some considerable time, but it did not prevent him from celebrating his 90th birthday on February 4th 1949. To mark this occasion, he pasted in the scrapbook a letter of birthday congratulations, received from the Old Etonian Association.

OLD ETONIAN ASSOCIATION

From Col. the Hon. J. J. Astor

Weston's Yard
Eton College
Windsor

3rd February 1949

Dear Mr. Cooke,

We notice with great pleasure that you are celebrating your 90th birthday anniversary and on behalf of all your fellow members I write to send to you our congratulations and good wishes.

We all wish you good health and happiness in the future.

We also note with satisfaction that the 3rd generation has recently passed through Eton.

Yours sincerely,

John F. Astor

Chairman of the Committee

H. R. Cooke, Esq.,
Dalicot House,
Bridgnorth,
Salop

The Final Years (1945-1951)

LAST SUCCESSES

In September of his 90th year, Mr. Cooke ran in the United Gundog Breeders Association's Retriever Trials on 7th and 8th October at Wetmore, Salop. Mr. Cooke won Reserve with his dog and this achievement, for a man over 90 years of age, must be worthy of admiration. His handwriting is now becoming shaky but still good enough to record his win on November 17th 1949 at the Flatcoated Retriever Society's Trial with Joy of Riverside, also having another dog, Nobby of Riverside, placed third in the same stake. The final entry in the last journal was made in February 1951, when Mr. Cooke was 92.

A CONCLUDING NOTE

H. Reginald Cooke kept a wonderful record of his life and the world of Retrievers, and I have personally deemed it a privilege to having access to them with the kind permission of his grandson Randle Cooke. I hope that I have managed to select just a few of the wonderful articles in those journals that will bring pleasure to others and give an insight into the History of our present day dogs.

Judi Seall

Better to hunt in fields for health unbought,
Than fee the doctor for a nauseous draught
The wise for cure on exercise depend
God never made his work for man to mend.

The History Of Retrievers